BLACK BALTIMO[RE]

By Ra[...]

HERITAGE BOOKS, INC.

Published 1987 By

HERITAGE BOOKS, INC.
3602 Maureen Lane, Bowie, Maryland 20715
301-464-1159

ISBN 1-55613-080-5

FOR DAD

"With God all things are possible"
(Matthew 19:26)

ACKNOWLEDGEMENTS

As is often the case in historical research the work of one evolves from the cooperation of many.

I'd like to express my gratitude to the Director of the Baltimore Enoch Pratt Free Library, Mrs. Anna Curry, and to the Assistant Director, Dr. John Blegen, for their continuing support.

I am particularly grateful to Wesley Wilson, head of Pratt's Maryland Department and to his entire staff.

Eva Slezak, librarian in charge of the Afro American Collection at Pratt, provided welcome assistance and moral support on a number of occassions.

My thanks to Ed Mantler, Dick Elder, Vince Snowden, and Karen Mewshaw.

A number of friends and associates rendered assistance in one form or another. Bill Forshaw, Agnes Callum, Alma Moore, Leroy Graham, Dean Krimmel of the Baltimore Peale Museum, and Jacques Kelly of the staff of the *Baltimore Evening Sun.*

A very special thanks to my dear friend and mentor, Edna Kanely, whose friendship, support, and expertise has meant so much to me in my life and in my work.

Ralph Clayton

Cover Photograph

Margaret Riddle Yoe and Nurse, circa 1864

Courtesy of the Peale Museum, Baltimore, Maryland

✶∧✶∧✶∧✶∧✶∧✶∧✶∧✶∧✶∧✶∧✶

SLAVES BY NAME originally appeared in *Flower of the Forest Black Genealogical Journal*, Vol. 1 #5 1986

SLAVEHOLDERS OF BALTIMORE, 1860 originally appeared in the *Maryland Genealogical Society Bulletin*, Vol. 25 #1 1984

THE EFFECT OF IMMIGRATION ON THE NEGRO IN BAL-TIMORE, 1850–1860 was first submitted as a paper for a University of Baltimore class, Introduction to Sociology

BALTIMORE FREE BLACK HOUSEHOLDS WITH SLAVES, 1820–1840 originally appeared in *Flower of the Forest Black Genealogical Journal*, Vol. 1 #4

LAUREL CEMETERY, 1852–1958 originally appeared in *Flower of the Forest Black Genealogical Journal*, Vol. 1 #3

TABLE OF CONTENTS

v

FOREWORD

Documents on a federal, state, and municipal level abound with information pertaining to the Nineteenth Century Black population of Baltimore.

Although these records are fragmented throughout a number of agencies statewide, the overwhelming majority are stored in the archives of three major institutions.

The Afro-American Collection and the Microform Center of the Baltimore Enoch Pratt Free Library store a series of clipping and query files, Baltimore City directories, newspapers, Federal Census Population Records, special collections, and thousands of volumes reflecting the life of the Black family in Maryland.

The collection of the Maryland Historical Society in Baltimore provides a number of primary source materials including a document room that houses indexed manuscripts referring to, in part, the slave and free Black population of Maryland.

The State Archives in the Annapolis Hall of Records has preserved the largest single repository of primary source materials in the area. Deeds or wills of manumission, orphans court records, indentures of apprenticeship, and applications for certificates of freedom are but a few of the manuscripts offering a unique insight into the lifestyles of Maryland's Afro-American population.

Although an obvious wealth of documents exist statewide, comparatively little work has been accomplished in the area of the indexing and compilization of primary source data.

It is my hope that the material collected in this book will present a starting point for further research and act as a catalyst for the initiation of new work in related fields.

THE EFFECT OF IMMIGRATION

ON THE NEGRO IN BALTIMORE 1850-1860

Introduction

Generalization is the major enemy of history. It remains the tempting forbidden fruit most often responsible for the downfall of a number of historians.

A look at the lifestyle of the American Negro in the Ante-Bellum Decade will serve to highlight the problems inherent in conducting historical research.

There are a number of differences in the condition of the free Negro and the slave in any given area of geographical focus. The life of a slave living on a cereal plantation in Carroll County was likely to be quite different from the life of a domestic slave residing in Mount Vernon Place, Baltimore.

Boundaries determining factors of lifestyle were not simply a division between urban and rural settings. A plantation slave on the cereal farm in Carroll County would find conditions considerably more tolerable than would the slave on a typical Louisiana sugar plantation. The free man of color residing in Mobile, Alabama, would face daily restrictions on his freedom uniquely different from the free man living in Lerew's alley, Baltimore.

The lifestyle of the slave and freeman could vary significantly, for a number of reasons, ward by ward in a sector of geographical focus the size of Baltimore.

There were a number of similarities in the life of the Negro, slave and free, regardless of residence. It is here where the temptation to generalize is greatest; where, at times, the historian loses sight of the vast differences between communities and the reasons for their uniqueness.

Therefore, the work of the "Local Historian" is extremely important in better determining areas of uniqueness reflected in lifestyles of any given race in the community.

1

It is incorrect to assume that past history is already laid before us in an open book. The pages are in constant revision and the epilogue as yet un-written.

From 1810 to the abolition of slavery in the state in November 1864, Maryland contained the largest free Negro population in the country. Intense competition between white, slave, and free Negro male laborers fostered growing feelings of belligerence between slaveholders and the free Negro. Adding to the slaveholders chagrin was the introduction, into the labor market, of thousands of white immigrant workers willing to toil for low wages.

Negro males found themselves at the bottom of the social and economic totem pole. Gradually forced from a number of occupations they had once excelled in, thousands were replaced in the labor market by cheap immigrant labor.

Slaveholders, particularly those of the Eastern Shore holding strong political influence in the Maryland State Legislature, seized upon this oppurtunity to initiate a series of campaigns aimed at the total annihilation of the free Negro.

State legislation was enacted throughout the 1850s that imposed severe restrictions on the free Negro in trade and labor. Seperate sanctions were set for crimes committed by free Negroes; sanctions which often resulted in the sale of the Negro into slavery.

Social restrictions were initiated or intensified. Travel restrictions were regulated and the meetings of large numbers of Negroes were forbidden unless supervised by a white person or approved by a justice.

When a community of people fails to revolt against unjust measures taken against it the obvious question we must ask ourselves is why?

Chapter 1

The Effect Of Immigration On The Negro In Baltimore
1850 – 1860

Any study of the effect of foreign labor on the Negro family in Maryland would have to include a careful study of two of Maryland's largest community of immigrants; The German and the Irish.

The mid and late 1840's were years of turmoil in Europe. There was revolution in the streets of Berlin, Hungarian revolt against Austrian domination, and the failure and destructive blight of the potato crop in Ireland in 1846. As a result,

2

hundreds of thousands of immigrants passed into this country between 1847 and 1857.

The effect of these events on labor in the Eastern Seaboard States, consequently on the free Negro and slave population of Maryland was enormous.

Immigrants began to drive the Negro male in increasing numbers from the labor market in Baltimore. Evidence of this phenomona can be obtained by comparing the wards circling the inner harbor area of Baltimore between 1850 and 1860 in the census[1]. The population of German immigrants in the first ward increased by over 100% from 1850 to 1860. The number of Germans, which stood at 4,339 constituted 30% of the entire population of the first ward by 1860.

	1850 Free	1850 Slave	1860 Free	1860 Slave
ward 1	1,091	79	460	54
ward 2	917	85	628	46
totals	29,075	2,946	25,680	2,218

Although the boundaries of wards had changed by 1860, making an exact comparison with 1850 impossible, the total population of Baltimore reflects a dramatic decrease in the Negro population. Population figures dropped from 32,021 in 1850 to 27,898 in 1860 (a decrease of 4,123). The white population, in the same period of time, had grown by 9,667.

The effect of labor competetion was much greater on the Negro male than on the Negro female. The overall effect on the Negro family, however, was considerable.

Many females had training and experience in various forms of domestic labor (i.e. cook, washerwoman, ironer)[2]. The demand for their services remained, for the most part, unaffected by immigration. Most whites demanded that their domestics live on or near the premises. As a result a number of families were seperated, at least a greater portion of time.

To help alleviate the problem of physical seperation Negro families attempted, whenever possible, to live as close to their source of employment as they could. As a consequence there was no segregation of neighborhoods by race. Housing for these families was often procured on small side streets or in alleys behind the houses of whites. A study of Baltimore City directories of the 1850's will provide evidence in the "Colored Section" of dozens of alleys inhabited by Negro families.

Slave families were also effected radically by the influx of immigrants. As the need for male slave labor decreased many males were sold to traders and sent to the New Orleans market. Here again the exception was the female slave.

The very nature of "Town Slavery" promoted the break-up of large numbers of families. Of 1,308 slaveholders in Baltimore in 1860, 962 or 73.5% were owners of one slave[3].

One of the ironies of "Town Slavery" was the inability of authority to prohibit a degree of intermingling of slave and free in the populace. Although state legislation forbid the gathering of large numbers of Negroes without the supervision of whites, peaceful corner gatherings were overlooked[4].

Another practice which allowed a great deal of mingling of the populace was the practice known as the "hiring out" of slaves. "The hiring out of slaves was accomplished in several ways. One, the owner signed a binding contract between himself and the employer; a contract which covered a specified time period and pre-arranged payments to the owner, with liability for the slave's welfare in the hands of the employer. Two, an owner allowed his or her slave to hire themselves out to an employer of their own choosing, provided the slave paid, out of his earnings, a pre-arranged amount to his owner on a regular basis."[5]

The practice of hiring out led to a greater sense of overall freedom of movement in the slave community. There were occassions when slaves were allowed to live with free family members in a household seperate from that of the owner. "As this practice evolved incidences of seperate habitation for slaves became apparent in the city. Some slaves were allowed....by their owners....to hire themselves out, and to keep a household of their own seperate from the property of the owner."[6]

The danger of forming close family ties in a house where one spouse was a slave was of course the possibility of the breakup of the family by the sale of that slave to a new owner. Nevertheless the practice was evident in a number of cities and towns throughout the South.

One way to study, in greater detail, the effect of immigration on Negro labor is to look at the demise of a single occupation, performed for decades, solely by the Negro.

Prior to 1850 the caulking of ships in Baltimore was accomplished by the Negro male. So great was their monopoly of the occupation that it was presumed that prior to 1858 there were no white caulkers in the city.[7]

The influence held by males of this profession provided a rare instance of real versus imagined power in an otherwise

4

powerless class of people.

Ships would not float, no matter how well they were built, without a good caulking job. A study of Baltimore's inner harbor ward 2 for the ante-bellum decade shows that of 168 Negro males holding jobs 112 were directly affected by or affected the shipping trade. It is easy to see that the profession of caulking was crucial to the economy of the city of Baltimore and the state of Maryland.

As a result, Negro males formed an association of caulkers to insure their control of the profession. Whites, strongly opposed to the unionization of any group of Negroes in their midst, swallowed their pride and fear. They had no other choice. By the late 1850's the situation had proved intolerable and radical changes were instituted.

Pressure was brought to bear on white shipbuilders by the association of Negro caulkers on several levels. One, they insisted on having the final say over who was to be hired for a particular job. Two, whites were outraged by the wages being demanded by the Negro caulkers. They were receiving a market high $1.75 a day while[8] white caulkers in other port cities were earning $1.25 a day.

Whites, not in the habit of being dictated to by Negroes, sought the labor of white caulkers working in other ports. A number of these workers were immigrants who had brought their trades with them from Germany and Ireland. This intrusion of whites into an occupation previously controlled[9] by the Negro brought about a number of labor riots in the city.

Labor problems were not unique to the Baltimore area in the ante-bellum decade. Labor militancy was rampant throughout the 1850's as labor riots ensued between whites and blacks struggling for the same jobs.[10]

One noted historian has stated "Whenever white and colored workers gathered in numbers, riots[11] were imminent during the middle of the nineteenth century."

By 1860 the job busting (for the most part by violent means) had excluded a great number of Negro caulkers from the shipyards. It is not difficult to see how occupations with little control by the Negro fell easlly into the hands of the white laborer. "The incoming Irish were quite willing to labor, haul merchandise or other material, or even work as porters and waiters as "job busting" became a normal tactic and made most jobs for Negroes scarce by 1860.[12]

A number of Negro males left tbe city in search of work, further fragmenting the family unit. Those not trained as domestics "Probably left the city to go to New York or Boston, if they were free, or were sold into the deep South, if they were slave."[13]

Why didn't the black male revolt against their exclusion from the labor market in Baltimore? Did he hold a means of rebellion or revolt and if so, why dld he fail to pursue those means?

Chapter 2

Slaveholders And The Law:
the failure of the Negro to unify

The Church evolved, in the Reconstruction period, as the most powerful institution in the life of the Negro in this country. The community unified behind church leaders, using the power of the vote, in an attempt to gain social, political, and economic advances. Such was not the case, however, in the ante-bellum decade. Although elements of the Black Church had formed by the middle of the nlneteenth century, it was by no means the powerful institution it was to become in the Reconstruction period. It was not yet elevated, for obvious reasons, to what was to become its post war status as central to the values and ideals of the community.

A community may act, or fail to act, motivated by the fear of the loss of an ideal or value crucial to its survival. The Negro Community had no power to legislate laws, little economic power, and the inability to do much of anything outside of white authorlty. What did the Negro fear losing as much, if not more, than his own life? The answer, of course, was the family.

A study of laws passed by the Maryland State Legislature will reflect the constant attempt to place restrictions on the rights of the Negro.

One example of this was legislation passed in 1832 as a response to the fear of slave insurrection.[14] The Nat Turner slave revolt in Southampton, Virginia in the summer of 1831 caused a wave of panic to spread throughout the South. As a result severe restrictons on the rights of the Negro were imposed.

In Maryland, for example, religious meetings not attended by whites were forbidden wlthout the permission of a justice. Negroes could not sell merchandise without a certificate issued by that same justice. The Sale of liquor and firearms to Negroes was forbidden. Restrictions were placed on travel into and out of the state.

The punishment often reflected in this legislation was the sale of an indlvidual into slavery. The terms of the sale would range from as little as one year to life. Sale into slavery often meant permanent exile from the family.

Although it is clear that immigration was the primary factor responsible for disruption of the labor market in Baltimore, slaveholders in Maryland continued to place the blame on the ever growing free Negro population.

As more and more Negro males lost their livelihood to whites, slaveholders pointed to what they perceived as the danger of a shiftless, lazy, idle free populace. As the situation deteriorated in the latter half of the decade, slave-holders attempted to unify their strength through a series of conventions designed at addressing the problem of a free, Negro community. Two courses of action, expulsion and re-enslavement, were debated by the members of the convention.

Slaveholders, particularly those of the Eastern Shore, exerted a significant influence on the proceedings of the State Legislature. They sought, through the introduction of new legislation and the revival of old vagrancy laws, to promote an atmosphere for the completion of their objective.

One example was legislation passed in 1858 which proposed[15] severe sanctions on Negroes for acts such as simple larceny. Acts of larceny as well as felonies brought terms of sale into slavery of from two to five years. Arson, on the other hand, brought the sentence of hanging or in some cases sale into slavery for life.

A study of the inmates of the Maryland State penitentiary in 1850 and 1860 will point to a marked contrast in the Negro population of the institution. Census schedules show a clear drop in the proportion of Negroes incarcerated in 1860 as opposed to 1850.[16]

	total pop.	Negro
1850	236	123
1860	428	109

These figures are certainly not a result of the improvement of conditions of the life of the Negro. They reflect, in my opinion, the tremendous increase in the sale into slavery of Negroes who had been charged with breaking the law.

Ironically, the conventions of slaveholders that had convened over a period of three years in the late 1850's voted against the expulsion or re-enslavement of the free Negro populace. Although they had branded the Negro as lazy and

7

idle, they found them to be crucial to the states economy and their expulsion impossible for several reasons:

1.) Thousands of Negroes were employed in the city of Baltimore as domestics or laborers in various departments of industry.
2.) In rural areas where help was not abundant they furnlshed a large supply of agricultural labor.
3.) Their removal would deduct 50% from and household labor provided by all Negroes, slave and free, statewide.
4.) It would break up businesses and destroy the property of a large number of landowners and renters.
5.) Legislation could not be secured or approval obtained from a large body of the people of Maryland.

The slaveholders resolved to use existing leglslation and to impose new, strict legislation, to control the Negro.

The slaveholder understood that the most important possession of the Negro was his family. Therefore much of the legislation was aimed at punishing the violater by sale into slavery and obvious fragmentation of the family unit.

Conclusion

In the Ante-Bellum Decade the Negro was in a vice gripping from all sides. White immigrants, who had poured into Maryland by the thousands in the early 1850's had, as aforementioned, forced many Negro males out of the labor market in the city of Baltimore. The inability to compete with white labor left many without visible means for support.

A number of male slaves were sold into the South, their services no longer needed in the city. Still others were hired out to employers. Both processes served to fragment the family unit.

Thousands of free Negro males left the city in an attempt to find employment elsewhere.

Slaveholders, realizing the threat that this growing free community imposed on the institution of slavery, moved to rid the state of the free Negro populatlon. Unable to accomplish their objectives through violence or existing legislation, they initiated new legislation aimed at imposing an even greater control over the Negro populace.

One of the means used to accomplish this goal was the threat of re-inslavement often initiated as a result of the failure to abide by the strict letter of the law.

The Negro could not unionize or rebel in any effective way against authority because of the danger this action might impose on the unity of the family.

Legislation was designed to prohibit the Negro from assembling or unionizing (outside of white authority) with the threat of slavery as a sanction imposed for the failure to comply.

Faced with the probability that unionization or rebellion of any kind would ultimately fail, the Negro resolved to maintain whatever sense of family unity he could.... Clearly it was an unstable unity often purchased at the expense of individual or community freedom.

Notes

[1] U.S. Government, Federal Population Census Schedules, 1850 and 1860, Baltimore.

[2] Ralph Clayton, "Slaveholders of Baltlmore 1860", *Maryland Genealogical Society Bulletin* vol. 25 #1 Winter 1984.

[3] Ibid

[4] Laws of Maryland, 1832, ch 323

[5] Ralph Clayton, "Slaveholders of Baltimore 1860," *Maryland Genealogical Society Bulletin*, vol. 25 #1 Winter 1984.

[6] Ralph Clayton, "Baltimore Free Black Households With Slaves 1820-1840", *Flower of The Forest*, vol. 1 #4 1985.

[7] Baltimore American, 7/9/58, p.1 and 7/8/58, p.1

[8] Ibid

[9] *Baltimore Sun*, 5/15/58, 7/5/58, 6/29/59, all p.1.

[10] *New York Tribune*, 1/13/51, 1/18/55, 2/15/55.

[11] Charles H. wesley Ph.D., *Negro Labor in The United States 1850 - 1925*, New York, Russell and Russell.

[12] Semmes, *Baltimore As Seen By Visitors*, p.170.

[13] Ray Della Jr., "Problems of Negro Labor.", *Maryland Historical Magazine*, vol. 66 #1 Spring 1971.

[14] Laws of Maryland, 1832, Ch 323.

[15] Laws of Maryland, 1858 ch 324

[16] U.S. Government, Federal population Census Schedules, 1850 and 1860, Baltimore.

Bibliography

1.) Fields, Barbara Jeanne, *Slavery and Freedom on the Middle Ground*, 1985, London, Yale University Press

2.) Katz, William Loren, *Eyewitness: The Negro in American History*, 1967, Pittman Corp., New York
3.) Owens, Leslie Howard, *This Species Of Property*, 1976, New York, Oxford University Press.
4.) Phillips, Ulrich B., *American Negro Slavery*, 1918, Baton Rouge, Louisiana State University Press.
5.) Wright, James M., *The Free Negro In Maryland 1634-1860*, 1971, New York, Octagon Books.

BALTIMORE FREE BLACK HOUSEHOLDS

WITH SLAVES 1820-1840

The following is an index of free black households with slaves in the city of Baltimore, Maryland as compiled from the Federal Population Census schedules of 1820, 1830, and 1840. Town slavery (more so than plantation slavery) encouraged the practice of the hiring out of slaves to businesses or individuals on a temporary basis. "Increased immigration" into the eastern seaboard states, coupled with a fast growing "free black" population flooded the labor market in Baltimore. As the need for slave labor in the city decreased, the practice of hiring out increased out of economic necessity. As this practice evolved incidences of separate habitation for slaves became apparent in the city. Some slaves were allowed...by their owners...to hire themselves out, and to keep a household of their own separatae from the property of the owner. Because of this practice, it is impossible to determine, strictly from the use of the census returns, which of these households are the households of free black slaveowners and whih are the households of white owned slaves allowed to live on separate premises. Nevertheless, an index such as this provides a good starting point for the researcher or genealogist interested in pursuing the study of slavery.

The index is organized as follows: Last name, first name or initial (if given), ward and page number (in parenthesis), and the number of female and male slaves. On occasion, there are several page numbers appearing on the left hand side of each page. One number is stamped and the other is handwritten. I have chosen to use the hand-written number because it is the only consistent numbering system of the two.

Baltimore Free Black Households With Slaves 1820

BARE, Susannah (1-3-) 1f
BARNES, James (8-295) 1m
BENNET, Jane (1-11) 5f
BOWLEY, Elizabeth (2-62) 2f
BROOK, Joliet (11-459) 1f
BROOKS, Nancy (10-431) 1m
BROUGHTON, William (11-434) 1f
BROWN, ? (10-395) 1m
 Charles (8-308) 2m
 Francis (8-317) 1m
BUDD, Julius (3-155) 1f
BURKE, James (3-144) 2f
BURNES, Fanny (7-277) 1m
 Theodore (1-11) 1f
BURNS, W. (10-406) 1f,1m
CANBY, Thomas (11-461) 2f
CHARLES, ? (11-458) 1f
CLARKE, Israel (2-80) 5f
CONNER, Rebeca (1-12) 2f
DAVIS, Carlos (11-426) 1m
DENTON, Resin (12-508) 1f, 2m
DICKSON, Jeremiah (7-275) 1m
DOUGLASS, Casandra (11-457) 1m
DOWDEN, Michael (8-304) 1m
DOWNS, Fanny (8-305) 1m
FIELDS, Henry (5-231) 1m
FRANCIS, John (5-218) 2f
FRISBY, George (3-145) 3m
GARNER, N. (10-398) 1m
HAIRS, Mary (3-139) 2f
HAMMOND, George (2-83) 1m
HARRIS, Elisa (11-462) 1f
HAWKINS, Benjamin (8-294) 2f, 1m
HILL, Hannah (4-183) 2f
JACKSON, Henry (11-461) 2m

JACKSON (continued)
 Peter (8-319) 1m
 Urias (11-426) 1m
JAMES, Frank (12-510) 1f
JOHNS, Primus (1-38) 3f
JOHNSON, Francis (8-310) 1m
 Jonathan (4-177) 1m
JOHNSTON, Samuel (3-132) 1f
JONES, Felis (12-482) 1f
 Senah (11-437) 1m
KANE, J. (10-387) 3f
LEE, N. (10-411) 1f, 1m
 Nancy (12-518) 1m
LEMAS, M. (10-395) 1m
LIMAS, ? (10-398) 1m
LOW, Margaret (3-112) 1m
LUSTON, Gracy (11-430) 1m
MAKEL, Benjamin (12-489) 1f
MAN, Allen Bailey C. (7-267) 1m
 Nicholas Douglass C. (7-269) 1f
MASURCT, Caprice (5-221) 1f
NICHOLAS, Elizabeth (12-506) 1m
OGLE, Samuel (3-151) 2f
PILLEY, Caleb (3-159) 1m
PUNCH, Mary (12-518) 1m
RAY, M. (10-403) 1f
 Thomas (3-140) 1f
RICHARDSON, Elizabeth (1-24) 1f
RIDGELEY, Lucy (11-428) 1m
RINGGOLD, Benjamin (11-429) 1m
ROBERTS, George (4-167) 2f, 1m
 George (11-458) 1f
 Jacob (4-176) 3f, 2m

SAMPSON, Isaac (8-301) 1m
SHERRALS, Gloss (8-319)
 1f, 1m
SMITH, J. (10-398) 1m
 John (1-21) 1f
 Mary (11-431) 1m
 Nancy (11-429) 1m
 Samuel (12-498) 2f
SNEEDS, Simon (8-306) 1m
SPARROW, Anthony (3-158)
 2f
SPRIGG, Henrey (12-522) 1m
STANSBURY, Susy (4-169) 1f
THOMAS, Sarah (1-25) 1f
 Charles (11-425) 1m

THOMPSON, Joseph (3-147)
 1m
WELLS, Nat (11-429) 1m
WHITTINGTON, Henny (8-
 300) 1f
 John (7-284) 1m
WILLIAMS, Benjamin (12-
 477) 1f, 1m
 J. (10-371) 2f
WILSON, Sophia (11-428) 1m
WON, J. (10-391) 1m
WRIGHT, Phillip (1-11) 2f,
 1m
YOUNG, F. (10-409) 1m

Baltimore Free Black Households With Slaves 1830

ALLEN, William (5-224) 1m
ANDERSON, James (12-494)
 1m
 Samuel (1-16) 2f, 1m
ASKINS, Christ (9-344) 1m
BANKS, Benjamin (1-17) 1m
BARNETT, Stephen (1-17)
 1m
BLAKE, Vincent (4-189) 1m
BOSTON, John (11-424) 1m
BRADLEY, Samuel (11-435)
 1f, 2m
BULT, Cirus (2-76) 4f, 2m
BURK, Thomas (1-21) 1m
BUTLER, Basil (9-343) 1m
CAIN, Elenor (2-85) 1m
CALHOUN, Peter (12-492)
 1m
CARROL, Peter (12-479) 1m
CASTLE, William (4-173)
 1m
CLARK, James (2-84) 1m
 Nancy (9-344) 1m
COOPER, Benjamin (3-138)
 1m
 Thomas (3-113) 1m

CURTIS, Henrey (10-361) 1m
DAILEY, Richard (10-361)
 1m
DIXSON, Perry (3-153) 1f
ELLIOTT, David (2-78) 1m
FISHER, Levin (3-141) 3f
FLEETWOOD, Thomas (3-
 124) 1m
FULLER, Clem (12-518) 1m
GAGE, Dina (7-269) 1f
GAMBLE, Peter (12-486) 2f
GIBSON, Jacob (11-419) 1m
GILLES, Ann (10-361) 1m
GRASON, Elizabeth (4-180)
 1f
GRAY, David (11-405) 1f, 2m
GREEN, Peter (3-132) 1m
GRIFFIN, Alexander (11-406)
 3f, 3m
 Maria (9-326) 1m
HAINS, Thomas (12-512) 1m
HALL, Peter (10-393) 1m
HARRISS, Cecelia (3-136)
 1m
HARDEN, James (3-110) 1m
HENSON, Emory (5-240) 1m

HICKS, Emanuel (9-341) 1f
HOLLOWDAY, Ann (4-192)
  1m
 James (4-197) 2m
HOWARD, Edward (10-361)
  1m
 James (12-499) 1f, 1m
JOHNSON, Job (12-471) 2m
 Richard (12-477) 1m
 Robert (12-460) 2f, 3m
JOHNSTON, Charles (10-385)
  4m
 Gustus (11-437) 1m
 Nicholas (2-61) 1f, 1m
KILL, David (9-346) 1f
LEWIS, John (6-256) 3f, 2m
LIMAS, Brudame (10-367) 1f
McKAY, Robert (10-367) 1m
MILLER, Henrey (10-377)
  3m
MITCHEL, Ann E. (12-515)
  1f, 1m
NELSON, Sarah (3-133) 1m
NOAL, John (10-383) 1m
PARKER, James (12-474)
  2m
PHILLIPS, Charles (2-78) 3f,
  3m
PINKNEY, William (7-271)
  1m
PRESCO, James (4-189) 1m
PRIMROSE, George (12-523)
  1m
RIDGELEY, Pompey (11-
  401) 6m
RIDGLEY, Charlotte (3-131)
  1m
RIDGELY, Loyed (7-270) 1f,
  3m
ROBINSON, Christine (2-54)
  1m
 Sarah (7-269) 1f
 Zachariah (2-66) 1m
SCOTT, Charlotte (11-403)
  1m

SCOTT (continued)
 Margaret (9-340) 1m
SHERRICK, John F. (9-338)
  1f
SHIVERS, Widow (10-377) 1f
SIMS, Henry (1-16) 2f
SMALLWOOD, Richard (3-
  119) 1f, 1m
SMITH, Edward (10-370) 1m
 James (1-5) 1f
 Perry (3-153) 1m
 Perry (12-479) 1f
 Rebecca (3-132) 1m
SNOWDEN, Peter (12-465) 1f
SPRIGG, Margaret (7-270)
  1m
STEPHENS, Littleton (12-
  461) 1f
STEWARD, Stephen (12-515)
  2f
STRUPPING, Priscilla (4-
  182) 1m
TALBOT, Benjamin (2-50)
  1m
THOMSON, Lewis (9-339)
  1m
THOMAS, Seth (1-12) 1f
THOMPSON, Richard (1-16)
  3m
TOLE, Hannah (12-474) 1f
VICTOIRE, Mary A. (11-417)
  1f
WALLACE, Charles (3-107)
  1f
WEST, Charles (10-358) 3f,
  2m
WILLIAMS, Nathaniel (4-
  171) 1m
 Senah (11-438) 2f
WILSON, William (12-490)
  1m
YOUNG, Benjamin (10-393)
  1m

Baltimore Free Black Households With Slaves 1840

ADAMS, Stephen (8-62) 1f
 Williams (12-312) 1m
ANDERSON, James (6-271)
 2m
AUGUSTUS, Charles (8-40)
 1m
BADGER, Richard R. (11-
 198) 1m
BAINS, Joseph (1-9) 3f
BORES, Lewis (11-197) 1f
BRISER, Lewis (11-232) 3m
BROWN, Joseph (1-46) 1f
 Richard (12-272) 1m
BUTLER, James (8-40) 2f,
 2m
CAMPBELL, Edward (12-
 298) 1m
CARROLL, Cesar (12-298) 1f
CONTEE, Philip (8-67) 1m
CORNISH, Charles (8-64) 2m
COSSELL, Edward (12-256)
 3f, 2m
DAVIS, Fanny (5-249) 1m
DICKEY, James (11-198) 1m
DORSEY, Bateman (8-81) 1f
GOULD, Richard (12-289) 1m
GRACE, Adam (1-16) 1f
GROSS, Lenard (11-211) 1m
HARDY, Samuel (12-257) 1f
HARRIS, Eliza (8-46) 1m
 James (8-61) 1f
HICKS, Robert (2-81) 1m
HILL, Pipin (6-281) 1m
HITCH, Charles (8-39) 1m
HODGES, Samuel (12-257) 1f
JACKSON, Christopher (8-67)
 1m
JANNEY, Sarah (11-198) 1m
JOHNSON, Cassey (8-46) 2f
 David (8-69) 1m
 Jesse (12-272) 2f
 Julia Ann (8-90) 1m
JONES, James (9-118) 1m
 Thomas (11-197) 1m

KEILER, George (8-82) 2m
KREHAM, Smithson (11-199)
 1m
LEE, Hugh (9-116) 1m
MARSHALL, Wesley (12-
 252) 1m
MINGO, James (1-34) 1f
MITCHELL, William (8-69)
 1m
MOORE, Ann (11-198) 1f, 1m
NEWMAN, William H. (10-
 159) 1m
OLNEY, Peter (9-114) 1m
PEER, Lydia (6-262) 1m
PERRON, Jerry (11-199) 1m
POWELL, John (12-306) 1m
ROBINS, Stephen (8-91) 1m
ROBINSON, Thomas (2-93)
 1m
ROGERS, Thomas (11-197)
 1m
SANDERS, Charles (5-207)
 1m
SEROUXOR, Ellen (6-285)
 1m
SEWELL, Perry, (8-50) 1f,
 1m
SEWELL, Pollydore (8-44)
 1f
SMALL, Ben (11-231) 1m
SMITH, Kitty (3-115) 1f
 Samuel (7-20) 1f, 1m
STEWART, Robert (10-139)
 1m
 William (8-81) 1f
TAYLOR, Henry (5-247) 1m
THOMAS, Lloyd (2-78) 1m
 Richard (12-319) 2m
 William (11-235) 2f
TYLER, Isaac (12-276) 1m
WALLACE, Samuel (8-74)
 1m
WALTON, Charles (10-159)
 1f

WILLIAMS, Rachael (11–
  197) 1m
 William (8–69) 2f, 1m
WRIGHT, Mary (10–183) 1m

SLAVES BY NAME

An Index to Advertisements for Runaway Slaves
in the *Baltimore Sun* 1837–1864

Stored in the archival records of various Maryland institutions are the full names (and in many cases descriptions) of thousands upon thousands of slaves and former slaves.

Among the sources available to the researcher are ledger and account books, applications for certificates of freedom, deeds or wills of manumission, family Bibles, slave inventories, and a number of daily and weekly newspapers placing advertisements for runaways.

These records provide information that is valuable to the historian and genealogist alike.

The following is an index to advertisements for runaways placed in the *Baltimore Sun* from May 1837 through October of 1864. The list represents only those ads in which the full name of the slave was indicated.

The index is constructred as follows: The slaves last name, first name, middle initial, age, date of ad (in Parenthesis), page number and alias. The absence of any of the above information indicates its failure to appear in the original ad.

This list represents 1,342 individuals and their aliases (1,380 names). Of that number 1,174 (87%) were male and 168 (13%) were female. Of 1,342 slaves 1,107 were listed with their ages.

The top five categories by age and sex were:

#1 males	21–30	(489)	44.0%
#2 males	10–20	(326)	29.0%
#3 males	31–45	(124)	11.2%
#4 Females	10–20	(60)	5.4%
#5 Females	21–30	(52)	4.0%

Although the overwhelming number of ads represent singular escapes or small groups of two or three, there are occasions when large groups escape at one time.

There is no consistency to the placement of ads with regard to paging or heading, i.e., *personal, absconded, reward, runaway.*

ADAMS, James 16
(9/16/50)–2
Joseph (6/1/47)–4
Mary 22 (8/25/57)–3 alias
Molly Adams
Mary Jane 20 (11/5/45)–2
Molly 22 (8/25/57)–3 alias
Mary Adams
Moses 40 (4/27/48)–2
Moses (3/12/51)–2
Otho (5/28/49)–2
William 20 (1/29/42)–2
ADDISON, John William
Tyler 19 (9/12/60)–3
William 12 (7/13/46)–3
ALEXANDER, John 16
(5/29/41)–4
Maria 26 (5/29/41)–4
Robert 20 (8/15/55)–4
ALLEN, Davy (2/25/46)–2
Sidney 19 (7/12/38)–2
AMER, Henry 16 (10/14/47)–
4
ANDERSON, James
(6/7/56)–2
Jim 20 (10/28/50)–2 alias
Jim Enderson
Joshua 18 (1/6/53)–2
Peter (6/27/51)–2
Reuben 18 (6/25/56)–2
Wesley 25 (11/25/56)–4
AYRES, Henry 20 (5/21/55)–
2 alias Henry Wilson
BADGER, Richard 25
(10/24/62)–3
BAILEY, George 22
(7/28/59)–3 alias George
Donaldson

BAILEY (continued)
Henry 12 (8/22/48)–2
Josiah 28 (11/25/56)–4
William (11/25/56)–4
BAILY, Andrew 15
(6/11/46)–4
BAINES, Alexander 19
(8/12/64)–3
BAKER, George 26
(9/17/53)–2
James 23 (10/29/42)–4
Windsor 26 (6/10/46)–2
BANKS, Henry Roe 18
(10/29/53)–2
Jim (10/20/58)–3
John (3/28/50)–3
Lloyd (8/25/58)–3
Peter 25 (5/23/63)–3
Tilghman 21 (8/25/58)–3
BANTUM, Rainee 32
(11/25/62)–3
BARBER, Phill 13
(4/22/56)–2
BARNES, Bill 24 (8/8/40)–3
alias Bill Meads
David Lloyd 12 (7/17/51)–2
Mary Ann 27 (8/12/64)–3
Nancy 20 (6/9/48)–2
BARNETT, Nathaniel 30
(7/8/51)–4
BARRETT, Horace 32
(10/3/49)–2
BARTON, Charles 17
(11/12/59)–3
BARTON, John 22 (9/23/56)–
2
BASHIELL, Albert 18
(8/2/38)–2

18

BASSINI, Berry (9/1/43)-2
BATTLE, Perry (12/4/47)-4
BATTY, George 22
  (9/14/61)-3
 Sam 20 (9/14/61)-3
BATY, George 20 (9/16/62)-
 3
 Ned 30 (9/16/62)-3
BAYLEY, Henry 14
  (4/17/49)-2
BAYNARD, John Wesley 31
  (8/19/57)-3
BEALE, Joe 34 (3/26/55)-2
BEALL, Frank (1/17/57)-2
 Isaac 30 (10/10/50)-2
 John 18 (10/14/57)-3
 Ross 25 (10/14/57)-3
BEATTY, Ann Elizabeth 18
  (10/22/61)-3
BECKET, Henry 18
  (10/8/62)-3
BECKUS, Charles 14
  (10/5/39)-3
BELL, Bill 26 (4/19/60)-3
 Bob (4/3/60)-3
 Cornelia 42 (10/22/59)-3
 Jim 22 (7/1/56)-4
 Lewis 19 (7/8/53)-2
BELLE, Jim 25 (7/28/57)-3
BELT, Madison (5/20/47)-4
 Robert 25 (10/25/54)-4
BENLY, William 25
  (11/5/47)-4
BENNET, Duglass 25
  (11/2/40)-3
BENTLEY, Margaret 22
  (10/16/49)-2
BERRY, Gabriel 23
  (5/23/51)-4
 Jacob 21 (10/6/47)-2
BIAS, Omer 27 (4/11/57)-3
BILLINGSLEY, Thomas 21
  (8/27/51)-2
BIRK, Lorenzo 23 (1/3/45)-2
BLACKISTONE, Isaac 40
  (9/17/47)-2

BLACKWELL, Lewis 25
  (9/24/63)-3
BLAKE, John 30 (6/23/47)-4
 alias John Mainiard
BOARDLY, Harry 28
  (8/18/49)-2
 Jesse 40 (7/27/55)-2
 Stephen 15 (7/1/59)-3
BOARMAN, Matilda 32
  (5/31/49)-2
 Stephen 38 (5/31/49)-2
 Stephen Jr. 4 (5/31/49)-2
BOMAN, John 25 (8/30/48)-2
BOND, Beckey (6/26/39)-3
 Jim (9/9/51)-2
 Joe 25 (7/29/56)-4
BOONE, Robert (10/11/58)-3
BOOTS, Israel 20 (7/15/57)-
 3
BORDLEY, Ben 28
  (8/18/49)-2
 Rachel 30 (3/4/57)-3 alias
  Rachel Taylor
BOSTON, Moses 28
  (6/25/47)-2
 Robert (1/24/54)-2
BOWEN, Davy 22
  (12/23/58)-3
 Josiah 10 (2/26/51)-2
 Lloyd 28 (5/12/54)-2
BOWIE, Benjamin 14
  (7/21/52)-4
 Jack 21 (1/9/58)-3
 Thomas 27 (3/29/50)-2
BOWMAN, Levi 15
  (9/15/52)-4
BOWSER, Henry 17
  (1/5/53)-2
 Henry 21 (8/14/52)-4
 James 30 (10/29/42)-4
BOYD, Abram 22 (8/21/55)-4
BRADFORD, Henny
  (8/19/42)-2 alias Hen-
  rietta Johnson
BRANNUM, Ned 28
  (7/10/56)-2

BRASHERS, Jim 19
(12/18/61)-3
BRAWNER, Lewis 35
(8/13/44)-2
BRENT, Charles Hamilton 13
(6/2/52)-4
BRICE, Henry 18 (9/16/44)-2
BRICKHOUSE, Lewis 21
(12/16/61)-3
BRIGHTWELL, Thomas 50
(2/6/54)-2 alias Thomas
Bryson
BRISCOE, David 16
(10/19/58)-3
John (5/25/55)-2
BROADLY, John 30
(4/12/62)-3
BROGDEN, George 26
(2/14/62)-3
Tom 20 (8/11/45)-2
BROOKS, Abraham
(7/28/43)-4
Augustus 16 (11/4/61)-3
Ben 23 (7/22/62)-3
Henry 45 (11/21/55)-4
Jerry 35 (4/7/48)-2
Jim 18 (10/18/59)-3
Margaret 22 (9/3/42)-4
Ned 35 (9/3/42)-4
Sam 33 (10/1/49)-2
Samuel 18 (8/27/58)-3
Saulsbury 40 (3/30/55)-2
Thomas (4/13/60)-3
Washington (12/19/61)-3
BROOM, David 25
(11/16/58)-3
BROWN, Alexander 14
(8/3/40)-4
Beck (1/8/53)-4
Bill 23 (11/26/55)-2
Bill 40 (3/5/57)-4
Bill (5/31/60)-3
Bill 55 (3/16/63)-3
Charles 18 (9/9/54)-2
Charles 19 (4/24/58)-3
David 24 (12/9/48)-2

BROWN (continued)
Eliza (9/28/47)-2
Elizabeth 19 (10/6/62)-3
Frederick 17 (9/14/61)-3
George (8/25/57)-3 alias
Joseph Brown
Henry 30 (12/23/52)-4
Henry (1/3/56)-2
Isaac 19 (10/18/49)-2
Isaac 38 (3/5/57)-4
Jacob 26 (10/12/50)-2
Jesse 21 (6/8/50)-4
Joe (6/18/60)-3
John (6/30/41)-4
John 18 (8/31/63)-3
Joseph (8/25/57)-3 alias
George Brown and Nat But-
ler
Joshua 18 (8/9/49)-2
Lazarus 22 (10/14/56)-2
Liz 22 (10/7/59)-3
Lloyd 28 (6/14/42)-4
Lloyd 28 (4/12/61)-3
Nick 38 (9/28/47)-2
Oliver 10 (1/18/39)-2
Peter 15 (11/10/43)-2
Phil 18 (12/31/56)-2
Richard 28 (11/18/58)-3
Samuel C. 21 (1/4/50)-2
Simon 25 (7/17/44)-2
Stephen 20 (11/16/59)-3
William 20 (10/18/49)-2
BROWNING, Joshua 45
(4/18/48)-2
BRUTUS, James (6/30/52)-2
alias Brutus Crought
BRYAN, Aleck 35 (1/1/51)-4
BRYANT, Louisa 19
(2/20/61)-3
BRYSON, Thomas 50
(2/6/54)-2 alias Thomas
Brightwell
BUCHANAN, Thomas 17
(3/24/40)-2
BULL, Abraham 17 (3/4/46)-
2

BULLER, Edward 19
  (8/29/40)-2
BUMBERRY, Richard 16
  (10/24/42)-3
BUMPER, Samuel 25
  (2/13/50)-2
BURGERSON, Elias 13
  (6/7/55)-2
BURGESS, Charles 32
  (10/14/42)-3
 Washington 53 (11/23/50)-2
 William 23 (7/12/50)-2
BURKE, Edward 25 (4/9/53)-
  2
BUTLER, Ann 28 (5/31/41)-
  4
 Henry (7/30/46)-2
 Jim 21 (6/8/59)-3
 Jim 25 (5/22/52)-2
 John 25 (6/21/56)-4
 Mat (3/10/57)-3
 Milton 22 (1/23/62)-3
 Nat (8/25/57)-3 alias
   Joseph or George Brown
 Nelly (1/11/43)-3
 Richard 14 (12/30/63)-3
 Stephen 22 (6/8/57)-3
BYRD, Levin 35 (11/21/57)-
  3
CADDIS, James 50
  (6/11/49)-4
CAMEL, Jacob 27 (3/27/46)-
  2
 Jacob (12/3/50)-3
CAMILL, Lewis 32
  (8/13/40)-3
CAMMEL, John 35 (5/2/62)-
  3
CAMPBELL, Amos 35
  (8/12/64)-3
 William 40 (7/26/61)-3
CAMPER, William 14
  (4/24/40)-2
CANTER, Lila 50 (4/17/63)-
  3

CAREY, Polly 25 (8/24/44)-
  2
CARR, James 25 (9/23/52)-4
 Robert 30 (1/2/58)-3
CARRELL, Isaac 20
  (11/3/63)-3
CARROLL, Anthony
  (3/28/50)-3
 Annie 24 (2/27/64)-3
 Bill 45 (5/20/46)-4
 Harry (6/25/49)-2
 Henry 20 (10/6/52)-4
 Jim 25 (9/10/53)-2
 Levin (9/15/47)-2
CARTER, Bill 21 (1/28/62)-
  3
 Bill 24 (8/20/62)-3
 George (9/30/52)-2
 Henry 20 (4/2/49)-2
 Henry 30 (7/16/61)-3
 Jim 18 (10/25/59)-3
 Robert 22 (1/11/59)-3
 William 35 (7/2/51)-2
CASSEL, Jacob 21
  (7/29/40)-3 alias Jacob
  Castle
CASTLE, Amanda 22
  (6/25/64)-3
 Jacob 21 (7/29/40)-3 alias
  Jacob Cassel
CECIL, Charles 22
  (12/5/61)-3
CENEY, William 15
  (11/21/55)-4
CHAPMAN, Henry 24
  (8/13/44)-2
CHASE, Bill 15 (8/13/46)-2
 Daniel 35 (7/1/61)-3
 George (7/13/63)-3
 Henry 28 (10/29/42)-4
 John (4/13/55)-2
 Richard 24 (1/12/52)-2
 Shermont 46 (6/21/59)-3
 William (7/20/48)-2
CHESLEY, John 27
  (3/10/49)-2

CHESTER, Robert 18
  (5/4/47)-2
CHRISTMAS, William 37
  (9/18/45)-2
CLARK, Albert 23 (5/22/50)-
  4 alias Alfred Clark
  Alfred 23 (5/22/50)-4 alias
  Albert Clark
  Amos 20 (7/3/58)-3
  Caleb 20 (7/3/58)-3
  Daniel 25 (7/30/44)-2
  Ellen 17 (1/14/61)-3
CLARKE, Miranda 22
  (10/15/49)-2
CLAXON, Perry 24
  (11/17/58)-3
CLAY, John 13 (12/3/46)-4
COALEN, Henry 24
  (10/9/50)-2
  Sandy 21 (10/9/50)-2
COBERT, Sandy 21
  (10/14/47)-4
COGER, Andrew 38
  (5/14/45)-2
COLBERT, Richard 19
  (10/25/61)-3
COLE, Bill 57 (9/9/57)-3
  Charles 18 (11/5/47)-2
  Ellen 18 (10/28/54)-4
  George (3/6/41)-3
  Mack 16 (3/30/39)-4
  Philip 40 (9/17/44)-2
  Richard 25 (1/8/59)-3
COLLINS, Charles 15
  (2/26/39)-2
  Charles (4/12/50)-2
  Henry (4/12/50)-2
COMIGERS, Nathaniel 8
  (12/11/39)-2
COMPTON, Henry 55
  (7/2/51)-2
CONAWAY, Tom (9/2/58)-3
CONTEE, Basil 26
  (11/29/39)-3
  George 25 (11/14/48)-2
  Harry 40 (4/7/59)-3

CONTEE (continued)
  Isaac 24 (2/20/51)-4
COOK, Bob 26 (7/29/59)-3
  Daniel 25 (6/29/61)-3
  James (11/30/61)-3
  John 24 (6/13/44)-2
  Wesley 17 (9/28/52)-2
COOPER, Charles 15
  (8/12/39)-1
CORDON, Jerry (12/27/56)-2
CORNISH, Anthony 25
  (8/14/47)-2
  Frances 22 (11/25/62)-3
  Henry 14 (8/3/54)-2
  Jerry 18 (5/6/63)-3
  Ned 29 (6/29/42)-2
  Stephen W. 20 (2/3/83)-3
  Vince 28 (8/14/47)-2
CORTS, Thomas 19
  (9/21/60)-3
COTES, James A. J.
  (19/14/51)-2
COTTEREL, Harrison 25
  (11/30/40)-4
COUNCIL, Daniel 18
  (4/6/58)-3
COVINGTON, Barney 22
  (10/2/56)-2
COWARD, Ann 19 (7/9/41)-4
COX, John 22 (6/13/49)-2
COY, William 22
  (12/13/54)-2 alias Wil-
  liam McCoy
CRAIG, Henry 30 (6/12/50)-4
CRAWFORD, Anthony 19
  (9/2/61)-3
CREGGS, Julia 40 (2/16/49)-
  2 alias Julia Holland
CROMWELL, James 35
  (7/4/55)-2
CROUGHT, Brutus
  (6/30/52)-2 alias James
  Brutus
CROWN, Frank (2/28/52)-2
CROWNER, Henry 25
  (5/1/47)-4 alias Henry

22

CROWNER (continued)
 Tunks
 William 25 (9/26/48)-2
CULVAY, William
 (3/24/59)-3
CULVER, Peter (7/26/55)-2
 Vach 36 (8/25/48)-2
 William 23 (3/7/61)-3
 William 35 (8/8/60)-3
CURREY, Isaac 18 (9/8/48)-2
 Jack (1/2/46)-3
CURRY, Eliza 25 (8/22/48)-2
 Orlando 25 (12/31/62)-3
CUSTIS, David 16 (5/7/52)-
DABNEY, George 35
 (10/8/44)-2
DAILY, Elizabeth
 (10/27/47)-4
DAMAN, Jane 18 (4/6/59)-3
DARIDGE, Bateman 21
 (5/9/49)-2
DASHIELL, Louise 23
 (6/21/41)-2
DAVIDSON, Allen 28
 (8/25/58)-3
 Bob 20 (8/25/58)-3
 Charles 15 (8/25/58)-3
 Horace 18 (8/25/58)-3
 Perry 20 (8/25/58)-3
 Priscilla 30 (8/25/58)-3
DAVIS, John 20 (8/26/45)-2
 Henry 14 (11/20/57)-3
 Tom 25 (4/27/47)-4
DEAN, Dennis 27 (6/30/56)-2
DENT, Camilla 24
 (3/10/42)-2
 Jim 28 (3/5/61)-3
 John 25 (2/10/49)-2
DICKERSON, Bill 28
 (9/29/53)-2
 John 30 (10/13/54)-2
DIGGES, Dick 28 (12/23/58)-3

DIGGES (continued)
 Thomas 30 (5/26/53)-2
DIGGS, James (8/24/44)-2
 Jim 40 (8/3/61)-3
 John 20 (4/2/40)-2
 John H. (5/28/47)-4
DIKES, William 10
 (5/24/50)-2
DINSEY, Frank 20
 (11/25/40)-3
DIXON, Ben 30 (9/16/41)-4
 Eliza (10/24/45)-2
 Henry 25 (5/11/60)-3
 Jim (8/28/40)-2
 Phil 35 (9/16/41)-4
 Washington 35 (8/27/60)-3
DOCKETT, Nathan 21
 (9/2/62)-3
DODDS, Mark (7/28/59)-3
DIDSON, Emanuel 18
 (7/28/59)-3
DODSON, John 21 (4/12/62)-3
 Thomas 13 (2/2/63)-3
 William 18 (2/2/63-3
DOGAN, Fred 21 (12/21/61)-3
DOLBY, Jim 30 (9/2/58)-3
DONALDSON, George 22
 (7/28/59)-3 alias George
 Bailey
DORSEY, Albert 18
 (12/31/61)-3
 Alfred 18 (6/4/50)-2
 Ben 20 (8/14/50)-2
 Caroline 45 (8/12/64)-3
 Celus 23 (12/22/48)-2
 Elizabeth 15 (12/24/57)-3
 Isaac 15 (12/9/51)-2
 John 30 (3/17/59)-3
 Lewis (12/13/50)-2
 Rachel 35 (4/22/63)-3 alias
 Rachel Taylor
 Robert 22 (3/15/56)-2
DOTSON, Isaac 19
 (9/24/56)-2

23

DOTTON, Tom 18 (8/29/39)-1

DOUGLAS, Ned 19 (9/3/55)-2

William 10 (7/12/58)-3

DOUGLASS, Frank 18 (10/29/42)-4

DOWNS, Joe 19 (3/30/59)-3

Samuel 25 (5/20/41)-3

DUCKET, Nathaniel 26 (3/17/56)-2

DUCKETT, Frank 30 (10/13/52)-4

DUKE, Henry 22 (7/27/49)-2

DUPEN, Jake 30 (8/19/56)-2

DUPIN, George Henry 30 (2/3/48)-4

DUVALL, Tobias 25 (5/11/43)-2

DYSON, Henry 16 (4/20/61)-3

EDELIN, Harry 50 (12/12/57)-3

EDINSEN, Toby 21 (11/12/49)-2

EMERSON, Toby 20 (9/18/49)-2

EDWARDS, Abram 26 (1/2/62)-3

David 23 (5/29/60)-3

Lewis 24 (7/3/58)-3

Sam 17 (2/4/45)-2

EGGLESTON, Nat 15 (4/18/62)-3

ELLIS, Joseph 25 (1/7/51)-2

EMORY, Aleck (3/20/62)-3

Dennis (3/20/62)-3

John (3/20/62)-3

ENDERSON, Jim 20 (10/28/50)-2 alias Jim Anderson

ENICE, Thomas 16 (9/14/63)-3

ENIS, Loyd (10/7/51)-2

ENNIS, Lloyd 20 (8/1/59)-3

Rachel Ann (4/3/54)-3

ESKRIDEGE, Daniel 25 (12/10/47)-2

EUSTACE, Lewis 19 (3/31/52)-4

EVANS, John Wesley 33 (12/31/57)-3

EYLE, John 19 (3/31/46)-2

EYLINT, Elizabeth 13 (8/25/41)-2

FAIRCHILD, Andrew 21 (4/2/57)-3

FAX, Charles 40 (8/25/58)-3

Ned (8/25/58)-3

Richard 40 (8/25/58)-3

FENICK, John 21 (9/17/47)-2

FERGUSON, David 33 (10/2/49)-2

FIELDS, James H. 14 (6/13/45)-2

Lucy Ann (11/30/47)-2

FISHER, Bob 37 (12/30/53)-2

Charlotte 12 (12/29/59)-3

Charlotte (10/28/63)-3

George Washington (11/4/62)-3

Jane 20 (10/28/63)-3

Lizzie 20 (10/28/63)-3

William 20 (10/28/63)-3

FLETCHER, John 17 (5/11/40)-2

John 18 (6/22/57)-3

FOLKS, Arnold (10/1/46)-4 alias Arnold E. Jones

FORD, George 20 (1/28/62)-3

Enoch 25 (8/31/61)-3

George 20 (5/29/61)-3

Levi 20 (12/10/53)-2

FOREMAN, John 12 (7/17/47)-2

John 17 (1/6/52)-2

FOSTER, Joseph 18 (9/8/52)-2

24

FOUSTER, Tom 19
    (7/16/51)-2
FOWLER, Fred 26
    (5/11/58)-3
FOX, Joseph 18 (10/6/47)-2
FRANCIS, John 16
    (7/13/57)-3
 Lewis, 40 (6/5/46)-4
FRANKLIN, Alley 25
    (9/14/49)-2
 George 20 (10/9/48)-2
 Phill 26 (1/24/62)-3
FREDERICK, William 35
    (5/27/46)-3
FREELAND, Bill 25
    (6/15/42)-2
 Jacob 63 (2/13/63)-3
 Jake 13 (9/14/59)-3
FRENY, John 18 (6/8/58)-3
FRISBY, Mary Jane
    (9/26/46)-3
FULLER, Jem (9/18/61)-3
GALLOWAY, Isaac
    (1/10/60)-3
 Joe 17 (7/21/57)-3
 Joe 35 (9/4/58)-3
 John 33 (5/28/39)-1
GAMBRILL, Alonzo 24
    (9/28/61)-3
GANTT, Andrew 32
    (1/22/48)-4
 Anthony 29 (4/19/50)-4
 Anthony 26 (9/7/50)-2
 Anthony 35 (1/12/55)-3
 John 34 (7/8/41)-4
 William 35 (4/22/63)-3
GARRET, Basil 18 (8/8/48)-
    2
GARRETT, Jim (3/6/44)-2
 Saul 21 (10/10/43)-2
 William 20 (1/2/54)-2
GARRISON, John 14
    (8/3/38)-3
 John 18 (10/29/42)-4 alias
    John Lloyd

GASKINS, Henry 40
    (6/25/49)-2
GASSAWAY, Caroline
    (9/30/58)-3
 Charles 23 (8/18/49)-2
 Henry 12 (8/18/49)-2
 Henry 40 (8/18/49)-2
 William 22 (12/24/49)-2
GASUA, George 25
    (1/18/60)-3
GATES, Henry 22 (7/22/51)-
    4
GAULT, William 25
    (2/3/45)-2
GENERALS, Elizabeth 21
    (10/27/63)-3
 William 22 (11/9/61)-3
GEORGE, John (8/25/58)-3
GIBSON, Alexander 21
    (4/11/39)-1
 Caroline 32 (8/15/48)-2
 Jacob 24 (11/22/44)-4
 John 22 (10/17/54)-2
 William 28 (11/22/44)-4
GIDDINGS, Charles 25
    (10/8/57)-3 alias Charles
    Matthews
GILES, Alec (5/15/49)-2
 David 15 (10/28/47)-4
 Hager (10/28/47)-4
GINAREAU, Alexander 22
    (2/22/53)-2
GINERALS, Isaac 23
    (5/23/50)-2
 Singleton 27 (5/23/50)-2
GINN, Maria 12 (12/10/40)-3
GODFREY, John 21
    (8/13/58)-3
GOOSEBERRY, Hannah 40
    (6/6/44)-2
 Judea 18 (6/6/44)-2
 Stephen 17 (6/6/44)-2
GORDON, Caroline 26
    (4/19/44)-4
 Charles 8 (4/19/44)-4

GORDON (continued)
Levi 21 (4/20/63)-3
Lucretia 18 (3/7/44)-2
Nancy 55 (4/19/44)-4
GORRELL, William
(6/17/57)-3
GOTT, Gassaway (4/6/48)-2
GOUGH, Alfred 26 (6/16/57)-3
Emanuel 25 (3/22/55)-2
Hamlet 28 (11/7/53)-2
Henry 21 (5/28/55)-2
GRAHAM, George 22
(11/6/55)-4
GRANDISON, Charles 11
(4/2/60)-3
GRANT, Strather 30
(1/26/58)-3
GRAVES, John Francis
(11/20/61)-3
GRAY, Charles 25 (2/6/54)-2
Eliza (3/5/63)-3
Jack 20 (6/20/60)-3 alias
John Gray
John 20 (6/20/60)-3 alias
Jack Gray
Levi 28 (8/27/61)-3
Redden 16 (2/2/63)-3
Robert 14 (10/4/52)-2
Tom 35 (11/5/59)-3
GRAYSON, John 26
(4/13/55)-2
GREEN, Alex 45 (6/17/47)-2
David (9/6/39)-2
David 13 (1/21/40)-1
David 24 (4/27/50)-2
David 27 (6/12/57)-3
Davy 27 (9/28/55)-4
George 29 (6/23/55)-2
Harry 36 (9/9/42)-2
Harry 36 (9/30/62)-3
Hazel 20 (6/9/47)-2
John Jr. 22 (1/5/53)-4
John Alfred (7/13/61)-3
Lear 18 (5/26/57)-3
Lucy 24 (12/27/49)-2

GREEN (continued)
Mary Ann 12 (5/17/47)-4
Miah 20 (9/3/59)-3
Richard 24 (6/23/55)-2
Robert 18 (5/13/53)-2
Sandy 22 (5/21/56)-2
Sarah 32 (9/20/44)-2
William 23 (2/20/60)-3
GRIFFIN, Metus 24
(10/1/50)-2
GRIMSHAW, Elizabeth G. 25
(4/30/46)-2
William 45 (4/30/46)-2
GROCE, Jim 55 (7/25/56)-2
GROSS, Charles 23 (5/3/52)-2
Isaac 21 (5/28/59)-3
Peter 33 (8/19/58)-3
Robert 18 (4/2/56)-2
Sam 38 (8/19/58)-3
GUSTIS, Adam (10/1/61)-3
HALE, Henry 26 (5/13/59)-3
HALL, Charles 25 (3/26/56)-2
John (8/3/49)-2
John (6/5/57)-3
John (2/27/60)-3
Lotte 18 (3/3/41)-3
Moses 25 (3/22/52)-2
Perry (8/2/52)-4
HAMILTON, Alexander 21
(2/10/83)-3
George 30 (6/24/46)-2
John 26 (8/12/46)-2
HAMMON, Otho 25 (6/9/46)-4
HAMMOND, Henry 29
(11/26/40)-3
Henson 16 (10/9/62)-3
Isaac 26 (5/27/42)-3
Margaret 22 (10/9/62)-3
HANDY, Washington 35
(6/21/41)-2
HANSON, Bill 24 (8/25/58)-3
James 30 (1/3/52)-2
Sam 25 (9/28/57)-3

HANSON (continued)
Wat 23 (10/15/39)-2
William 21 (9/7/47)-2
HARDEN, Charles
(10/30/57)-3
HARDING, Alexander
(1/26/53)-2
HARDY, Benjamin Marshall
26 (10/15/49)-2
Lewis 21 (4/8/58)-3
HARKNESS, John 30
(10/12/58)-3
HARMOND, Caeser 40
(10/2/62)-3
HARRIS, Abraham (4/9/51)-2
Anthony 20 (8/16/60)-3
Ben 35 (12/23/58)-3
Bill 26 (1/7/45)-2
Charles 15 (10/28/56)-2
Edmond 45 (9/5/57)-3
Frances Ann 18 (10/27/48)-
2
George (6/25/40)-2
George 22 (4/20/63)-3
Henry (4/27/60)-3
James 19 (1/1/42)-4
John 15 (5/31/55)-2
Nace 21 (12/30/53)-2
Samuel 56 (9/2/61)-3
Solomon 19 (2/2/64)-3
Theodore 20 (5/28/59)-3
HARRISON, Dennis Lowe 27
(5/19/57)-3
Edmund 25 (1/16/62)-3
Sandy 18 (7/25/42)-3
Thomas James 11
(1/20/55)-4
HARROD, Jackson
(10/19/61)-3
Len 31 (8/28/56)-4
Martha 19 (12/8/62)-3
HART, James 20 (7/26/50)-2
Peter 25 (6/11/63)-3
HARVEY, Nace 30
(6/14/41)-4

HARWOOD, Jim 26
(6/28/52)-2
HASON, Emily 28
(11/22/60)-3
HAWKINS, George 24
(4/3/49)-2
George 30 (1/4/51)-2
George 16 (3/17/53)-2
Hanson 25 (5/25/50)-2
Harry 24 (1/1/63)-3
Henry (7/6/42)-3
John (1/23/45)-2
Nace (7/19/58)-3
Sandy 29 (8/11/55)-2
Tom (1/1/56)-2
HAYES, Washington 27
(5/26/42)-3
HAYMAN, Absalom 20
(2/8/51)-2 alias Henry
Hayman
Henry 20 (2/8/51)-2 alias
Absalom Hayman
HAYS, Jack 25 (7/8/47)-2
HAYWARD, William Henry
19 (4/8/40)-2
Henry (12/31/61)-3
HAYWOOD, Bill 23
(4/27/50)-2
HELMS, Andrew (12/1/41)-3
HEMSLEY, Levi 14
(3/18/58)-3 alias Ned
Hemsley
Ned 14 (3/18/58)-3 alias
Levi Hemsley
HENDERSON, Oscar 20
(9/16/57)-3
HENRY, Charles 22
(4/8/46)-4
Dennis 28 (6/5/46)-4
Ely (10/16/55)-2
James 30 (7/26/56)-2
John 12 (3/27/61)-3
John 42 (7/5/58)-3
Patrick 20 (8/31/60)-3
William 20 (9/19/54)-2

27

HENSON, James 30
(9/8/57)-3
Jim 32 (6/1/60)-3
Sam 25 (9/9/57)-3
Andrew 18 (5/27/46)-3
Bob 15 (9/28/47)-2
George 25 (5/27/46)-3
Jacob 28 (9/19/60)-3
Lloyd 20 (5/27/46)-3
Thomas 30 (5/27/46)-3
HERDEN, Henry 36 (9/2/61)-
3
HERROD, Benjamin 40
(11/14/57)-3
HILL, Eliza 15 (7/26/64)-3
Lloyd 18 (8/31/63)-3
Martha 15 (8/4/62)-3
HILLEARY, Perry 18
(9/24/53)-2 alias Perry
Ridgely
HILTON, Harriet (4/20/60)-3
Henry 19 (12/3/45)-3
HOGE, Nase 16 (5/25/57)-3
HOLADY, Howard (9/22/49)-
2
HOLLAND, Bill 18
(5/22/54)-
Julia 40 (2/16/49)-2 alias
Julia Creggs
Tom 30 (9/23/62)-3
William 22 (4/9/61)-3
HOLLIDAY, Bill 12
(4/28/46)-4
George 16 (8/29/48)-2
Henry 26 (9/30/42)-4
HOLLINGSHEAD, George 23
(11/5/47)-4
HOOPER, Hopewell
(1/23/57)-2
John 19 (7/2/42)-3
HOPEWELL, Alexius 24
(10/15/56)-2
HOPKINS, Liddy 11
(9/10/40)-2
HOPLEY, Chance 35
(5/22/48)-2

HORNER, Josh 20 (5/10/61)-
3
HOWARD, Alleck 35
(7/23/62)-3
John 23 (4/16/39)-2
Washington 18 (2/25/46)-2
HUBBARD, John (2/27/61)-3
Robert 17 (3/11/57)-3
HUGHES, Jinn (10/15/39)-2
HUGHSON, Tom 24
(12/24/47)-4
Tom 28 (1/4/48)-4
HUMPHREYS, Humphrey 18
(8/6/46)-2
HUNTER, James 27
(9/17/50)-2
William (12/12/61)-3
HUSE, Jin 30 (6/19/40)-2
HUTCHINSON, Jim
(5/31/47)-2 alias Jim
Johnson
HUTTON, Bill 45 (4/25/57)-
3
HYAS, Peter 25 (5/15/49)-2
William 30 (5/15/49)-2
HYNSON, Peggy 24
(3/31/41)-4
IJAM, Phill 27 (8/21/55)-2
ISAACKS, Joshua 26
(6/5/44)-4 alias Tom
Walker
ISAACS, Chance 31
(9/14/39)-3
Jack 23 (9/15/52)-4
Joshua 23 (10/4/41)-3
JACKSON, Arnold 20
(4/9/40)-2
Charles (5/27/57)-3
Ellen 22 (10/20/46)-3
Henry 18 (9/18/61)-3
Henry 23 (6/21/41)-2
Henry 30 (3/17/53)-2
Isaac (1/27/58)-3
Nackey (10/6/49)-2
Oliver 19 (5/15/57)-3
Randolph 18 (7/6/53)-2

JACKSON (continued)
Randolph 22 (8/16/55)-2
Samuel 18 (11/1/51)-2
Samuel 18 (11/23/61)-3
Thomas 30 (12/9/48)-2
William 18 (6/26/61)-3
JAMERSON, Abraham 21
    (8/8/45)-2
JAMES, Betsy (9/12/62)-3
Hannibal 23 (6/8//58)-3
James 27 (6/8/58)-3
JANE, Mary 19 (10/15/53)-4
JANEY, John 22 (8/19/58)-3
JEFFERSON, Thomas 24
    (1/13/43)-3
JENEY, William 15
    (11/20/55)-2
JENIFER, John 28 (9/2/62)-
3
Prince 17 (9/2/62)-3
JENKINS, Andy 28
    (12/11/56)-2 alias Handy
    Jenkins
Bill 21 (11/2/61)-3
Handy 28 (12/11/56)-2 alias
    Andy Jenkins
Jane 18 (3/22/41)-4
JENNIFER, George 25
    (9/2/62)-3
JENRELS, John 14 (2/8/62)-
3
JETT, Richard 21 (5/28/41)-
4
JILES, George 24
    (12/21/48)-4
JOHNS, Ann Louisa 18
    (1/4/49)-2
Joe 15 (5/6/63)-3
JOHNSON, Bill 15 (11/4/5)
Caroline 33 (7/28/42)-3
Casander 13 (9/20/49)-2
Charles (9/21/60)-3
Charles 19 (5/9/62)-3
Charles 31 (4/8/58)-3
Charlotte 19 (9/7/44)-4
Dick 18 (8/3/44)-2

JOHNSON (continued)
Dick (12/25/50)-4
Dick 18 (2/20/57)-4
Frederick (8/25/58)-3
George 35 (10/2/49)-2
George 35 (8/31/55)-2
Henry 25 (10/2/49)-2
Henrietta (8/19/42)-2 alias
    Henny Bradford
Henry 10 (12/29/40)-3
Henry 19 (6/8/57)-3
Horace (4/3/50)-2
Jacob 26 (11/1/53)-2
Jake 24 (1/21/58)-3
James 23 (10/2/49)-2
Jesse 26 (1/28/46)-2
Jim 17 (5/31/47)-2 alias
    Jim Hutchinson
Jim 27 (10/25/47)-2
Joe 27 (1/21/58)-3
John 10 (12/18/51)-2
John 18 (3/19/42)-4
John 21 (4/22/58)-3
John Nelson 24 (3/6/62)-3
John R. (1/30/52)-2
John Thomas (7/31/49)-2
Johns (3/22/52)-2
Levi (5/18/64)-3
Laura 16 (6/29/60)-3
Lewis 28 (4/3/49)-2
Louis 30 (1/4/51)-2
Major 33 (3/14/54)-2
Margaret (9/22/63)-3
Mary Elizabeth 15 (8/8/60)-
3
Nathaniel (9/28/48)-2
Nicholas 22 (1/18/59)-3
Oliver 17 (10/26/52)-4
Richard 20 (5/11/39)-3
Richard 30 (3/31/45)-2
Robert (7/29/63)-3
Ruth 18 (9/18/47)-3
Samuel 21 (12/10/46)-2
Samuel 29 (6/3/48)-2
Samuel 33 (6/29/57)-3
Talbott 35 (8/19/58)-3

JOHNSON (continued)
Tilghman 40 (4/30/59)-3
Tom 13 (6/4/50)-2 alias
Felix Reed
Tom 23 (5/10/56)-2
Wesley (5/2/60)-3
William (12/18/55)-2 alias
Black Ball
William 30 (8/2/45)-2
William H. (3/23/60)-3
William Henry 18
(6/25/49)-2
William Henry 15
(11/20/54)-4
JOHNSTON, George 25
(9/3/57)-3
William 17 (3/7/57)-4 alias
Black Ball (see William
Johnson)
JOICK, Edwards 35
(10/31/57)-3
JOLLY, Henry 16 (9/11/52)-
2
JONES, Abraham (4/18/56)-4
Abram (11/22/54)-4
Arnold E. (10/1/46)-4 alias
Arnold Folks
Caroline 15 (5/20/47)-4
Dansey 22 (10/7/51)-4
Davy 15 (3/31/46)-2
Felix 34 (7/10/43)-4
Hebrietta 24 (8/14/62)-3
Henry 25 (3/30/53)-4
Henry 34 (10/12/61)-3
Jacob 25 (9/23/61)-3
James (10/27/56)-2
John 10 (1/14/43)-2
John 40 (10/10/44)-2
John 23 (12/8/55)-2
John I. 13 (5/2/63)-3
Madison 20 (9/2/61)-3
Margaret 15 (1/6/62)-3
Martha 15 (11/21/61)-3
Samuel 21 (7/4/55)-2
Talbot 23 (7/4/55)-2
Thomas 24 (11/1/61)-3

JONES (continued)
William 15 (1/12/42)-3
William (1/1/49)-2
KANE, Alfred 30 (11/30/59)-
3
KELLY, David 17 (5/18/61)-
3
Henson 25 (5/12/60)-3
Nace 17 (10/8/51)-2
Oliver 20 (8/22/48)-2
Remus (5/27/42)-3
KELSON, Isaac 28
(10/29/50)-2
KEMP, Henry 30 (10/6/53)-3
KENNARD, Henry (1/25/39)-
2
KENNIARD, Eveline 19
(11/15/43)-4
KENT, John (9/2/58)-3
KERCHNER, John Adam 17
(9/29/57)-3
KETTLE, John 21 (4/11/60)-
3
KEYER, Bill 19 (7/6/42)-3
KING, Jane 18 (2/18/50)-2
John 21 (9/13/55)-2
William H. 18 (4/15/52)-2
KITELY, Sam 35 (3/8/53)-2
LANCASTER, George 50
(11/14/60)-3
LANE, Bill 25 (12/8/62)-3
LARKIN, Henry (9/23/62)-3
LARKINS, David 23
(4/18/62)-3
LAWRENCE, John 40
(9/17/56)-2
William 12 (10/1/53)-2
LAWRY, Mely 18
(11/28)42)-4
LEE, Aaron 22 (2/12/53)-2
Ben 17 (6/29/61)-3
Columbus 23 (2/7/59)-3
Jonathan 23 (4/8/39)-3
LEEMS, Tom (9/18/61)-3
LENN, Frank 60 (6/26/58)-3
LEWIS, Caroline (9/11/55)-2

LEWIS (continued)
Jarvis 38 (4/26/45)-2
Jim 17 (6/20/42)-4
Major 28 (8/26/45)-2
Thomas (9/11/55)-2
LIMPEN, Isaac 21 (9/2/61)-3
LINGER, John 22
  (11/14/48)-2
LINGRAM, Abram 14
  (2/11/52)-2
LLOYD, John 18 (10/29/42)-4 alias John Garrison
LOCKS, Samuel (9/9/51)-2
LOOGOOD, Ann 16
  (1/24/62)-3
LORMAN, Kitty 24
  (10/28/40)-3
LOWE, Dennis 24 (9/9/54)-2
MACKALL, David 21
  (10/20/42)-3
 William 24 (7/9/47)-2
MACKAY, Jane 26
  (5/25/63)-3
 Mary Adeline 9 months
  (5/25/63)-3 (escaped with mother..Jane)
MADEN, Tom 21 (10/19/54)-4
MADISON, James 14
  (8/14/41)-4
MAGOINS, Dennis (1/15/62)-3
MAINIARD, John 30
  (6/23/47)-4 alias John Blake
MANYEL, Dixon Silas
  (6/17/57)-3
MARBURY, John 30
  (5/11/60)-3
MARRIOT, Josh (11/10/63)-3
MASON, Austin (11/10/62)-3
 James 19 (11/18/39)-2
 William Annanias 18
  (7/2/62)-3

MASTIN, Charles 30
  (8/13/44)-2
MATHEWS, George 25
  (5/15/50)-2
MATTHEWS, Tom 25
  (3/27/56)-2
 Abe 47 (9/26/62)-3
 Betty 18 (10/31/61)-3
 Bill 20 (5/10/61)-3
 Charles 25 (10/8/57)-3 alias
  Charles Giddings
 Dennis 25 (5/16/60)-3
 Peter 27 (7/27/42)-3
MATTOX, Eby 21 (2/24/47)-2
MAYNARD, Edward
  (8/20/50)-2
 Jim 25 (9/7/59)-3
McCOY, William 22
  (12/13/54)-2 alias William Coy
McGEE, Minerva 20
  (5/5/58)-3
McGOWANS, Eliza 30
  (11/3/58)-3
McLEAN, Toby 12 (7/7/55)-2
MEADS, Bill 24 (8/8/40)-3
  alias Bill Barnes
MIDDLETON, Ann 35
  (9/8/43)-2
MILBURN, John 21
  (2/21/59)-3
MILES, Peter 21 (8/6/60)-3
 William 18 (10/1/46)-4
MILLER, Garrison 45
  (9/9/62)-3
 Hanson 22 (10/29/51)-2
 Mary (6/22/57)-3
MILLIGAN, Elijah
  (12/29/52)-4
MILLS, Alex 22 (7/15/63)-3
 William (8/23/53)-2
MINOR, James 26 (6/6/39)-3
 Sam 21 (6/6/39)-3
MONDAY, Allen (5/31/42)-3

MONDAY (continued)
    alias Allen Snowden
MONROE, George 19
    (1/7/51)-2
  Joe 25 (9/3/58)-3
MONTGOMERY, Augustus 17
    (4/21/41)-4
  Jess 30 (5/24/47)-2
MOODY, Charles 19
    (12/18/61)-3
MOOR, Melchior (6/26/56)-2
MOORE, Alexander 20
    (9/21/48)-2
  Alexander 28 (11/13/44)-2
  Charlotte 22 (7/25/42)-3
    alias Mary Moore
  Fanny (1/13/64)-3
  J. 19 (8/30/47)-2
  Mary 22 (7/25/42)-3 alias
    Charlotte Moore
  William Andrew 27
    (10/6/63)-3
MORGAN, Edward 21
    (6/8/57)-3
MORRIS, Clara 23 (9/22/63)-
    3
MORSELL, Henry 45
    (4/25/57)-3
MURDOCK, Green (9/27/56)-
    2
MURPHY, John 21 (9/2/50)-
    4
MURRAY, Caleb 23
    (5/6/63)-3
  Ellen 11 (8/1/42)-3
  George 21 (5/6/63)-3
  Henry 35 (4/21/59)-3
  Henry (11/20/61)-3
  Jacob 25 (10/18/48)-2
  Jacob 31 (3/19/51)-2
  Lemuel (11/4/62)-3
  Moses 18 (1/6/63)-3
  Peter 23 (10/21/61)-3
  William 24 (3/18/62)-3
  Henry 30 (4/16/51)-2

MURREY, Samuel 21
    (9/3/55)-2
MURRY, Ellen 10 (9/18/40)-
    2
MYERS, Adam 25 (8/12/61)-
    3
  Alexander 17 (1/14/54)-2
  Isaac 18 (7/30/52)-2
MYRES, Independent 30
    (11/11/58)-3
NACE, Charloty 35
    (10/2/49)-2
NAILOR, Ben 27 (9/22/49)-2
  Jack 50 (7/3/44)-4 alias
    John Nailor
  John 50 (7/3/44)-4 alias
    Jack Nailor
NASH, Charles (6/24/57)-3
NAYLOR, Sam (4/14/59)-3
NEAL, George 17 (9/3/53)-2
  Martha 14 (4/20/57)-3
  Thomas 20 (7/21/57)-3
NELSON, Isaac 18
    (9/21/60)-3
NEWELL, James Francis 19
    (6/25/56)-2
NICHOLS, George 19
    (7/1/59)-3
NICHOLSON, Bell 17
    (9/14/48)-2
  George 18 (10/19/58)-3
NORTON, Charles 21
    (1/15/59)-3
NOWLAND, Ned 20
    (8/27/51)-2
OBLESE, Dick (7/24/49)-2
ODEN, Charles 22 (3/23/47)-
    2
  Charles 25 (6/18/60)-3
  Charles 40 (5/6/47)-2
OFFLEY, George 25
    (9/29/58)-3
OGLE, Charles 22 (1/23/62)-
    3
  Joshua 27 (8/8/44)-2

OGLE (continued)
Joshua 30 (5/23/50)-2
Massam 20 (1/3/53)-4
Tom (6/13/62)-3
OLIVA, Charlotte 15
(2/1/62)-3
OLIVER, Henry 14
(6/26/52)-2
OLLNA, Milly 20 (9/14/43)-2
ORMES, Jim 24 (6/23/45)-2
OSBORNE, Dick 16 (4/3/41)-3
Lunnon 25 (11/25/54)-2
OSLE, Masson 21
(12/23/52)-4
OWENS, James Henry 21
(2/10/44)-3
William 19 (8/25/41)-2
OWINGS, Charity 25
(4/5/44/)-4
OXFORD, William 22
(4/12/60)-3
PACK, John 18 (9/1/48)-2
Nace (11/12/61)-3
PAINE, Daniel 25 (8/13/44)-2
Lawrence 29 (10/24/42)-3
PANE, Rufus 25 (8/6/62)-3
PARDY, Tom 22 (8/14/48)-2
PARKER, George (8/3/49)-2
Jacob 24 (9/7/58)-3
Jim 25 (4/25/57)-3
Joseph 20 (3/18/59)-3
Leah 3 (5/10/48)-3
Milly 26 (5/10/48)-3
Richard 23 (9/2/50)-2
Sarah 20 (3/2/54)-2
PARKS, Alfred (8/8/55)-2
Jack 40 (9/16/41)-4
William 25 (8/26/46)-3
PATTERSON, George 20
(1/4/45)-2
Robert 46 (1/2/56)-2
PAYMAN, William 22
(5/23/51)-4

PAYNE, Oscar 30 (7/19/58)-3
PEACH, Henry 38 (9/17/58)-3
William Jr. 20 (9/4/45)-2
PEAL, Isaac 23 (10/20/45)-3
PECK, Lewis 40 (5/30/60)-3
Tom (8/7/54)-2
PENINGTON, Peter 25
(11/25/56)-4
PENNINGTON, Jane 20
(5/27/54)-4
PEOMAN, Robert 21
(6/14/54)-4
PERRY, James 21
(8/20/47)-4
PHILIPS, Henry 20
(3/11/59)-3
Henry 26 (8/30/51)-2
Rosetta (3/20/57)-3
PHILLIPS, Charles 30
(10/18/51)-2
Moses 26 (10/18/51)-2
PIE, Leary 25 (6/1/57)-3
PINKNEY, David 19
(3/5/63)-3
Eliza 35 (11/2/49)-2
Henry 27 (3/5/63)-3
Mary Ann (8/21/60)-3
PLATE, George 58
(8/27/55)-2
PLATHEY, Lloyd 20
(9/18/51)-2
PORTER, Phil (5/31/64)-3
William Lewis 10
(2/24/57)-3
POSEY, George (8/20/51)-2
POTTS, William Wesley 24
(12/6/50)-4
POWELL, Elick 29
(10/28/47)-4
POWELS, Tony (4/25/62)-3
PRATT, Rebecca 16
(11/5/59)-3
PRETTYMAN, George 21
(5/29/58)-3

PRICE, William 35
(10/28/61)-3
PROUT, Abraham 22
(9/13/44)-4
PUGH, George 10
(10/14/61)-3
PURNAN, lewis 21
(8/18/51)-4
QUEEN, Henrietta 30
(4/26/48)-2
 Henry 28 (3/2/59)-3
 John 19 (9/28/50)-2
 William 25 (3/6/58)-3
RADLEY, Anthony
(8/25/57)-3
RAINS, Evelina (10/20/46)-3
RAYMAN, William 23
(10/7/51)-2
REED, Felix 13 (6/4/50)-2
 alias Tom Johnson
 Henry 18 (4/17/58)-3
 Jeremiah (7/7/40)-3
 Richard 12 (8/10/52)-4
REESE, Mary Jane 11
(3/6/45)-2
REEVES, Jim 22 (5/15/57)-3
RESIN, Bill 15 (11/11/50)-2
RHODES, Mary Ann
(12/4/46)-4
 Remus 25 (2/13/50)-2
RICE, Hannah 21 (12/16/61)-
3
RICHARDSON, Emory 30
(5/5/51)-2
RIDGELY, Perry 18
(9/24/53)-2 alias Perry
Hilleary
RIDOUT, George 28
(7/2/47)-2
RILENOUR, Daniel 26
(8/31/58)-3
RILEY, William 17
(8/27/58)-3
RILY, George 18 (8/17/57)-3
RING, William Henry 20
(5/2/54)-2

RINGGOLD, John 24
(10/27/48)-2
RINGOLD, Maria 23
(7/15/63)-3
 William Henry (10/22/45)-2
RITTER, Tom 21 (1/14/48)-
4
ROBERSON, Mat 30
(1/12/58)-3
ROBONSON, Edward 19
(7/5/41)-4
ROBINSON, Elizabeth Ann
(10/24/57)-3
RODGERS, Andrews
(7/16/46)-3
ROGERS, Margaret
(8/10/52)-2
 Sarah E. 13 (8/13/63)-3
ROLLAND, David 17
(7/16/46)-3
ROLLINS, Caleb 26
(8/18/49)-2
ROSHIER, Frank 19
(6/28/50)-2
ROSS, Robert 25 (5/6/63)-3
 William 12 (7/20/57)-3
RUSE, Jane (5/20/46)-4
RUSSELL, Isaiah 12
(1/1/39)-3
 Philip 23 (4/25/53)-4
 Philip 26 (11/11/58)-3
SANDERS, Amos 15
(9/2/46)-3
SAUNDERS, Ben 25
(9/21/61)-3
SAUNDERS, Henry
(6/30/48)-2
SAVOY, Daniel (11/5/61)-3
SCHLEY, Belinda Sophia 30
(8/20/42)-3
SCOOT, Jo (4/8/64)-3
SCOTT, Charles 17
(8/28/49)-2
 Charles 19 (3/18/58)-3
 Harriet (9/12/64)-3
 John 22 (5/23/51)-4

SCOTT (continued)
Richard 26 (6/21/55)-2
Singleton 23 (11/8/47)-2
Tilghman Hilleary
(9/10/57)-3
SEALS, George (5/4/59)-3
SEDWICH, Henry 25
(4/11/46)-2
SEEMS, Tom (10/19/61)-3
SELINER, Jacob (6/17/57)-3
SEMMES, Ben 45 (6/23/54)-
2
SEWELL, Nace 35
(10/2/56)-2
SHADDON, Henny 24
(12/6/43)-4
SHARP, Jim 19 (9/7/58)-3
SHAW, Cornelius 25
(9/21/46)-4
Dennis 25 (8/30/42)-3
Gustavus 24 (5/23/54)-2
Jacob 20 (7/13/49)-2
John 24 (5/13/58)-3
Nace 45 (9/15/58)-3
SHIPLEY, Daniel 22
(3/16/46)-3
Joe 33 (12/20/61)-3
SHOPE, Jerry 19 (10/16/54)-
2
SHORTER, Jacob 21
(6/10/57)-3
Tom 17 (7/13/49)-2 alias
Tom and Jacob Thomas
SHUMATE, Serena 21
(11/4/40)-2
SIDDONS, Jerry 12 (6/6/57)-
3
SIMMONS, Addison
(9/30/56)-2
Fielder 23 (4/19/50)-4
SIMMS, Bill 25 (12/18/61)-3
Daniel (2/21/57)-2
Gustavus 20 (12/21/60)-3
Tom (9/9/51)-2
Thomas 25 (9/17/53)-2
SIMONS, Adam (10/21/51)-2

SIMS, Samuel 30 (9/24/56)-2
SINGER, Bill 50 (9/17/51)-2
SKINNER, Thomas 18
(4/14/58)-3
SLAUGHTER, Edgar 26
(5/26/63)-3
SMALL, Jake (4/24/47)-4
Mary 27 (11/7/42)-2 alias
Mary Turner
SMALLWOOD, Matthew 36
(5/21/55)-2
Mat 43 (6/7/61)-3
SMITE, Anne 4 (9/16/63)-3
alias Anne Wright
Charlot (9/16/63)-3 alias
Charlot Wright
SMITH, Adam 30 (8/27/57)-3
Benjamin Ringgold 11
(2/19/57)-2
Bill 30 (9/7/46)-2
Bill 24 (10/11/50)-2
Dennis 28 (11/1/58)-3
Esther 50 (1/20/59)-3
Fanny 28 (4/20/40)-2
Ferdinand (12/23/53)-2
Flavella 34 (9/8/42)-3
Frederick (1/11/59)-3
George (8/27/51)-4
Henry (5/23/49)-2
Henry 22 (3/28/56)-4
Henry 26 (6/12/50)-2
Henry 27 (5/26/63)-3
Hester 40 (3/23/60)-3
John 25 (7/15/46)-2
John 25 (4/24/54)-2
John 27 (8/24/54)-2
John Henry 21 (3/19/62)-3
Kate 15 (1/23/64)-3
Lewis 30 (10/28/63)-3
Ned 30 (12/27/43)-2
Patty 14 (6/4/46)-2
Tom 13 (9/19/49)-2
William Henry 18
(11/13/45)-2
Wilmot (3/7/63)-3

SMOOT, George 22 (6/7/41)-
4
SMOTHERS, Dick 25
(1/2/46)-2
Sam 23 (1/2/46)-2
William 23 (11/11/58)-3
SNOWDEN, Allen 29
(5/31/42)-3 alias Allen
Monday
Andrew 27 (8/28/54)-4
Elias 25 (7/6/49)-2
Hazel 35 (10/22/45)-2
Josephine 24 (10/9/41)-4
Mary 32 (10/3/49)-2
SOUTHARD,Nace 30
(10/15/42)-4
SOUTHWOOD, Isaac 20
(2/11/43)-3
SPRIGG, Charles 21
(6/28/56)-2
Edward 24 (5/2/50)-2
Frank (9/4/60)-3
SPRIGS, Dick 17 (5/10/60)-3
STANMORE, Basel
(9/16/45)-2
Bazel 19 (6/21/53)-4
STANSBERRY, Selina 20
(10/5/47)-4
STAVE, Seward 26
(10/8/45)-2
STEARNS, Bill 25 (4/26/62)-
3
STEPNEY, Tom (5/15/49)-2
STEVENSON, George 24
(5/25/61)-3
STEWARD, Charles 50
(6/2/41)-4
STEWART, Alexander
(4/23/57)-3
Amanda 25 (8/2/42)-2
Edward 38 (4/24/40)-2
George 20 (9/18/52)-2
George 24 (7/15/46)-2
Harry 25 (10/19/61)-3 alias
Henry Stewart

STEWART (continued)
Henry 25 (10/19/61)-3 alias
Harry Stewart
Jacob 23 (5/22/51)-2
John 19 (3/12/62)-3
Saul 21 (7/28/59)-3
Tom 18 (11/28/53)-2
William (9/24/49)-2
William 18 (11/3/52)-4
STODDARD, Dick 30
(8/16/44)-2
Henry 35 (8/20/41)-2
STOKELY, Henry (4/29/58)-
3
STORARD, William 18
(12/19/61)-3
STOUT, Emaline 18
(5/9/60)-3
STUART, Adam 19
(8/30/48)-2
SUTTON, Ben 25 (4/4/49)-2
Bill (8/6/47)-2
TABBS, Hezekiah 40
(5/21/55)-4
TACK, Maria (11/11/61)-3
TALBERT, Jim 34
(9/20/54)-2
TALBOTT, Daniel 24
(1/25/60)-3
TASKER, John 24
(10/31/61)-3
Virgil (3/5/60)-3
TATE, Edwin 32 (10/22/59)-
3
Jane 35 (10/22/59)-3
TAYLOR, Adriadne 26
(5/26/42)-3
George (9/26/54)-2
Ned 20 (6/22/52)-2
Rachel 35 (4/22/63)-3 alias
Rachel Dorsey
Roberta 22 (3/27/58)-3
Sanford (9/1/59)-3
Thomas (6/30/49)-2
Thomas (8/25/52)-4 alias
John T. H. Williams

TAYLOR (continued)
William Alexander 14
(7/19/45)-2
TEAS, William H. 13
(7/8/52)-2
TENDER, Augustus 13
(11/15/43)-4
THOMAS, Charles 29
(9/12/49)-2
George 22 (5/9/56)-4
Henry 19 (6/5/44)-4
Jack 29 (6/5/57)-3
Jacob 17 (7/13/49)-2 alias
Tom Thomas and Tom
Shorter
John (11/6/56)-2
Lewis 35 (8/1/61)-3
Martha 22 (4/23/63)-3
Mary (6/30/41)-4
Robert 24 (6/3/53)-2
Samuel 12 (10/10/60)-3
Tom 17 (7/13/49)-2 alias
Jacob Thomas and Tom
Shorter
William 15 (12/31/52)-4
Wilson 18 (11/30/61)-3
THOMPSON, George 19
(2/11/51)-2
Jacob 23 (10/28/41)-3
Nimrod 21 (9/28/40)-2
Sophia (8/4/41)-2
TIBBS, William 25
(11/22/39)-1
TIBS, William 25
(11/25/39)-1
TILBALL, Stephen 22
(9/16/47)-3
TILDEN, Betsey 23
(3/27/41)-3
TILGHMAN, Clara 18
(10/22/59)-3
George 24 (5/28/52)-
Nace (7/1/42)-4
TIPPINS, Jack 30 (1/14/61)-
3
TITUS, Henry 29 (1/2/47)-2

TITUS (continued)
Henry 30 (12/5/43)-2
Henry 35 (3/24/48)-2
TONGUS, Isaac (9/13/53)-2
TOOGOOD, Alfred 18
(10/12/39)-2
James 25 (6/12/57)-3
Mary Ann 18 (12/30/61)-3
TRAVERS, Jim 11
(10/3/40)-3
TRIPLETT, William 23
(8/27/57)-3
TRIPP, James 12 (4/14/48)-
2
TROTT, Rachel 26
(12/16/45)-3
TUCKER, Tom 30 (11/8/42)-
4
TUNKS, Henry 25 (5/1/47)-4
alias Henry Crowner
TURLEY, Daniel 19
(11/14/42)-3
Martha 19 (8/5/43)-4
TURNER, Charles 33
(3/26/46)-2
Charles 32 (1/25/48)-4
Dick (12/13/61)-3
Emanuel 22 (3/15/56)-4
Joshua (5/26/43)-3
Mary 27 (11/7/42)-2 alias
Mary Small
Mary 31 (3/26/46)-2
Matthew 35 (6/26/55)-4
Oliver 25 (8/22/50)-2
William 30 (2/26/45)-2
TYLER, John (8/25/58)-3
Robert 19 (11/29/54)-2
Tom (8/25/58)-3
TYSON, John 16 (6/28/44)-2
VANDEVERT, Ann Maria 15
(4/3/41)-3
VANHORN, Jerry 23
(9/15/47)-2
VEIL, Daniel 25 (10/6/63)-3
VERMILION, Tom 22
(12/17/49)-2

WALKER, Hanson 30
(9/6/49)-4
Tom 26 (6/5/44)-4 alias
Joshua Isaacks
WALLACE, John 21
(4/17/45)-4
Maria 23 (11/28/43)-4
WALTER, George 22
(9/2/63)-3
WARD, Jim 17 (6/8/52)-4
Josiah H. (6/30/49)-2
Polly Levenia 11
(10/28/40)-3
WARFIELD, George 21
(9/11/50)-2
Leonard 24 (3/19/44)-2
WARICK, Charles 25
(10/29/42)-4
WARRING, Harry 25
(10/25/42)-3
WASHINGTON, Ned
(8/3/44)-2
Stephen 19 (5/27/46)-3
WATERS, Bill 28 (6/16/47)-4
Bill 25 (2/6/51)-2
Charles 16 (11/5/45)-2
Isaac 12 (6/21/41)-2
John 34 (9/14/59)-3
Levin 15 (6/21/41)-2
William Upsher 20
(6/21/41)-2
William (12/12/53)-2
WATKINS, George W. 17
(2/2/64)-3
Henry 28 (8/25/49)-2
Philip 20 (7/2/47)-2
WARSON, Bill 20 (12/7/60)-3
WATTS, Henry 30
(10/30/48)-2
Hinson 24 (9/10/53)-2
John 25 (5/24/50)-2
WEAVER, Zenus 17
(4/1/63)-3

WELLS, Billy 40
(11/22/53)-4
WERNSLY, Levi 14
(3/10/58)-3
WESLEY, John 14
(7/19/64)-3
WEST, Allen 19 (9/23/54)-2
Alsey 50 (5/12/49)-4
David 21 (5/8/60)-3
James (11/26/40)-1
WETHERBY, John 35
(10/7/42)-3
WHITE, Alexander
(2/23/64)-3
Amanda 19 (11/30/59)-3
Basil 24 (1/6/53)-2
Joseph 18 (8/22/51)-2
Lewis 25 (12/8/62)-3
William (3/19/44)-2
WHITEHEAD, Martha 23
(8/11/49)-2
WHITTINGTON, Sophia
(1/31/44)-3
WILEY, John 16 (8/14/62)-3
WILLET, Lewis 24
(2/18/61)-3
WILLIAMS, Aleck
(6/13/64)-3
Charles 17 (1/13/57)-2
Charles 17 (5/13/63)-3
David 10 (7/4/38)-3
Elias 10 (11/10/26)-2
Emory 25 (11/5/55)-3
Henry (9/2/58)-3
Jason 40 (8/28/54)-4
Joshua 35 (11/9/51)-2
John 34 (9/4/55)-2
John T. H. (8/25/52)-4 alias
Thomas Taylor
Luke 23 (8/11/51)-2
Mandy (7/5/41)-4
Matilda 26 (5/20/41)-3
Nace 25 (8/26/61)-3
Sam 22 (6/14/48)-2
Sandy 25 (6/11/61)-3

WILLIS, Berkley 24
(10/10/44)–2
WILSON, Alexander
(1/2/62)–3
Charles (9/9/42)–3
Henry 6 (9/20/52)–2
Henry 20 (5/21/55)–2 alias
Henry Ayres
Henry 24 (4/5/56)–2
Isaiah 23 (8/7/55)–2
Jacob 17 (7/8/46)–2
John 8 (9/23/62)–3
John 28 (9/23/62)–3
John (3/20/49)–2
Joseph 22 (8/29/54)–2
Laura (9/23/62)–3
Louis 50 (9/14/59)–3
Perry Henry (3/7/55)–2
WISE, Harry 24 (8/29/57)–3
WOOD, Isaac 30 (5/15/57)–3
John 20 (10/27/53)–2
Tom 18 (8/28/39)–3
WOODARD, Bill 45
(9/13/53)–2
WOODLAND, Lewis 22
(12/8/59)–3

WOODS, Lewis 16 (7/2/44)–
2
WOODYARD, Jared 25
(8/24/60)–3
WOOTEN, Thomas 21
(11/30/61)–3
WOOTON, Charles
(12/16/61)–3
James (12/16/61)–3
WRIGHT, Anne 4 (9/16/63)–
3 alias Anne Smite
Charlot (9/16/63)–3 alias
Charlot Smite
Clinton 17 (5/28/41)–4
Elias (8/23/61)–3
Griffin 28 (5/28/41)–4
YOUNG, Betsey 30
(10/24/53)–2
Charles 23 (10/27/58)–3
George 22 (9/21/46)–4
James 30 (9/21/60)–3
Jim 38 (7/24/50)–2
Joe 22 (1/1/57)–2
Juba 51 (8/23/47)–4
Richard 17 (9/3/47)–4
William 28 (1/26/48)–2

SLAVES WANTED!

We are at all times PURCHASING SLAVES, paying the HIGHEST CASH PRICES. Persons wishing to sell will please call at

282 Pratt Street,

Communications addressed to

B. M. & W. L. CAMPBELL.

Advertisement taken from the *Baltimore City Directory 1860*, p. 27 (John W. Woods, publisher).

LAUREL CEMETERY 1852 - 1958

As late as the 1840's in the Baltimore area many Blacks were, at their deaths, buried in plots of ground provided by their respective churches.

A number of church burial grounds bordered Belle Air Avenue (now Gay Street) from East Chase Street north to Lanvale Street.

Drawings filed at the Maryland Historical Society name at least four of these plots as early as 1822. They were Bethel A.M.E. (African Methodist Episcopal), First Independent, Second Presbyterian, and Trinity.

A map filed in 1876 shows, along with the four previously mentioned, a colored burial ground (owned by the Sharp Street Methodist Church) at the corner of East Lanvale Street and Belle Air Avenue.

The initial legal transaction that led to the formation of Laurel Cemetery took place in September of 1851. Thomas Burgan Jr., a wealthy land owner of Baltimore County, sold a parcel of his land on Belle Air Avenue to three men.

According to the transfer of property the land was to be "Converted into a burial ground under the name and style of Laurel Cemetery for the benefit of the colored people of the city and county of Baltimore."

The choice seemed a logical one for several reasons. First, the land was privately owned and would serve as an attractive alternative to Blacks who wished to bury their loved ones in a place other than that provided by the church. Secondly, the hill had been used for years as a burial ground for the Black servants of local merchants and landowners.

On July 14, 1852 the cemetery was incorporated and a charter filed under the name of the Laurel Cemetery Company of Baltimore. The area now had its first non-sectarian cemetery for the exclusive use of Blacks.

Although at the beginning of the Civil War organized Black regiments were not allowed to take part in the fighting, the situatuion soon changed. As many as 200,000 Black soldiers

41

served during the period from 1862 to 1865.

The Federal Government was faced with the problem of where to bury Black Union veterans with honor. Portions of cemeteries were seized and converted to National Cemeteries, in many cases without the consent of the owners.

Laurel Cemetery was no exception. More than 230 Black Clvil War Veterans were interred at the cemetery between September 1863 and February 1866.

A plan to widen Belle Air road was initiated and approved in 1911. While widening the road the city, without the permission of the Federal Government or the owners of the cemetery, disinterred the remains of the Civil War veterans from the Laurel property owned by the Federal Government.

The remains were re-interred at the Loudon National Cemetery on Frederick Road.

Between 1919 and 1920 a road (Elmley Avenue) was constructed on the southern boundary of Laurel. Not long after moving into their new homes the residents began dumping refuse over their back yard fences into the cemetery.

This, along with the lack of perpetual care on the part of lot owners in the cemetery, led to the demise of one of the most beautiful cemeteries the Baltimore area had ever known.

Efforts for a solution to the problems at Laurel continued for the next four decades.

In a maze of legal maneuvers conducted by members of the city law department in 1957 and 1958 the cemetery was destroyed without prior knowledge of the lot owners.

A small number of bodies (approximately three hundred to four hundred) were re-interred in a cornfield in Carrol County.

Litigation initiated by the N.A.A.C.P. (National Association For The Advancement Of Colored People) on behalf of several lot owners at Laurel failed to resolve the injustice that had been done.

Approximately five years later a Two Guys department store and parking lot was constructed on the site, over the remains of at least 2,000 of the people who had been buried there. (For the complete history of Laurel Cemetery you are invited to read "Laurel Hill Cemetery 1852-1958" by Ralph Clayton and Alma Moore in the *Flower of The Forest Black Genealogical Journal* vol. 1 #3 1984.)

Partial List of Internments At Laurel Hill Cemetery

(LC) - Follows name and/or date listed on the tombstone located at the new site of the cemetery in Eldersburg. When a date was obliterated only the name of the deceased will appear followed by the symbol (LC).

(CW) - Follows name Civil War veteran interred at Laurel (now re-interred at Loudon National Cemetery in Baltimore).

(AF) - Follows the date of the obituary or death notice appearing in the *Afro-American Newspaper*.

(MS) - Follows the date of the death notice that appeared in the *The Morning Sun* (Baltimore).

month/day/year

ADAMS, Mary B. 7/28/1935 (LC)
William (CW)
ALEXANDER, Rev. William 4/14/1919 (MS)
ALKORN, Rebecca D. 12/?/1885 (LC)
ALLEN, Rev. Dr. J. C. 7/1/1905 (AF)
ANDERSON, Edward 2/10/1906 (AF)
Emma 4/?/1889 (LC)
John C. b. 8/21/1841 d. 3/2/1903 (LC) (12/3/04) (AF)
ARCHER, Mary E. 7/25/1880 (LC)
AYERS, John 1/29/16 (AF)
BAILEY, Elizabeth B. 10/3/1793 d. 8/7/1878 (LC)
BANISTER, Mary E. 5/17/18 (AF)
BANKS, Burwell ? (LC)
Isabella 6/13/14 (AF)
Lucinda b. 4/7/1836 d. 8/7/1878 (LC)
BANNISTER, Goldie A. 10/18/18 (AF)

BARBER, Washington 4/25/1864 (CW)
BARRETT, James H. b. 3/11/1832 d. ? (AF)
BELL, Benjamin 8/14/1864 (CW)
Charles 9/6/1863 (CW)
BENIE, Benedict 8/4/1864 (CW)
BENNETT, Elizabeth W. 2/16/07 (AF)
Florence R. 1867 - 1964 (LC)
Osborne S. 1863 - 1895 (LC)
BERKELY, Shorter Saunders ? (LC)
BERRY, George 12/23/1915 (LC)
BILLINGSBY, Henry 4/23/1864 (CW)
BISHOP, Elizabeth 8/2/1886 (LC)
BLACK, Franklin 11/7/1864 (CW)
BLAKE, Sarah E. 5/31/1883 (LC)
BLAND, Peter 7/11/03 (AF)
BODLAY, R. H. 3/22/1864 (CW)

BOOTH, Henry 3/20/1864 (CW)
BOWEN, Jarrett 5/7/1904 (AF)
Jennie R. 4/8/05 (AF)
BOYD, Bird 1/26/1865 (CW)
BRADSHAW, Jackson 4/27/1865 (CW)
BRECENRIDGE, Milton 5/18/1865 (CW)
BREWINGTON, Richard 3/30/1864 (CW)
BRICE, William 3/11/1864 (CW)
BRISTOL, John 8/?/1864 (CW)
BROOKS, Simon 3/6/1909 (AF)
Wilson 10/24/1863 (CW)
BROWN, Dr. M. b. 9/24/1863 d. 9/19/1920 (LC)
Elizabeth B. 2/12/16 (AF)
Elizabeth E. 1/2916 (AF)
Fannie C. 1/14/11 (AF)
John F. 12/30/1905 (AF)
BROWNE, William H. 2/18/1889 (LC)
BUCHANAN, Elizabeth 1/1903 (LC)
BURGESS, John D. 6/30/06 (AF)
BURKETT, Lewis 10/25/1911 (LC)
BURNETT, William 3/5/1864 (CW)
BUTLER, Anna 10/12/1864 (CW)
Elizabeth 2/14/1853 (LC)
Ethel 7/11/14 (AF)
George 4/18/1864 (CW)
James T. 6/12/1879 (LC)
John G. 12/7/1912 (AF)
Louis C. 8/12/1905 (AF)
Lulie ? (LC)

CALDWELL, Charles H. 1891 (LC)
CALVERT, William 3/8/1864 (CW)
CAMPER, Washington 5/26/1864 (CW)
CAREY, James 11/3/1865 (CW)
CARR, Milbert 4/15/1916 (AF)
CARROLL, George Washington 9/26/1903 (AF)
CARTER, Emily 4/8/1916 (AF)
William b. 1/1/1859 d. 1/2/1883 (LC)
CARY, Clay 6/4/1864 (CW)
CECELIA, Helen S. 1886 – 1905 (LC)
Jann 1854 – 1905 (LC)
John L. 1847 – 1923 (LC)
CEUTIS, George 10/5/1865 (CW)
CHAMBERS, Rachel Wells Pumphrey 2/18/1911 (AF)
CHANDLER, George F. 12/11/1909 (AF)
CHINN, Addison 6/12/1878 (LC)
CHIPMAN, John 10/23/1864 (CW)
CHUBB, Mary Ann ? (LC)
CLARK, Mary Catherine 11/1/1918 (AF)
CLASH, John 5/4/1907 (AF)
CLOVER, Daniel 5/4/1864 (CW)
COATES, Major 3/7/1864 (CW)
COLLETT, Rev. John H. b. 2/19/1852 d. 4/8/1909 (LC)
COLLICK, I. 3/14/1864 (CW)

COLLINS, Rubins 8/15/1865
(CW)
COOK, Benjamin 11/22/1865
(CW)
John W. Jr. b. 5/28/1848 d.
10/10/1864 (LC)
COOPER, Henrieta B.
12/30/1911 (AF)
Horace 8/?/1864 (CW)
CORNISH, Joseph 4/30/1904
(AF)
CONOR, Samuel 4/18/1864
(CW)
COVEY, William 3/23/1864
(CW)
CREDITT, Mary L. 1/4/1913
(AF)
CREEK, Dr. J. W. no date
available (LC)
CROMWELL, Albert
3/20/1864 (CW)
CULLIGAN, Charles
3/?/1865 (CW)
CULLY, Emma Stevens 1871
- 1901 (LC)
Lottie Barbon 1899 - 1905
(LC)
Lucille Stevens b.
1/25/1897 d. 7/18/1898
(LC)
CURRIN, Isaac 4/23/1864
(CW)
DAILEY, John W. 7/24/1864
(CW)
DAVIS, John H. 12/29/06
(AF)
Nellie 1/2/1904 (AF)
DECKSON, William
2/11/1865 (CW)
DEJARNER, Henry
3/13/1865 (CW)
DEMLY, William 3/?/1865
(CW)
DENNIS, Aaron 6/6/1865
(CW)

DICKERSON, Charles A.
4/20/1912 (AF)
DICKSON, David D.
2/24/1908 (AF)
DIGGS, Thomas 2/18/1905
(AF)
DOCKEN, Robert 2/1/1865
(CW)
DOLSON, Samuel ? (LC)
DOONANE, Henry 1/30/1865
(CW)
DORSEY, Charles H. no date
available (LC)
Grace 8/6/1910 (AF)
Martha b. 9/30/1840 d.
7/8/1918 (LC)
DRAPER, Rev. Daniel
7/5/1902 (AF)
Emily J. 9/19/1914 (AF)
DRAPPER, Garrison
2/3/1865 (CW)
DRY, Robert 2/20/1865 (CW)
DUFFIN, Addie 2/5/1910
(AF)
DUNGEE, John H. B.
7/30/1904 (AF)
Mary 5/9/1914 (AF)
DYER, Dr. Levin D.
1/28/1911 (AF)
Sarah A. 10/3/1914 (AF)
DYETT, Isaac M. 1887 (LC)
DYETT, Mager 1/1/1877
(LC)
Mary 7/6/1890 (LC)
Sarah A. 1878 (LC)
DYSON, Robert 3/19/1864
(CW)
EDWARD, Serena 1/27/1906
(AF)
ELLIOTT, Robert A.
4/8/1916 (AF)
ELLIS, Henry 5/28/1865
(CW)
Sophia L. 11/15/1881 (LC)
ELY, John B. 2/13/1865
(CW)

ENNIS, John 3/5/1864 (CW)
EWING, Amos 7/4/1865
(CW)
FATEN, Mary 8/12/1905
(AF)
FERGUSON, Thornton
9/1/1865 (CW)
FISHER, Francis A.
10/13/17 (AF)
FLETT, Lillian A.
9/12/1908 (AF)
FLEMING, Amanda R.
12/29/1888 (LC)
FLETCHER, Nicholas
10/10/1920 (LC)
FLORENCE, Mary b.
8/27/1875 (LC)
FOOT, James 10/11/1863
(CW)
FORD, Walter 2/?/1863
(CW)
FOSSETT, James 1864 –
1937 (LC)
FRANKLIN, Sarah 5/?/1909
(LC)
FRAZIER, Albert 7/14/1865
(CW)
FRENCH, Margaret
3/21/1885 (LC)
FREY, Jennie E. b.
8/25/1863 d. 1/26/1915
(LC)
GAINES, Nash 2/8/1902 (AF)
GARDINER, William H.
3/24/1865 (CW)
GARNER, Henry 1/20/1865
(CW)
GARRISON, George
1/20/1865 (CW)
GAULK, Joseph b. 5/10/1840
d. 1/26/1915 (LC)
GAYLOR, John 10/31/1864
(CW)
GERDEN, Anderson
1/20/1866 (CW)

GIBBS, Robert H. 11/26/1910
(AF)
GIBSON, Ed 8/?/1864 (CW)
Emma 12/16/1890 (LC)
Jefferson 6/18/1864 (CW)
John C. 3/11/1864 (CW)
GILES, Charles H. b.
1/18/1842 d. 3/16/1907
(LC) 3/16/1907 (AF)
Derius b. 12/24/1862 d.
6/4/1908 (LC)
John B. 6/21/1902 (AF)
Mollie ? (LC)
GINN, Jerry 2/7/1865 (CW)
GORDEN, Anderson
1/20/1866 (CW)
GORDON, Catherine
3/6/1909 (AF)
GRAFTON, Allen 4/24/1864
(CW)
GRANT, Nancy ? (LC)
GRASON, Minnie J. 8/9/1913
(AF)
GRAVES, Marseline ? (LC)
GREEN, Alexander
7/12/1864 (CW)
Atha V. 12/26/1903 (AF)
James M. 5/6/1864 (CW)
GRENNIGE, Rev. E. P.
2/18/1905 (AF)
GREENWOOD, Dennis
5/9/1865 (CW)
GRETCHELL, Fred C.
12/31/1864 (CW)
GRIFFIN, James E.
4/6/1912 (AF)
GROSS, Benjamin 4/5/1864
(CW)
GUHE, William 4/2/1864
(CW)
HALL, Amelia E. 1820 –
1904 (LC)
Emeline 1822 – 1892 (LC)
James 6/6/1865 (CW)
Dr. Reverdy ? (LC)

46

HALL (continued)
William H. 1820 – 1889
(LC)
HAMES, Rebecca F. b.
1/7/1865 d. 4/1/1914 (LC)
HAMMOND, Dr. William
4/22/1905 (AF)
HANDS, Samuel J. 5/7/1910
(AF)
HANDT, Isabell ? (LC)
HANDY, Alfred 3/27/1864
(CW)
Frances 8/1/1914 (AF)
Ishmael 1/11/1850 (LC)
Bishop James A. 1911 (LC)
HARDMAN, Thomas
3/27/1864 (CW)
HARRIS, Emily b. 9/20/1835
d. 10/11/1875 (LC)
Irving 10/24/1864 (CW)
James 10/13/1864 (CW)
Susan 1/16/1909 (AF)
HARRISON, Henry 2/16/1865
(CW)
HAZARD, Jacob 11/3/1864
(CW)
HEADING, Zachariah
2/?/1865 (CW)
HEBRON, Oliver 7/12/1913
(AF)
HENDERSON, John W. b.
4/20/1860 d. 11/21/1928
(AF)
Rosa 5/8/1929 (LC)
HENRY, Nancy A. 6/14/1913
(AF)
HENSON, Emma 12/7/1903
(AF)
Mary A. 2/18/1896 (LC)
HICKS, James 4/15/1865
(CW)
HILL, Charles 7/26/1865
(CW)
Louisa 3/20/1915 (AF)
Sarah 2/23/1887 (LC)

HILLIARD, Martha
8/19/1905 (AF)
Thomas J. 2/26/1914 (LC)
HODGES, Henry 1/26/1865
(CW)
HOLLAND, J. 3/19/1864
(CW)
HOLLIDAY, Marshall
3/27/1865 (CW)
HOLLIS, George 12/7/1863
(CW)
HOLSTON, Philip 3/7/1864
(CW)
HOMPSON, John 3/3/1865
(CW)
HOMSLEY, Robert 9/13/1863
(CW)
HORSEY, Moses 4/9/1865
(CW)
HOWARD, Ben 3/11/1864
(CW)
Isaac 11/21/1864 (CW)
W. H. 3/16/1864 (CW)
HUDDLESTON, Richard
5/28/1864 (CW)
HUDGINS, Cornelius
1/27/1912 (AF)
HUMSTEAD, Lillian
10/11/1918 (AF)
HUSA, Ferdinand 3/27/1864
(CW)
HUTCHINS, Annie M. ? (LC)
Samuel B. 1814 – 1889 (LC)
HUTCHINSON, Robert N. b.
6/21/1841 d. ? (LC)
HUTTON, Rev. Henry
3/27/1897 (AF)
INES, Emma 9/23/1911 (AF)
JACKSON, Adel 7/9/1904
(AF)
Alfred 1/26/1865 (CW)
Burrel 3/20/1865 (CW)
Carrie 11/22/1918 (AF)
Daniel 3/23/1864 (CW)
Elizabeth ? (LC)

JACKSON (continued)
Henry 12/12/1869 (LC)
John M. 8/?/1864 (CW)
John W. 10/?/1865 (CW)
Josiah 3/4/1864 (CW)
Peter 3/25/1864 (CW)
Whittington 7/11/1879 (LC)
JAMES, A. 3/18/1864 (CW)
Theodore 10/6/1863 (CW)
JEFFERSON, Margaret S.
10/27/1904 (LC)
Thomas b. 11/25/1843 d.
12/6/1896 (LC)
JENIFER, Alice 8/2/1902
(AF)
JENKINS, George 6/21/1902
(AF)
Noah 7/17/1864 (CW)
William 3/13/1864 (CW)
JEWELL, Willis 1/25/1865
(CW)
JOHNS, Levi 3/13/1864
(CW)
JOHNSON, Amelia E. 1858 –
1922 (LC)
Annie 6/6/1908 (AF)
Bettie 3/3/1906 (AF)
Charles A. 9/13/1913 (AF)
Daniel b. 10/28/1848 d.
12/17/1897 (LC)
Ed 4/21/1864 (CW)
Elijah 3/13/1904 (LC)
Elliott Newton 9/5/1914
(LC)
Rev. Harvey 1843 – 1923
(LC)
Horace 11/5/1863 (CW)
Jane 9/1885 (LC)
Jennie 12/4/1915 (AF)
Joyoforth 4/2/1864 (CW)
Lucy 9/8/1906 (AF)
Mary 5/19/1913 (LC)
Mary C. 7/25/1908 (LC)
R. 4/6/1864 (CW)
Thomas ? (CW)
Virgil 1/20/1865 (CW)

JOHNSON (continued)
Wihlelmina 1/31/1901 (LC)
JOHNSTON, Amelia
8/23/1915 (LC)
JONES, Allen 5/14/1864
(CW)
Elizabeth A. 4/25/1907 (LC)
Ella 2/15/1896 (AF)
Isaac 11/18/1911 (AF)
James H. 12/10/1893 (LC)
Maggie ? (LC)
Robert E. 3/30/1907 (AF)
William 7/11/1865 (CW)
JORDAN, Cora E. 8/12/1911
(AF)
Daniel 11/2/1864 (CW)
Elizabeth ? (LC)
Rev. John 7/30/1884 (LC)
KEELY, George W. 11/10/06
(AF)
KELLEY, Washington
10/30/1864 (LC)
KENNARD, Dr. George W. ?
(LC)
Margaret 3/24/1906 (LC)
KEYS, Nobel H. 1845 – 1935
(LC)
KING, Fannie B. b.
9/12/1883 d. 11/12/1906
(LC)
Samuel J. b. 9/13/1877 d.
1/21/1905 (LC)
Susan Ellen 3/25/1911 (AF)
Thomas G. b. 8/25/1847 d.
8/1/1908 (LC)
KIRKFOLD, W. 1/29/1912
(AF)
LANE, George 6/29/1912
(AF)
LANGFORD, Robert
4/28/1864 (CW)
LANGLEY, Hazel M. b.
7/8/1907 d. 7/11/1909
(LC)
LAWLER, Richard
1/19/1865 (CW)

LEE, Clarence 7/2/1904
    (AF)
Cornelia 5/26/1888 (LC)
Joseph H. 7/10/1909 (AF)
LEWIS, Henry 8/11/1865
    (CW)
LITTINGS, ? 7/7/1879 (LC)
LIVELY, William H.
    11/1/1918 (AF)
LODO, John 11/20/1865
    (CW)
LOGAN, James 1/19/1866
    (CW)
LOUISA, M. L. ? (LC)
MADDOX, James 6/27/1865
    (CW)
MAHAMMITT, Charles E.
    6/24/1911 (AF)
MARKHAM, Willis
    1/18/1865 (CW)
MARTIN, Caroline 1/18/1889
    (LC)
George 9/21/1864 (CW)
Jane b. 1805 d. 1/28/1880
    (LC)
Laura V. b. 10/15/1856 d.
    4/25/1930 (LC)
MASON, Laura b. 12/15/1864
    d. 4/25/1930 (LC)
R. P. 3/16/1912 (AF)
MATTHEWS, Howard J.
    6/11/1887 (LC)
Jones 1/15/1886 (LC)
Joseph F. 5/15/1909 (AF)
Marie 7/2/1889 (LC)
William E. 11/22/1889 (LC)
William E. 5/4/1894 (LC)
McDONALD, John 9/18/1865
    (CW)
McKINER, I. N. 3/12/1864
    (CW)
MOBERLY, Ed 3/16/1865
    (CW)
MONTGOMERY, James
    4/21/1864 (CW)

MOODY, William 1/11/1864
    (CW)
MOORE, Henry 3/7/1865
    (CW)
John W. 8/18/1906 (AF)
Joseph 4/13/1912 (AF)
Martha 7/19/1918 (AF)
William 4/11/1864 (CW)
MORRIS, Luther L.
    7/23/1904 (AF)
MORSELL, ? ? (LC)
MORTON, Samuel
    10/31/1864 (CW)
MYERS, Abraham 6/15/1864
    (CW)
Galedonai 12/24/1910 (AF)
NEAL, Emma 11/25/1901
    (LC)
Rev. P. Carter ? (LC)
Spicer 7/29/1901 (LC)
NEWBY, Annie 2/1892 (LC)
NEWCOME, Henry 7/2/1865
    (CW)
NICHOLSON, Belle
    4/15/1911 (AF)
Isabella L. 4/15/1911 (AF)
NICHON, Rev. St. George
    11/11/1911 (AF)
NINNINGS, Elisha
    10/15/1864 (CW)
NOBLE, Howard W. 1882 –
    1929 (LC)
Louisa 1858 – 1922 (LC)
NOLAN, James G. 5/7/1910
    (AF)
NORRIS, Augusta 3/15/1864
    (CW)
John 3/20/1864 (CW)
OATS, Mark 6/22/1865 (CW)
OLIVER, Emma F. 7/4/1903
    (AF)
Lewis 3/22/1913 (AF)
ORSBURY, Adaline b.
    12/5/1817 d. 12/5/1865
    (LC)

OWINGS, Samuel 4/8/1911
  (AF)
PACK, Eli 5/17/1864 (CW)
PARKER, Benjamin
  4/24/1864 (CW)
PASSON, Jessie 1/22/1865
  (CW)
PATRICK, Lewis 6/21/1889
  (LC)
PAUL, James M. 11/16/1919
  (LC)
 Morris ? (LC)
 Sarah M. 11/4/1927 (LC)
PAYNE, Bishop Daniel A.
  1893 (LC)
PERKINS, Lelia P.
  7/15/1911 (AF)
PERRY, John 10/15/1910
  (AF)
PETERS, James W. b.
  5/7/1840 d. 12/31/1873
  (LC)
PITTS, Roberts 4/20/1864
  (CW)
 Sarah 3/7/1911 (LC) &
  3/18/1911 (AF)
PLATER, Lizzie 7/4/1914
  (AF)
POSEY, Margret 8/1862 (LC)
PRICE, Catherine 2/21/1903
  (AF)
 Thomas 9/21/1865 (CW)
QUAM, William 3/18/1865
  (CW)
RALPH, Viola R. 10/3/1908
  (AF)
REDDING, L. M. 4/3/1864
  (CW)
REID, James H. 10/31/1908
  (AF)
RICHARDSON, William
  4/18/1864 (CW)
RIDDLE, John 6/13/1864
  (CW)
RIDEOUT, Anna M. 1814 –
  1908 (LC)

RIDEOUT (continued)
 Wellington 1829 – 1900 (LC)
RILEY, Frank 12/3/1864
  (CW)
ROBERTS, Harriet A.
  7/18/1914 (AF)
 John 2/8/1866 (CW)
ROBERTSON, A. 10/10/1864
  (CW)
ROBINSON, Newton
  10/24/1864 (CW)
ROSIER, Robert 3/29/1864
  (CW)
ROSS, Rev. Hurcules
  9/12/1903 (AF)
 Mary E. 3/7/1861 (CW)
 Priscilla ? (LC)
 Richard 4/27/1864 (CW)
RULKER, Benjamin
  8/14/1865 (CW)
RUTHERFORD, Henry
  1/29/1865 (CW)
SAUNDERS, Hilda Louise
  5/7/1910 (AF)
 Russell A. 3/18/1916 (AF)
SCOTT, Charles 5/3/1864
  (CW)
 George 9/30/1863 (CW)
 Joshua 11/3/1865 (CW)
 Robert 4/7/1864 (CW)
 William 4/13/1864 (CW)
 William H. 1/30/1909 (AF)
SEATON, Jacob A. 7/1/1905
  (AF)
 John L. 10/23/1863 (CW)
SHARP, Basil 5/17/1864
  (CW)
SHIPLEY, Moses 9/4/1909
  (AF)
SIMON, Henry 3/20/1864
  (CW)
 Samuel 9/13/1864 (CW)
SKINNER, Gilbert 9/25/1864
  (CW)
SLAUGHTER, Nicholas
  10/1/1863 (CW)

SLOWAR, Henry S. ? (LC)
SLOWER, Harriett E. ? (LC)
 Martha A. ? (LC)
 William C. ? (LC)
SMITH, Ann Eliza 5/2/1821
  (LC)
 Hestor A. 6/5/1909 (AF)
 Hester H. 11/24/1943 ?
 Howard ? (LC)
 John 3/8/1864 (CW)
 John H. 3/11/1864 (CW)
 Joseph L. H. 11/18/1911
  (AF)
 Julia Ann 8/25/1888 (LC)
 M. Blanch 1882 - 1918 (LC)
 Morris F. 1884 - 1914 (LC)
 Peter 5/8/1864 (CW)
 Veronica ? (LC)
 William Anthony 2/12/1916
  (AF)
SMOOT, Marshall 4/5/1866
  (CW)
SMYTHE, Enda–Hall
  12/3/1904 (AF)
SNOWDEN, Elizabeth
  4/23/1904 (AF)
 John W. 1/29/1916 (AF)
 Robert 7/18/1866 (LC)
SOUTHGATE, John A.
  11/16/1864 (CW)
SPEARS, Washington
  2/9/1865 (CW)
SPENCER, John 1/20/1865
  (CW)
STAFORD, Jacob 3/8/1865
  (CW)
 Jacob ? (CW)
STARKE, Charles W.
  1/26/1865 (CW)
STEEL, William 3/9/1865
  (CW)
STEPHENSON, Allen
  2/2/1865 (CW)
STEVENSON, Jacob
  2/21/1865 (CW)
 William 4/2/1864 (CW)

STEWARD, Beverly
  4/1/1865 (CW)
STIVERSON, Thomas
  3/28/1864 (CW)
STOKES, Edward V. b.
  12/25/1857 d. 12/28/1915
  (LC)
 Hatie 2/15/1909 (LC)
STOOKS, William 4/6/1869
  (CW)
TASKA, Amanda 2/1868 (LC)
TASKER, Mary ? (LC)
TAYLOR, Edward 5/17/1913
  (AF)
 I. H. 4/23/1864 (CW)
 James ? (LC)
 Lyston M. 9/15/1917 (AF)
 William F. 1/9/1909 (AF)
THOMAS, Adam 5/7/1890
  (LC)
 Ann 6/9/1952 (LC)
 Elizabeth 4/12/1879 (LC)
 George 3/22/1864 (CW)
 Harry C. 4/17/1909 (AF)
 Henry 3/6/1864 (CW)
 Jane 3/21/1903 (AF)
 Joseph ? (LC)
 Perry ? (LC)
 William 4/25/1864 (CW)
THOMPSON, John 3/28/1865
  (CW)
 Oscar S. b. 3/8/1878 d.
  2/22/1904 (LC)
 Philip 11/26/1865 (CW)
 Rev. William (LC)
TIMCH, Edward 6/20/1864
  (CW)
TONEY, William 9/29/1864
  (CW)
TOWNSEND, Samuel
  4/24/1909 (AF)
TUBMAN, John T. Sr.
  4/6/1895 (LC)
 Moses Z. 11/1895 (LC)
 Priscilla 7/1/1835 (LC)

TUCKER, John W. 2/1865 (LC)
TYLER, John 4/1865 (CW)
VORN, Allen 1/22/1865 (CW)
WALKER, Abigha 11/25/1905 (AF)
WALLACE, Greenburg 5/12/1864 (CW)
WARD, John 3/16/1864 (CW)
✓ WASHINGTON, Eliza 5/17/1918 (AF)
Josiah 12/15/1864 (CW)
L. 3/23/1864 (CW)
Mary E. 2/19/1916 (AF)
WATTY, Hiram 10/28/1905 (AF)
WAYMAN, Bishop Alexander 1895 (LC)
WEAVER, Benjamin 7/1/1905 (AF)
William 9/11/1895 (LC)
William H. Dr. ? (LC)
WEBB, J. E. G. 6/30/1906 (AF)
WESLEY, James 3/23/1864 (CW)
John 12/11/1864 (CW)
WHALEY, Sidney 3/8/1864 (CW)
WHITAKER, John 3/27/1864 (CW)
WHITE, Dennison 8/1864 (CW)
Lewis 11/16/1864 (CW)
Sophia 7/11/1885 (LC)
WHITNEY, Edward 11/26/1864 (CW)
WILKINSON, P. 3/3/1864 (CW)
WILLIAMS, Daniel 5/51864 (CW)
Ella b. 7/25/1850 d. ? (LC)
Rev. Frank R. b. 5/9/1857 d. 11/11/1929 (LC)

✓ WILLIAMS (continued)
G. 4/5/1864 (CW)
Grace 9/26/1908 ?
Henry C. 3/27/1883 (LC)
John 5/15/1864 (CW)
Jqhn H. 1/28/1911 (AF)
Joseph 12/10/1910 (LC)
Joseph 10/31/1864 (CW)
Mary E. 1/28/1911 (code not available)
Minnie N. d. 3/14/1914 (LC)
Nelson 7/2/1906 (LC)
Richard 11/3/1864 (CW)
Rosa 8/12/1905 (AF)
WILLIAMSON, Joseph 3/7/1865 (CW)
WILSON, Charles 9/23/1864 (CW)
Fanie D. ? (LC)
Frank 3/17/1865 (CW)
Philip 8/1864 (CW)
Priscilla 11/26/1910 (code not available)
WINDS, Francis 4/20/1864 (CW)
WINSEY, Bertha ? (LC)
WONGER, Charles 5/28/1864 (CW)
WOODHOUSE, Mary C. 9/16/1911 (AF)
WOODSON, Cornelius 1846 – 1910 (LC)
WORTHAM, Plummer W. (Rev.) 5/10/1918 (AF)
WRIGHT, G. 11/10/1863 (CW)
YOUNG, Isaac 11/24/1864 (CW)
James 1/25/1865 (CW)
Robert A. 9/25/1909 (AF)
Thomas 9/24/1863 (CW)

SLAVEHOLDERS OF BALTIMORE 1860

"Oh get you ready, childron,
don't you get weary
Get you ready, children,
don't you get weary
Dere's a great camp-meetin
in de promised land."
                Old slave song[1]

    Although slave trading was on the decline in Baltimore prior to the outbreak of the Civil War, slave owners were far from becoming a vanishing breed. The following index, which was compiled from Federal Census slave schedules for Baltimore in 1860, points to, by its sheer magnitude, the veracity of that statement. Any study of a primary source such as the census is beset with several problems. One is the use of terminologies that remain unexplained in that source. In order to discern their meaning one must use a combination of available historical data and assumption based on "good common sense". (Hopefully more of the former than the latter). Secondly, one must contend with enumerators' varying styles of handwriting. There are several ways to overcome this problem. When the records deal with city residents (as in this case), a study of Baltimore city directories may provide clues to spelling. A close look at the individual style of each enumerator's handwriting is helpful in determining subtle differences in letters of similar formation. Finally, a thorough double-check of all names is extremely important.
    Included with this index is a chart the author has devised, displaying an accurate statistical breakdown of slaves and their owners in Baltimore in 1860. One conclusion we can draw from this study is the predominance of female slaves in the Balatimore area (80%). Most of these had domestic chores to perform i.e. washer-woman, cook, ironer, etc. Interestingly, a study of the Cecil County slave population of the same time period reveals 951 slaves, 483 of which are female (50.5%). The rigors of plantation life obviously demanded the employment of a greater number of male slaves. This is not to say

that life was easy for the slave in the urban setting. A thesis set forth by M. Ray Della, Jr.[2] proposed that the great influx of German and Irish immigrants in the 1850's drove many free blacks as well as slaves from the northern labor market, both in semi-skilled and unskilled jobs. According to Della those not trained as domestics "Probably left the city to go to New York or Boston, if they were free, or were sold into the deep South, if they were slave."[3]

Owners with the foresight to train their slaves in domestic labor were able, to a degree, to offset the loss of demand in the labor force resulting from the influx of the immigrants. This helped to bring about an increase in the practice known as hiring-out. The hiring out of slaves was accomplished in several ways. One, the owner signed a binding contract between himself and the employer; a contract which covered a specified time period and pre-arranged payments to the owner, with liability for the slave's welfare in the hands of the employer. Two, an owner allowed his or her slave to hire themselves out to an employer of their own choosing, provided the slave paid, out of his earnings a pre-arranged amount to his owner on a regular basis. Any money left over was his for the keeping.

The slave schedules will, in some cases, name the owner and, in the event his slave was hired out, the employer who did the hiring. I have included in this index the names of owners only since a check of that schedule will reveal the employers' names if it be so desired. The case where an owner's name is followed by the term, Estate Of, probably indicates that the owner is deceased and his slave property has not yet changed hands through the execution of his will. The term, In Trust, can have several meanings. It may indicate that slaves are being held by a second party for the owner while he or she is out of town. The other possibility is that the second party is holding slaves temporarily until the deceased owner's will is executed. For example, in the following ad that ran in a Baltimore paper in July 1860 Owen Cecil, Administrator of the will of the deceased may have held the slaves prior to execution of the will.

"The negroes belonging to the estate of William Cecil- slaves for life. Immediately after the sale of the household furniture, as above, the undersigned, administrator of the estate of William Cecil, deceased, will sell by order of the Orphans Court of Baltimore City. The negroes belonging to the estate of William Cecil, most of whom are slaves for life. As follows:

NEGRO MAN, David 18 years of age – slave for life
NEGRO MAN named William, about 48 years of age – slave
for life
NEGRO WOMAN named Sarah – slave for life
NEGRO GIRL named Jane, 23 years of age – slave for eight
years
NEGRO named Andrew – slave for life

We call the attention of those wanting Negroes to the above sale. Terms as prescribed by the court – One third cash, and the balance in two equal payments, on credits of four and eight months, with interest from the day of the sale, and that where credit is given, bond with good security. shall be taken."
Owen Cecil, Administrator of William Cecil, deceased
ADREON and Co. Aucts."

The slave schedules of 1860 list him with twenty-four female and twenty-six male slaves. His slave depot, located at 282 West Pratt Street (now 224 W. Pratt), was close to the slave jail owned by another of Baltimore's largest slave dealers, Hope H. Slatter. Slatter's jail held slaves who were often sold on the auction block in the courthouse behind the building. "The building which housed the slaves at night was a two story brick affair with barred windows, and its appearance was not unlike that of a stockade. The women slaves occupied the second floor, the men the ground floor. During the daytime they did a little work, but generally loitered about the yard playing cards, singing and dancing to tunes fiddled by some of their fellows."
Another dealer, Joseph S. Donavan, kept his slave jail on the southwest corner of Camden and Eutaw Streets. Although he is listed with only eighteen slaves in the schedules, it is safe to assume that hundreds of them passed through his hands on their way to the South.

NOTES

[1] Cabin and Plantation Songs, arranged by Thomas P. Fenner and Frederic G. Rothbun, 1891.
[2] Della, M. Ray, Jr. "Problems of Negro Labor," *Maryland Historical Magazine*, v. 66, no. 1, Spring 1971.
[3] Ibid., p. 19.
[4] *Baltimore American*, July 3, 1860, p.3.

[5] *Baltimore and Ohio Magazine*, v. 27, no. 2, February 1941, p.25.

[6] Scharf, J. Thomas. *History of Baltimore City and County* (Philadelphia:Louis H. Everts, 1881) p. 145.

| No. of Entry | Names | —Sex— | | Age | —Height— | | Whether Negro Mulatto or Person of color | Owner or shipper | |
		Male	Female		Feet	Inches		Name	Residence
27.	Mary Dorsey		"	18	5	1	Black	Hope	
28.	Charlotte Morgan		"	26	5	5	"	H.	
29.	Edward Nelson	"		Infant			"	Slatter	
30.	Adaline Francis		"	6	3	7	"	(shipper)	
31.	Catherine Hogan		"	4	3	1	"		
32.	Elisha Shorter		"	30	5	4	"		
33.	Asbury Shorter	"	.	11	4	6	"		

Examined and found correct
S. W. Pops April 9, 1845
G. M. Browsfrich
Brig. Off.

District of Baltimore-Port of Baltimore
22nd day of March, 1845

Hope H. Slatter, owner and shipper of the persons named and particularly described in the *above* manifest of *Slaves* and *W..J. Watts*, Master of the *Barque Home*, do solemnly, sincerely, and truly swear, each of us to the best of our knowledge and belief that the *above slaves have* not been imported into the United States since the first day of January, one thousand, eight hundred and eight; and that under the laws of the State of Maryland, *are* held to service or labor as—slaves and *are* not entitled to freedom under these laws at a certain time and after a known period of service—so help *you* God.

Sworn to this 22nd day of March, 1845.

W. H. Marrot, Collector.

Hope H. Slatter
Wm. J. Watts

Slave Manifest (*Manifests of Slave Shipments Along the Waterways, 1808-1864* by Charles H. Wesley, p. 171)

The Index

The index to the Federal Census Slave Schedules is set up as follows:

Last name, first name, middle initial if given (question mark indicates initial is not discernible), number of female slaves, number of male slaves, ward number, and the page number in the ward's schedule.

BAYLIES, Charles (?) 1 F 7-2

George H. 1 F 7-2

BAYNE, William 3 F, 2 M 14-1

BEALE, Ellen E. 1 F 1-1

BEAM, Mrs. 2 F, 1 M 14-2

BEAN, John H. 1 F 1-1

BEARD, Mr. 1 F 18-6

Thomas H. 1 F 15-1

BEATTY, S. Lewis 1 F 11-3

BECKER, C.T. 3 F, 2 M 20-1

BEELMER, Catherine 1 F 9-1

BEHLER, W. 1 M 3-2

BELL, Frances W. 1 F 11-1

T. H. 1 F 9-1

BELMORE, Catherine 3 F 11-2

BENNET, Ann E. 1 F 20-1

BENNETT, George W. (1 fugitive) 8-6

John 1 F 7-1

BERKELY, Edris 3 F 20-1

BERRY, Charles D. 1 F, 1 M 12-1

George W. 1 F 5-6-1

Joseph W. 1 F 15-2

Walter W. 2 F 15-2

BEVAN, Francis 5 F, 5 M 20-3

BEVANS, William 1 M 9-1

BIAS, Joseph 1 F 15-2

Joseph 1 F 18-5

BIGHAM, Maria 1 M 20-2

BILMERS, Mrs. 1 M 9-1

BIRD, James A. 3 F, 1 M 18-8

Marriot 2 F 16-1

Stephen 1 F 14-2

Steven L. 1 F 11-3

BLACKISTON, Mary 1 F 18-8

William 1 F 15-2

BLAIR, Michael M. 1 F 8-5

BLAKE, S. V. 1 F 15-2

BLOCKER, Daniel 1 F 18-6

BOGGS, Susan G. 2 F 11-3

BOND, George 1 M 18-5

BOONE, Mary 1 F, 1 M 18-8

BORDLEY, James 2 F, 12 M 9-2

BOSTON, Cecilia 1 F 18-6

Esau 1 F 11-4

John 1 F, 1 M 3-1

BOULDER, Owen 2 F 4-1

BOULDIN, Anna 1 F 5-6-1

BOUNDS, Mrs. 1 F 4-1

BOWEN, Mary 1 F 8-5

BOWLING, Thomas W. 1 F 14-1

BOWMAN, Rebecca 1 M 18-5

BOYD, J. J. 1 F 18-7

BRADFORD, Margaret 1 M 11-2

BRENER, Matilda 1 F 20-1

BRENNER, Cecelia 1 M 8-6

BRENT, George 1 F 5-6-2

BRIAN, Deborah 1 F 5-6-2

William S. 1 F 11-4

BRICE, George H. 1 M 20-1

BRISCOE, Elizabeth 1 F, 2 M 18-8

BRISCOE, William 1 F 11-4

BROMWELL, H.J. 1 F 14-2

BROOKS, Mary C. 1 F 15-2

Walter 1 M 14-1

BROWN, Basil 2 M 13-1

Elizabeth 1 F 14-1

Elizabeth 2 F 20-3

Garret 1 F 20-3

George 1 F 5-6-2

I. F. 1 F 14-1

John W. 1 F 11-3

Lewis 3 F, 4 M 5-6-2

M. 1 F 3-2

Martha 2 F 18-7

Thomas R. 1 F 20-1

BRUFF, John 2 F, 1 M 18-5
BRUNDRIDGE, William 3 F, 3 M
BRUSCUSS, Sally 1 F 4-1
BUCK, Adelaide 1 F, 1 M 4-1
 Bill 1 F 14-1
 William 1 F 20-1
BURNETT, Lewis H. 1 F, 3 M 20-3
BURNS, L. 1 F 3-2
 Samiel 1 F 11-3
BUSBY, Abraham 1 F 20-2
BUTLER, Thomas 1 F 3 M 4-1
BYM, William F. 1 F 2-1
BYRNES, Elizabeth 1 F 7-2
CALLADAY, B.C. 1 F 18-5
CALLAWAY, William S. 1 M 7-2
CALVERT, William S. 1 F 20-2
CAMPBELL, Bernard 24 F, 26 M
CANFIELD, James 1 M 3-1
CANN, Daniel M. 4 F 11-4
CANNON, Mary A. 1 M 9-1
CARBACK, Sarah 2 F 20-1
CARCAN, Gerber 1 F 20-1
CARLISLE, William C. 2 F, 1 M
CARR, Martha 1 M 19-1
 Robert H. 3 F, 1 M 11-3
CARROLL, Charles R. 3 M 11-4
 Harry 1 M 9-1
 Harry D.G. 1 F 11-1
 Judith C. 2 F 11-3
CARSON, John 1 F 18-8
 Thomas J. 3 F, 1 M 11-5
CARVIN, Thomas 1 F 11-3
CATOR, Benjamin F. 4 F 11-2
 Clarissa 1 F, 1 M 15-1
 Elizabeth 2 F, 2 M 15-1
 M. 1 F 15-1

CATOR (continued)
 Robinson W. 1 F, 1 M 11-1
CAUGHY, Ellen 1 F, 2 M 12-1
 Michael 2 F 5-6-1
 Patrick 2 F 12-1
CECIL, W. 1 F 15-1
CHANDLER, David 1 F 18-6
 George 1 F 18-8
CHANLER, Sarah 1 F 7-2
CHASE, Daniel 1 F 20-3
 Daniel 5 F, 2 M 20-3
 Daniel 1 F, 1 M 20-3
CHESNUTT, William 1 F, 2 M 4-1
CHURCHMAN, Francis 1 F 11-3
CHURNE, John 2 F 20-3
CLAGGETT, Mary 2 F, 3 M 20-2
CLARK, Benjamin 1 F 15-1
 Elizabeth 1 F 11-2
 Henry 1 M 12-1
 Maria 1 M 11-4
 Mary A. 3 F 15-3
 Mathew 1 F 18-8
 Temperance 1 F 18-7
 William 1 M 15-1
CLARKE, Charles R. 2 F 20-2
 Martha M. 1 F 11-4
 Zackariah 2 F, 5 M 1-1
CLARY, Aaron 2 F 8-5
CLAWON, Mary 1 F 15-1
CLIFFORD, John 1 F 14-1
 Sylvester 2 M 16-1
COCHRAN, John 1 F 5-6-1
COCKEY, Ed 3 F, 2 M 1-1
 Elizabeth 1 F 11-1
 Peter 1 F 5-6-2
COLBURNER, L.D. 2 F, 1 M 15-2
 L. D. 1 F 15-2
COLE, Ellen 2 F, 1 M 14-1
 Ellen G. 1 F 20-1
 Martha 2 F 18-7

59

COLE (continued)
Nancy 1 F 5-6-2
William 1 F 3-1
William 1 F 5-6-2
COLEMAN, Gezno 1 F 7-2
James 1 M 18-7
COLLIER, Jane A. 1 F 8-5
COMPTON, Eliza 1 F 5-6-1
CONLEY, Emma 1 F 8-5
CONN, James C. 1 F 11-1
CONNOR, Richard 1 F 15-1
CONRAD, George 1 F 4-1
Nelson 2 F 14-2
CONWAY, Columbus (?) 2 F, 2-1
James 1 M 15-2
John R. 1 M 15-3
COOK, Catherine 2 F, 1 M 9-1
Stephen 1 F 9-2
COOPER, Elector 2 F 7-2
Elector E. 1 F 7-2
Hugh H. 2 F 2-1
James 1 F 15-3
CORNER, Solomon 1 F 11-2
COTTMAN, James s. 1 F 11-1
James S. 2 F 11-4
COY, Benjamin F. 1-F 11-3
CRANE, Mary 1 F 20-1
CRASH, Mary 1 F 3-1
CRAWFORD, Arabella 1 F 18-5
George 1 F 12-1
Mrs. 1 F 18-6
CREBS, Julia 1 F, 1 M 7-2
CREY, Elizabeth 1 F 8-6
CRICHTON, William 1 F 11-1
CROMWELL, Richard 3 F 12-1
CROOK, Caroline 1 F 19-1
CROSS, John M. 1 F, 1 M 7-2
CUNNINGHAM, James W. 1 F 5-6-1

CUNNINGHAM (continued)
Martha 1 F, 1 M 4-1
Sarah 1 F 18-8
CUSHING, Francis 1 F, 1 M 14-2
DAIL, Daniel 4 F, 2 M 2-1
DAIRY, George 1 F 3-1
DALLAM, Edward B. 1 F 11-4
DALLAS, Mary 2 F 19-2
DANIELS, John D. 2 F 11-1
DARBY, Benjamin 1 F 18-5
DARKINS, Miss 1 F 11-2
DASHIEL, Dr. Nicholas L. 1 M 2-1
DASHIELDS, Henry 3 F, 1 M 18-5
DASHIELL, Mary 4 F, 2 M 2-1
DAVIDSON, B. 1 F 3-1
DAVIS, John F. 1 F 13-1
Priscilla 2 F, 1 M 12-1
William 1 M 3-1
DAY, John 1 F 5-6-1
John G. 1 M 11-1
DEAL, George J. 1 F 20-2
Mary 1 F 3-1
DEBOW, Harriet 1 F, 2 M 20-3
DEFFENDAFFER, Mrs. 1 F 9-1
DEFORD, Benjamin 1 M 11-3
DEMPSEY, John 1 F 3-1
DENHAM, Maria 1 F 11-3
DENMEAD, Ann 1 M 11-3
DENNY, Ann 1 F 11-2
James 1 F 3-1
DERLIN, Ann M. 1 F 2-1
DESHON, Mary 1 F 14-1
DICKERSON, Mrs. 1 M 14-1
DICKSON, William 1 F 18-7
DIFFEL, George 1 F 20-2
DIFFENDAFER, Sarah 1 M 20-2
DIFFENDAFFER, Sarah 4 F,

DIFFENDAFFER (continued)
3 M 9-1
DIGGS, Richard 2 F, 1 M 3-1
DISNEY, William 1 F 20-3
DOAKLEY, Henry M. 1 F 9-1
DOANE, Mary 1 F 11-4
 Mrs. 1 F 14-2
DONI, Julia 1 F 9-1
 Miss 1 F 9-1
DONOVAN, Joseph S. 8 F, 10
 M 16-1
DORSEY, Allen 1 F, 1 M 14-
2
 Amanda 1 F 5-6-1
 Comfort 2 F, 3 M 10-1
 Edward 3 F 4-1
 Grace 2 F 20-1
 Mary A. 1 F 20-4
 Matilda 1 F 18-5
 Michael 1 F 15-2
 Samuel 1 F 18-7
 Trueman 1 F 20-1
 W. 1 F 3-2
DOUGHERTY, James W. 2
 F, 1 M 15-2
DOWNES, M. 2 F 9-1
DOWNS, Clara 1 F 16-1
DRILL, Mary 1 F 20-3
DUDLEY, Mary 1 F 3-2
DUNCAL, George 2 F, 2 M
 19-2
DUNNICK, Samuel 1 F 15-1
DUSHANE, J.A. 1 F 15-2
DUVALL, William 2 M 20-2
EARHART, George 1 F 20-2
EDMONDS, Rebecca 3 F 19-
1
EDMONDSON, H.L. 1 F, 1 M
 18-6
 Horace 1 F 11-2
EGERTON, John B. 1 F 11-3
EHLER, John H. 1 F, 1 M
 12-1
ELICOTT, Elias 1 F 19-1
ELLMORE, James 3 F 1-1
ELY, John 1 F 1-1

EMMICH, Christian 1 M 18-7
EMORY, Arthur 1 F 5-6-2
 Catherine 1 M 11-2
 Henry M. 1 M 11-2
 John B. 1 F, 1 M 16-1
 Mary 1 F 20-3
ENSOR, John 1 M 18-6
ERRICKSON, J. 1 F 3-2
 Mrs. 1 F 4-1
ESCHBACH, Joseph A. 1 F,
 1 M 8-5
EVANS, Henry W. 1 F 12-2
 Mrs. 1 M 4-1
 William 2 F, 18-8
 William H. 1 F, 1 M 15-1
EZY, Letia 2 F, 1 M 9-1
FAIRALL, Alex 1 F 20-1
FAIRBANKS, W. 1 M 3-2
 William 1 F 3-1
FAITHFUL, Ann 4 F, 4 M
 18-6
 Mrs. 1 F 18-5
FALLS, Moore N. 1 F 20-3
 Sarah 1 F 20-2
FANKERSON, Emily 1 F, 3
 M 12-1
FEILMAN, Capt. Richard 1 F
 12-1
FELGMAN, William P. 2 F
 12-1
FELL, Mary 1 F, 1 M 8-6
FERGUSON, J.C.H. 3 F 18-6
FERNANDIS, Walter 1 F 11-
1
FINDALL, Philip 1 M 20-3
FISHER, Fannie 2 F 14-1
FITZGERALD, Robert B. 1
 F, 2 M 12-2
FLACK, Thomas I. Sr. 2 F
 14-1
FLAHARTY, William R. 1 F
 18-5
FOLLANSBER, Joseph (?) 1
 M 18-5
FORBES, James 1 F 20-3
FORBES, Mathias 3 F 18-7

FORD, James 1 F 3-1
 John 2 F 18-6
 Josiah 1 F 11-3
 Mr. 1 F 14-1
FORREST, Moreau 1 M 11-3
FORSYTHE, Alex 2 F, 2 M
 20-1
FOSBENNER, William G. 1
 F 15-3
FRAILEY, Leonard 2 F 14-1
FRANCE, John 1 F 3-1
 Richard 1 M 11-1
 Richard 3 F, 1 M 11-3
FRANK, Mary 1 F, 1 M 4-1
FRAZIER, John 1 M 18-7
FREEBURGER, Lytha 1 M
 15-1
FREEMAN, Sophia 1 F 5-6-1
FRICKS, George P. 1 M 20-1
FRYER, Gunblet 1 F, 1 M 3-
 1
 James 1 F 3-1
FULLER, Richard 4 F, 2 M
 11-4
FULTON, Louis 1 F 18-6
GAILINGLY, Harmam 3 F, 1
 M 12-1
GALE, Elizabeth 1 F 20-3
 Polena 1 F 1-1
 Robert W. 1 F 16-1
 Sarah 2 F, 1 M 20-4
 Susan 2 F 20-3
GAMBRILL, Charles 2 F, 1
 M 14-1
GANTZ, Mary 2 F, 4 M 19-1
GARDINER, Dr. 2 F 12-2
GARRETT, Emiley 1 F, 2 M
 19-1
 William 7 F, 8 M 16-1
GARVIL, C. 1 F 3-2
GARVIN, Robert 1 F 9-1
GAULT, Ann Eliza 1 F 5-6-1
 Dickson 1 F 5-6-2
GEORGE, Mary 1 M 3-2
 Philip T. 1 F, 1 M 11-3
GIBBS, Mary 1 F 18-6

GIBSON, George S. 1 F 11-4
 George S. 1 M 11-4
GILMORE, Nancy 1 F 5-6-2
GIST, Ellenor 1 F 18-7
GITTINGS, James 1 M 8-6
 James (In Trust) 3 F 20-1
 John S. 1 F 11-4
 John S. 1 M 11-4
 Margaret 1 M 5-6-1
 Miss 1 F 9-1
 Williams S. 1 M 11-2
GIVIN, James 1 M 12-1
GLADSTONE, Rebecca 1 F
 8-6
GLENN, Henrietta 1 F, 11-3
 Henrietta 1 F, 2 M 13-1
GOLDSBOROUGH, Dr. 1 M
 9-1
 Mrs. 1 F 9-1
 Mrs. 2 F, 2 M 11-4
GOODACHRE, John 1 F, 1 M
 3-2
GOODLOW, Mary 1 F 18-7
GOODRICH, Henry 3 F, 1 M
 5-6-1
GOODWIN, Achsha 1 F, 1 M
 8-6
 Charles 1 F 14-2
GOOLL, Elizabeth 1 F 18-5
GORDON, William 1 F 11-2
GOSNELL, Douglas 1 F 19-1
 Phillip 1 F 14-1
 Phillip H 1 F 14-2
GOTEE, Sarah A. 2 F 1-1
GOUGH, Ann 1 F 11-4
 Henry 1 F 11-1
GRAFTON, Samuel 1 F 18-7
GRAHAM, Amanda 1 F, 1 M
 5-6-2
 Mrs. 1 M 9-2
GRANGER, George 1 M 14-1
 Henry 1 M 14-1
GRANT, George 1 F 2-1
GREEN, Amon 1 F 8-5
 Ann 1 F 11-4
 Mrs. 1 F 9-1

GREEN (continued)
Sarah 1 M 11-4
GREENWELL, James 1 F 14-2
GREGG, James 2 F 11-4
GREY, Francis 1 M 3-1
GRIFFIN Robert B. 1 F 12-1
GRIFFITH, Capt. 1 F 18-5
Chanleth 1 M 16-1
Emily 1 F 12-2
John 4 F, 1 M 11-3
Mary E. 1 M 20-1
Michael 2 F, 1 M 11-1
GRIFFITHS, Maria 1 F 20-3
GRIMES, Mrs. 1 F 13-1
S. 4 F 3-2
GRINDALL, John T. 1 F 15-1
GROGAN, Henry 1 M 11-5
GROVE, Daniel 1 F, 1 M 18-6
GROVERMAN, Anthony 3 F, 1 M 11-1
Henry 1 F 18-6
Samuel 1 F 11-2
GUNTHER, Lewis 1 F 18-5
HACKETT, Mrs. James 1 M 11-4
HADAWAY, John 2 F 15-2
HALL, Eliza 1 M 11-3
Hester 1 F 3-1
Margaret 1 F, 1 M 10-1
Sarah 1 F, 12-2
Sarah B. 1 F 18-7
Susan 1 F 3-2
William 1 F, 1 M 15-2
HALLADAY, Robert B. 1 M 11-5
HALLER, Elizabeth 1 M 4-1
HAMB, Pondence 3 M 16-1
HAMEY, Joseph 1 M 14-2
HAMILTON, Edward 1 F 18-6
Mr. 1 F 10-1
Mary C. 1 F 11-3
Sarah 1 F, 1 M 18-6

HAMILTON (continued)
Thomas E. 1 F 11-2
William 1 F 20-2
HAMMOND, George 1 F 18-7
Col. Thomas 1 F 12-2
HAMON, J.C. 1 F 18-8
HANAWAY, James 1 F 8-5
HANDY, Thomas 1 F 11-4
HANNEL, Dr. James 2 F 12-1
HANSE, George 1 F 9-1
HANSON, John 2 F 10-1
Maria 1 F 18-6
HARDESTY, Mary 1 M 15-1
Richard S. 1 F 11-1
HARDON, Joseph 2 F 18-5
HARDY, Thomas 1 F, 3 M 19-1
HARE, Maria 1 F 8-6
HARKER, John J. 1 M 8-6
HARMON, Enos 1 F, 1 M 18-5
HARR, Mary E. 1 F 18-7
HARRINGTON, Mary 1 M 16-1
HARRIS, Mary 1 F 12-1
Morrison 1 M 11-4
HARRISON, James 1 F 3-1
Margaret 3 F, 1 M 18-5
Mary A. 1 F 7-2
Samuel A. 1 F, 1 M 11-1
Sarah (In Trust) 1 F 20-4
HASLOP, Ruth 2 F 18-7
HASLUPH, Reason 2 F, 1 M 9-1
HAUCK, Albert 1 F 3-1
Daniel 1 M 3-1
Joseph 1 M 3-1
HAWKINS, Caroline 1 F 19-1
HAYMORE, Alice 1 M 3-2
HAYNE, Eliza 1 F 11-1
HAZELITT, James 1 M 14-2
HEALD, John H. 1 F 11-1
HEIGH, Benjamin 2 F, 1 M 11-4
HEIRN, Anna 1 F 12-1

HENDERSON, Alice 1 F 8-5
Eliza 1 F 13-1
J. Frisby 1 M 11-4
James 1 F, 1 M 4-1
Mrs. 1 M 4-1
Thomas 1 F 5-6-1
HENSLEY, John 1 M 10-1
HERNAN, Peter 1 F 11-1
HERRING, Mrs. 1 F 4-1
HEY, Charles H. 3 F 11-1
HIGGANS, Dr. James 1 M
11-2
HIGGINS, Asa 1 M 18-7
HIGHLAND, John 1 M 9-1
HILDT, George C. 1 F, 1 M
2-1
HILLEN, Rebecca A. 1 F 11-
3
HINDES, Mary 2 F 14-2
HINDS, G. 4 F 15-2
Margaret 1 F 15-2
HISER, Henry W. 2 F 14-1
HITCH, John 1 F 4-1
William 1 F 18-7
William 2 F, 1 M 19-1
HITCHCOCK, Joshou F. 1 F
11-1
HOBBS, Samuel 1 M 12-1
HOBLITZELL, James 2 F, 1
M 14-1
HODGES, Mary 1 F 3-1
HODGKINS, Thomas 1 M 9-1
HOFFMAN, Aaron 1 M 20-1
Charles 1 F 14-2
H. K. 4 F 14-1
HOLLAND, Amanda 3 F 14-2
Sarah 1 F 5-6-1
HOLMS, Victor 1 F 20-3
HOOPER, Elizabeth 1 F 11-2
Elizabeth 3 F 19-1
Joseph 1 F 15-2
Joseph J. 3 F 18-5
Rachael 1 F 20-3
T. (Estate of) 1 F, 2 M 15-1
Thomas 1 M 12-1
Zepola 1 M 9-1

HOPKINS, Ann 1 M 14-1
Dr. 1 M 10-1
James 2 F 16-1
Lavina 1 M 11-1
Martha 1 F 12-1
HOUCK, John 4 F, 2 M 4-1
HOUGH, Dixon 2 F 15-2
Robert 1 M 11-1
William 1 M 11-1
HOULTON, Mary 1 F, 1 M
19-1
William 1 F 19-1
HOWARD, Benjamin C. 5 F,
4 M 11-5
Charles 1 F, 1 M 11-1
Charles 1 M 20-1
Harriet 2 F 3-1
Henretta 1 F 11-2
James 1 M 20-1
Mary 1 F 11-3
HUDSON, Rebecca 1 F, 1 M
20-2
Sarah 2 F 20-2
HUGGINS, Mary 1 F 16-1
HUNT, John w. 2 F 5-6-2
Julia 1 M 19-1
HUNTER, Ellen M. 2 F 11-2
HURBERT, Henry C. 1 F, 1
M 13-1
HUTCHINS, John 1 F 15-2
Thomas T. 3 F 11-4
HUTTON, Isaac 2 F 18-6
Jane 1 F 11-2
HYATT, Mary 2 F 15-3
Richard 2 F 15-1
HYLAND, George 1 F 11-1
Mary 1 F 11-3
IAGO, Michael 1 F 11-3
IGLEHART, James 1 F 15-2
IMMOKE, John 1 M 7-2
IRELAND, Edward 2 F 11-2
ISAACS, Richard 1 M 15-1
IVETT, Eliza 1 F 14-1
JACKSON , Mollie E. 1 M
11-2
JACOBS, Samuel 2 F 15-2

JAMES, Ann 2 F 3-1
George 1 F 5-6-1
JAMESON, Charles C. 3 F, 2
    M 11-4
John 1 M 11-2
JAMISON, John 3 F, 8 M 5-
    6-1
JENKINS, Alfred 1 F 12-1
Ann M. 2 F, 11-3
Austin 1 F 11-5
Heigh 1 F 20-2
Mary A. 1 M 11-2
T. Robert 1 F 11-3
JESSOP, James 1 F 19-1
JESSUP, George 1 F 8-5
JESUITS, Order of 1 F 11-1
JOHNSON, George 1 F 15-2
George 1 F 20-2
Mary 1 F, 1 M 15-1
Sarah 5 M 19-1
Thomas 1 F 20-2
W. L. 1 F 14-1
William 1 F 5-6-2
JOHNSTON, Elizabeth 1 F
    11-3
JONES, Abraham 2 F 3-1
Charles 1 F 5-6-2
Dr. 1 M 20-3
Henry 1 F 11-1
James 1 M 15-1
Levi 1 F 15-2
Mrs. 1 F 4-1
Sarah 1 F, 1 M 15-1
JOYCE, Henry 1 F 5-6-1
KAFLINSKI, Susan 1 F, 1 M
    13-1
KAIN, Amelia 1 F 15-2
KALLFAUS, Margaret 1 F, 1
    M 12-2
KANE, George P. 2 M 11-3
Mary 1 F 5-6-1
KEENE, Benjamin 1 F 18-7
Benjamin 2 F, 1 M 20-3
Benjamin 2 F 20-3
Elanora 2 F 14-1
John R. 2 F 12-2

KEENE (continued)
Mrs. 1 M 18-8
Richard 1 F 11-4
Susan 2 F 14-1
KEIGLE, David 1 F 12-1
KELLY, Timothy 1 F 13-1
Harriet 1 F 3-1
Mrs. 2 F 18-6
KEMP, Frederick C. 1 F 8-5
John N. 1 F 11-4
KENLY, Edward 2 F 14-2
KENNARD, George 1 F 5-6-1
KETTLEWELL, A.L. 1 F
    15-2
KILTY, Augustus 1 F 11-3
KIMBERLY, Henry 1 F 1-1
Henry 1 F 8-6
James 1 M 18-7
KING, Anna 1 M 9-1 [co
    owns with George
    Merryman]
Benjamin F. 1 F 2-1
John 2 F 18-7
KIRBY, John 2 F, 1 M 19-2
KIRK, Ellen 1 F 5-6-1
KIRT, Amelia 1 F 20-3
KOON, C.H. 1 M 14-1
KOORSMAN, William H. 1
    F, 1 M
KYLE, Adam B. 1 M 15-2
LAMDIN, Ann 1 F 7-1
S. 1 F 3-2
William K. 2 F, 2 M 8-6
LANAHAN, William 1 M 14-
    1
LANGE, Mary 2 F 12-2
LANGFORD, Henry S. 2 F
    11-2
LAWARENCE, Catherine 6
    M 12-1
LEACH, Matilda 1 F 5-6-2
Mrs. 1 F 9-1
William 1 F 11-3
LEARY, W. 1 F 15-1
LEBRON, Mary 2 M 1-1
LEE, Thomas 2 F 20-2

LEONARD, Mary 1 F 15-3
 William 1 F 10-1
LEVERING, Samuel S. 1 M
 11-4
 Thomas W. 1 F, 2 M 11-1
LEWIS, William 1 M 4-1
LILBRIAN, John Y. 1 F 8-5
LILBRUN, John 1 F 5-6-1
LILGHAM, Cap 1 F 14-2
LINDEY, Mary 1 F 12-1
LINTHICUM, Sweetzer 1 F
 16-1
LLOYD, Thomas 1 M 2-1
LOCKWOOD, Robert 1 F 18-
 8
LOGEN, James 1 F 20-1
LONEY, William 1 F 11-4
 William 1 F 20-2
LONG, H.A. 2 F 15-2
LORD, Josiah 2 F 11-2
LOVE, Robert H. 4 F 11-1
LOWE, Mrs. 1 F 4-1
LUCKABAUGH, Mary 1 F
 20-1
LURNBULL, Mr. 1 F 14-2
LYNCH, Emma 1 F 18-7
 Ruth 1 F 5-6-1
MACE, Frances 1 F 8-6
 Virginia 1 F 8-6
MACKENZIE, Colon 2 F 11-
 1
MADDOX, Charles T. 1 M
 11-3
 Elizabeth 3 F 10-1
 Mary 1 F 11-2
 Miss 1 M 20-3
MAGRUDER Eliza 2 F, 1 M
 13-1
 Sarah 1 F 20-3
MAKEPIECE, Susan 1 M 11-
 1
MALSOY, Hannah 1 M 10-1
MANBIA, Isaac 1 F 18-6
MANKIN, John (?) 1 F, 3 M
 2-1
MANLY, John 2 F 16-1

MANNING, Elizabeth 1 F 16-
 1
MANSFIELD, Sarah 2 F, 1 M
 7-2
MANSOW, Manor 1 M 14-2
MANSOW, Rachael 1 F, 1 M
 14-2
MARENA, Thomas P. 1 F, 1
 M 9-1
MARKLAND, William 1 F, 1
 M 16-1
MARRIOTT, J. McKim 1 F,
 1 M 11-1
 Mrs. 1 F 12-2
MARTER, James 1 F 7-2
MARTIN, Lucretia 1 F 20-1
 Samuel 1 M 3-2
 Thomas 1 F 20-2
 William 1 F, 1 M 4-1
 William 1 F, 11-2
 William 1 F, 15-1
MASON, Mary 1 F, 20-1
MASS, Hamilton 2 F 7-2
MATHEW, James B. 1 F 12-
 1
MATLOCK, Elizabaeth 1 M
 10-1
MATTHEW, Susan 1 F 9-2
MATTHEWS, Isaac 1 F 18-5
MATTHIOT, Augustas 1 M
 11-4
McADAMS, Edward 1 F 11-3
McCABE, John C. 1 F 11-3
McCLELLAN, William W. 1
 F 11-1
McCLEMEN, Carey 1 F, 1 M
 18-6
McCLEMENS, Laura 1 F 3-1
McCORMICK, Dr. 1 F 14-2
 William 1 F 5-6-1
McCOY, Mary 1 M 11-4
McDANIEL, James 1 F, 1M
 20-2
McDERMOT, Elizabeth 1 F,
 1 M 15-2
 Mrs. 1 F 18-6

McDEVITT, John 1 F 11-3
McELDERRY, Henry 1 F 18-7
Margaret 2 F, 2 M 11-3
McGREW, J. 1 F 3-2
McKAY, Miss 1 M 9-1
McKEW, D.J. 1 F 5-2
Elizabeth 1 F 2-1
McKIM, John S. 1 F 11-1
McLAVISH, Emily 1 F 11-1
McMULLAN, John 1 F 10-1
McMURRAY, Sallie 1 F 20-1
McNEAL, Sarah 1 F, 1 M 2-1
McPHERSON, Samuel 1 M 1-1
McTAVISH, Emily 1 M 11-3
Emiy 1 F 18-7
MEDCALFE, Henrietta 1 M 11-3
MEDINGER, Charles W. 2 F, 1 M, 19-1
MEILLER, John 1 F 15-3
MEKER, Charel 1 F 12-1
MERRITT, George 1 F 18-6
MERRYMAN, George 1 M 9-1 [Anna King co owner]
MEYERS, George 1 F 18-5
MICAL, Mrs. 2 F 4-1
MILBURN, Susan 2 F 20-2
MILES, Samuel G. 4 F 14-1
MILLER, Adam M. 1 F 12-1
Caroline 1 F 19-1
Decator 2 F 11-3
Margaret 2 F 14-2
Mary 1 M 9-1
Samuel 1 F 5-6-1
MILLS, Ann 1 F 5-6-1
Catherine 2 F 16-1
Joshua 1 F 18-7
Mary 2 F 15-2
MINCE, Eleanor 1 F 2-1
MITCHEL, Mary H. 1 F 7-2
MITCHELL, Elizabeth 1 F 18-5
Henry 3 F, 1 M 20-2
John 1 F 19-1

MITCHELL (continued)
Lucy 1 F 18-6
MOMAC, Francis C. 1 F, 2 M 9-1
MONMONIER, John 1 F 3-1
MONTAGUE, H.B. 4 F, 5 M 13-1
Mary 1 F 12-2
Sallie H. 1 M 11-4
MONTGOMERY, James 1 M 12-1
MOON, Edward 1 F, 1 M 18-7
Ruth 1 F 18-6
MOORE, Francis 2 F 12-1
Rachael 2 F 14-2
MORELAND, O. 1 F 15-1
MORRIS, Biddy 1 F 7-1
John B. 3 F, 1 M 11-3
John B. 1 F 20-1
MORROW, John 1 F 15-1
MORTON, George 1 F 12-1
Mary 2 F 15-2
Nicholas 1 F 20-2
MOULTON, James M. 1 F 14-2
MOWELL, Peter 1 F 1-1
MUCKLEROY, John 1 F 1-1
MULES, Thomas H. 1 M 19-1
MUNROE, Catheine 1 F 15-1
Richard 1 M 11-1
MURRAY, Herron, 1 F, 3 M 20-3
James 1 F 15-1
MUSSING, John 1 F 20-2
NEALE, Thomas Z. 3 F 11-2
NEATELL, George W. 1 F 5-6-1
NELSON, H. C. 1 F 18-5
Thomas 1 F 18-5
NEWTON, William M. 1 F 1-1
NICHOLS, Margaret 3 F 20-3
NICHOLSON, James M. 4 F, 3 M 11-1

NICHOLSON (continued)
John 1 F 18-7
Margaret 1 F 11-2
NORMAN, Michael 1 F 20-2
NORRIS, C. 1 F 20-2
Kennedy O. 1 F 11-3
Mary 1 F 3-1
Thomas 1 F, 1 M 19-1
William H. 2 F 1 M 11-3
OGLE, R. C. 1 F 20-2
OITLER, Moris 1 F 15-2
OLER, William H. 1 F 20-1
ONION, Lloyd D. 1 F 8-5
ORENDORF, Samuel 1 F, 1
M 12-1
OWENS, Ann 2 F 20-2
Ellen 1 M 18-6
James 1 F 18-5
Sally 1 F 18-6
Sarah 2 F 18-7
Sophia 1 F 18-6
Thomas J. 1 F 19-1
William H. 3 F 19-1
OWINGS, Sophia 1 F 10-1
PADGETT, William 2 F, 2
M 12-1
PAIRI, C.W. 1 F 20-1
PAPLER, George W. 2 F 1-1
Jacob 1 F, 2 M 1-1
PARKER, Rebecca 1 F, 2 M
18-7
PARKS, Laura 1 F 3-2
PASCOLT, William 1 M 19-
1
PASTERFORD, Matthew 1 M
8-6
PATERSON, Winder 1 F 15-
2
PATTEN, Adelaid 1 F, 1 M
5-6-2
PATTERSON, Ann 3 F, 2 M
15-1
Edward 3 F 9-1
Isabella 1 F 3-1
Sarah 1 F 15-2
PEARCE, Mary 1 F 20-3

PEARCE (continued)
S. A. 1 M 9-1
PEARSON, Joseph 2 F, 1 M
PEICKMAN Mary 1 F, 1 M
12-2
PENDLETON, Robert 2 F, 1
M 11-2
PENTZ, Samuel (?) 2 F 5-6-
1
PEREGOY, J.L.M. 1 F 18-5
PERESTON, Eliza 1 F 3-2
PERIN, Thomas 1 F, 1 M
16-1
PERKINS, B.T. 1 F 18-8
Jane 2 F 11-1
William 1 M 11-2
PERRY, James B. 1 F 15-1
PHELPS, Elmira 2 F, 2 M
20-2
Mrs. 1 M 9-1
PHILLIPS, J.N. 1 F, 1 M 18-
7
PIE, Caroline 1 F 19-2
PIERCE, Letitia 1 F 20-3
S. A. 1 F, 4 M 20-1
PIERSON, John 1 F 15-2
PIET, John B. 1 F 11-3
PIGMAN, Mrs. 1 F 14-1
PINDALL, Samuel 1 F 18-5
PINDELL, J. 1 F 3-2
PITCHER, Thomas 2 F, 1 M
16-1
PITTMAN, Catherine 1 M
14-2
PLATON, Ed 2 F, 1 M 18-8
PLATOR, Charles M. 2 F
11-4
PLUMMER, John F. 1 F 5-
6-1
PLY, Mrs. 1 F 18-8
POINDEXTER, Henry 2 F
11-1
Thomas 1 F 20-1
POLK, James 1 F, 1 M 20-3
PORTER, Maria 1 M 11-1
Robert 1 F 18-5

POSEY, John 1 F 5-6-1
POWELL, Mary 1 F 5-6-1
 Mary 1 M 5-6-2
PRACHT, August 1 F 20-1
PRATT, Mary 2 F, 1 M 18-7
PRESTON, James 1 M 5-6-2
PRICE, Ann 1 F 20-3
 George 2 F 18-6
 Marion 1 F 11-3
 William 1 M 8-6
 William E. 1 M 8-5
PRITCHARD, Joseph 1 F 18-
 7
 William 2 F, 1 M 15-1
PURDY, John Mrs. 1 F, 1 M
 4-1
PURNELL [no first name] 1
 F 20-1
 Maria 1 F 20-3
PURVIANCE, Henry Y. 1 M
 11-1
PURVIS, William F. 1 M 8-6
RABORG, Charles 1 M 16-1
 Harriett 1 F, 1 M 16-1
RADDELL, George 1 M 18-6
RANKIN, Dr. 1 F 18-8
RASIN, Mary R. 1 F 8-5
 Mary R. 2 F, 2 M 8-6
RATCLIFFE, Quintin 1 M
 19-1
READ, William G. 2 F, 1 M
 11-3
REDDING, Octavia 1 M 15-1
REDGRAVE, S. 1 M 15-1
 Samiel, H. 2 F 16-1
REED, Calvin 2 F 18-7
 Ellen 1 F 5-6-1
 James 2 F 4-1
 James A. 1 F 8-5
 Sarah 2 F 18-7
REILLY, George 1 F 18-5
REIMAN, Henry 1 F, 1 M 19-
 2
REINECKER, George 1 F, 2
 M 20-2

RESSO, Elizabeth 1 F, 1 M
 15-2
RHODES, Margaret 1 M 13-1
RICE, Henry 1 F 3-1
 Jacob 1 F, 1 M 19-1
RICHARDSON, Anna 1 F 12-
 2
 B. H. 1 F, 1 M 12-1
 George 1 F, 15-1
RIDGELY, Andrew S. 1 F,
 11-2
 Mary L. 1 M 11-1
RIDGEWAY, John 2 F 4-1
RIDGLEY, John R. 1 F 19-1
RIETHOLZ, William 1 F 18-
 5
RIGGINS, Ann 1 F 20-3
 Annie 2 F 20-3
RIGGS, George 2 M 19-1
RINGNOSE, J.W. 1 F 18-7
 John 1 F, 1 M 14-1
RITCHER, Thomas 3 M 18-6
ROBBINS, Henry 1 F 19-2
ROBERTS, Elizabeth 1 M 8-
 5
ROBERTSON, Charles 1 F
 14-2
ROBINSON, Dr. 6 F 13-2
 Harriett 1 F 18-5
ROBISON, John 1 F 19-1
RODEMYER, Mary 1 F 19-1
 John 1 F 14-2
RODGERS, William 1 F 18-7
ROGERS, Charles 3 F 7-2
ROLLINS, Eliza 1 F, 3 M
 13-1
 Mary 2 M 13-1
 Mary 4 F, 2 M 19-1
ROSE, Peter 3 F 15-2
 William H. 2 F, 3 M 10-1
ROSS, Rachel 1 F, 2 M 15-1
 William 1 F 20-1
RUDDISH, Mary 1 F 15-2
RUSKELL, Elenora 4 F, 3 M
 5-6-1

69

RUSKELL (continued)
John 3 F, 3 M 10-1
RUST, Peter 2 F, 1 M 18-5
RUTLEDGE, Ignatius 1 F
18-5
SANBORN, David M. 1 F 5-
6-1
SANDS, Hannah 1 F 20-1
SANK, Nicholas 1 F, 1 M 12-
1
SAPPINGTON, Jane 4 F 18-7
Mrs. 1 F 18-6
Dr. Thomas 1 F 12-2
SAYERS, Ariana 1 F 1-1
SCARF, John 3 F 3-1
SCARFF, Thomas 3 F, 1 M
18-5
SCHAEFER, William A. 1 M
18-6
SCHAEFFER, David 1 F 3-1
SCHOFIELD, Jesse S. 2 F
11-2
SCHRIVER, John 2 F 20-2
SCHWARTZ, Edward 2 M
18-5
SCOTT, Frances H. 1 F 18-7
SCRIMGER, Peter 1 F 15-3
SEARES, Julia A. 3 F, 3 M
2-1
SEARS, Amanda A. 1 F 1-1
SEATON, John L. 1 F 5-6-2
SEEVERS, Augustus F. 1 F
11-1
SEIDENSTRICKER, John B.
1 F 8-6
SELBY, John W. 1 F 20-1
SELDON, Mary 1 F 11-2
SEMMES, Mary J.T. 1 F 8-5
SEWARD, Eliza 1 F 15-1
SEWELL, Emily G. 2 F 20-1
SEWELL, Thomas 2 F 20-1
SHACKETT, Thomas 1 F 15-
2
SHANE, Morris 1 F 8-6
SHANKS, James 1 M 18-7

SHARP, William 1 F, 1 M
15-2
SHAVEN, John 1 F 3-2
SHAW, Elizabeth 1 F 1-1
Hugh 1 F 12-1
Matthew 1 F, 1 M 5-6-2
SHEFFY, Henry W. 1 F 11-1
SHERWOOD, Richard P. 3 F,
1 M 10-1
SHETHTON, A. 1 F 3-2
SHIELDS, John 1 F 11-3
Mrs. 1 F 14-2
SHIMP, H.A. 1 F 14-2
SHIPLEY, Enoch 1 F 14-1
SHIRK, Henry 1 F 12-1
SHOEMAKER, Samuel M. 2
F 11-2
William 2 F, 2 M 3-1
SHORB, Dr. 1 F 11-2
SHRIVER, Andrew 1 M 11-2
SHUCK, Julia A. 1 M 8-5
SHUTHOFF, Catherine 1 F
5-6-2
SIKS, William 1 F 3-1
SIMPKINS, R.G. 1 F 18-7
SIMPSON, John 1 F 3-1
SISSON, Hugh 1 F, 1 M 11-4
SKINNER, James A. 3 F 15-
1
Rachel 1 F 5-6-2
SLADE, John E. 1 F 11-4
SLATER, James 1 F, 1 M 3-
1
SLEE, Eliza 1 F 5-6-1
Eliza 1 F 7-1
SLINGLUFF, Charles D. 2 F
14-2
SLY, Mary 1 F 3-1
SLYDELL, Nathan 1 M 3-1
SMITH, Asa H. 1 F, 1 M 14-
2
Eliza A. 1 F 1-1
George M. 1 F 15-1
George M. 1 F 15-3
George M. 1 F 15-3

SMITH (continued)
Jacob 1 M 12-1
James 1 F 5-6-2
John D. 2 F, 2 M 18-6
M. 2 F, 2 M 15-2
Sally 2 F, 1 M 20-2
Thomas 1 M 4-1
Treadwell 1 F 20-1
Walter 1 F, 1 M 15-2
William 1 F 18-7
SOFFIT, Mrs. 2 F 18-6
SOLLERS, Thomas 1 F 14-2
SOMERHAUT, S. 1 F 3-2
SORRELL, Stephen 1 F 11-4
SORROW, Mary 1 M 3-1
SPANGLER, Mathias 1 F 5-6-1
SPATES, Alfred 1 M 9-1
Richard 1 F 14-1
SPENCE, William 1 F 3-1
SPENCER, Eliza 1 F 7-1
Mrs. 1 M 14-2
SPRAIGHTS, R. (Estate Of) 1 F, 1 M 11-4
SPRIGG, Daniel 1 F, 1 M 20-2
STALLINGS, Samuel B. 1 F 8-5
STAMISON, Benjamin 1 F 15-2
STANSBERG, Nathaniel 1 M 10-1
STANSBURY, Ann 2 F 18-6
Elijah 1 M 2-1
John 2 F, 1 M 7-2
John E. 2 F 5-6-1
Nathaniel 1 M 1-1
STEINER, Elizabeth 1 F 14-1
STEM, Mrs. 2 F, 2 M 9-1
STEM, Samuel 1 F 5-6-2
STEPHENS, Alexander 1 F, 2 M 16-1
Wesley 1 M 12-1
STERINE, Rosa 1 F 12-1
STERITT, Mary 1 F 12-1

STEVENS, John A. 2 M 15-1
STEVENSON, E. (Estate Of) 1 F 20-3
Elizabeth 1 M 5-6-1
STEWART, Charles 1 F 4-1
Edwin 1 F 3-2
J. T. 1 F 9-1
James A. 1 M 9-1
Maria 1 F 20-1
Mary 1 F 20-2
Mrs. 1 M 14-2
Sydney 1 F 5-6-1
STINLEY, J. 1 F 3-2
STOCKETT, Frank 20-3
STODDARD, J.T. 1 F 18-7
STOREY, Mrs. 1 F 4-1
STORY, Ann R. 1 F, 1 M 16-1
STREET, Thomas 3 F, 1 M 8-5
STRONG, Laurence 1 F 20-3
STURGEON, Edward 1 M 18-7
SULLIVAN, Abba 1 M 15-1
Betsy 1 F 3-1
SUMMERCANT, Sophia 1 F 5-6-2
SUMMERVILLE, Mrs. 1 F 14-1
SUTER, Henry 1 F, 1 M 5-6-1
SUTTON, Andrew 1 F 14-2
Andrew 1 M 1-1
SWAN, T. H. 1 M 9-1
SWANN, Horace 1 F 5-6-1
SWARTZ, Mary 1 F 5-6-2
SWIND, John 1 F, 1 M 1-1
TAGART, Edward 2 F, 1 M 11-2
TALIAFASO, Elizabeth 2 F 18-8
TALL, Washington 1 F 15-1
TAMS, Mary E. 1 F 18-5
TASKINS, Catherine 1 F 11-2
TAVISH, Emily M. 5 F, 2 M 11-2

71

TAYLOR, Ann 1 F 11-1
Mrs. Bushrod (In Trust) 2 F 20-1
Fanny 1 F 19-1
M. 2 M 9-1
Nicholas 1 F 15-1
Owen 1 F 15-1
William 1 F 5-6-1
THOMAS, Edwin 1 F, 2 M 2-1
J. Hanson 2 F 11-5
John 1 F 3-1
John 6 F 16-1
Lewis 2 F 8-6
Maria 1 M 18-7
Maria 2 F, 1 M 18-7
Mrs. William 1 F 20-2
THOMPSON, Sarah 3 F, 1 M 10-1
Susan 1 F 11-5
Susan 1 F 14-2
William 1 F 11-5
THOMSON, Peter 1 F 15-2
THURSTON, David 1 F 20-3
TIBBONS, Mr. 1 F 14-2
TIERMAN, Charles 1 F, 2 M 11-2
TILGHMAN, Charles 1 F 11-2
Mary J. 1 F 11-2
TILGMAN, Henry 1 F 11-3
TOWNES, Darius 1 F 18-7
TOWNSEND, Edward 1 F 3-1
John 5 F 18-7
Mary 1 F 18-5
Samuel 1 F 20-1
Sarah 1 F, 1 M 14-1
TOWSON, Mrs, 1 F 18-6
TRAVERS, Martha 1 F 15-1
TRAVERSE, Mason 1 M 8-6
TRIP, William 1 M 9-1
TROTTING, Thomas 2 F, 1 M 3-1
TRUST, Jacob 1 F 19-1
TUBMAN, Benjamin 1 F 11-4

TUBMAN (continued)
Mary E. 1 F 20-4
TUCKER, G. 2 F 3-2
TULL, Wesley 1 F 18-7
William 1 F 9-1
TUMWALL, Thomas 1 F, 1 M 15-2
TURNER, Charlotte 1 F 14-1
Frederick 2 M 1-1
James 1 F 5-6-2
John 1 M 20-2
Joseph 1 F, 1 M 5-6-1
Mary 1 M 3-1
VAN WYCH, William H. 2 F, 1 M 18-5
VARDEN, Robert B. 1 F 5-6-1
VEAZEY, Eliza 1 F 11-2
WAGNER, George 1 F 3-1
WAGUARMAN, Elizabeth 1 F 11-1
WALKER, Isaac 1 F 18-6
John 3 F 12-1
Joshua 1 F, 1 M 14-1
Josiah 1 M 11-2
Noah 1 F, 1 M 5-5-1
Richard B. 2 F 15-2
WALL, Edward 1 M 12-1
Martin 3 M 17-2
Mr. 1 F 14-1
WALLIS, Ann J. 3 F, 4 M 20-1
WALSH, Annie 1 M 18-6
WALTERS, Edward 1 F 18-8
Mary 1 F 4-1
WALTON, Mary 2 F 18-7
Susan 1 F 18-6
WARD, Caroline 1 F 5-6-1
George W. 1 M 11-2
Lewis 1 F 19-2
William 1 F 4-1
WARFIELD, Daniel 4 F 9-1
Susan 1 F 20-2
WARWICK, D. 3 F, 2 M 14-2
WATERS, Mrs. 2 F 20-2

72

WATERS (continued)
Rebecca 2 M 11-3
Robert C. J. 5 F, 1 M 11-4
Thomas L. 3 F, 1 M 10-1
Dr. William 1 F 11-3
WATKINS, Edward 1 F 3-2
H. 1 F 18-6
John W. 1 M 20-1
WATKINSON, Samuel 1 F
12-1
WATSON, W.W. 1 F 15-3
WATTS, Eliza 1 F 18-7
Henry 1 M 3-1
Henry 1 F 8-5
WAUGH, James F. 1 F 14-2
WAY, Kate 1 F 20-1
WEBB, Catherine 1 F, 1 M
14-2
Charles 1 M 5-6-1
Sarah 1 F 18-5
WEEKS, John (In Trust) 1 F
20-1
WEEMS, George M. 1 F, 1 M
18-8
Mason 2 F, 1 M 18-6
Mrs. 1 F 14-1
Nathan 1 F, 1 M 15-2
WEIDON, James H. 1 F 20-1
WELCH, Joseph 3 F, 1 M 4-
1
WELLING, Michael 1 M 11-
3
WELLS, Mary 3 F, 1 M 19-1
WELSH, Robert 2 F, 1 M 18-
6
Robert 1 F 18-6
WEST, John 1 M 5-6-1
Sarah C. 1 F 19-1
WESTFORD, John 1 F, 1 M
5-6-1
WHEEDEN, James 1 F 3-1
WHITEHOUSE, George 1 F
20-1
WHITRIDGE, John 1 F 9-1
WHITTAKER, Thomas 1 F
8-6

WICKERSHAM, J. 1 F 3-2
WIELAN, Washington 1 F
18-7
WILCOX, Thomas S. 1 F 5-
6-2
WILHELM, Daniel 1 F 18-7
John M. 2 F 20-3
William 1 M 18-7
WILKESON, John 3 F 3-1
WILKINSON, Samuel 1 F 7-2
WILKS, Francis 1 F 4-1
WILLIAM, E. 1 F 14-2
WILLIAMS, George H. 1 F, 1
M 11-2
John 2 F, 2 M 11-4
John (Estate Of) 1 F 14-1
Lewis 2 F, 1 M 11-4
P. C. 2 F 20-2
Thomas 2 M 11-2
Thomas 3 F 11-5
Virginia 1 F 11-1
William 1 F 5-6-1
William 1 F 12-1
WILLIS, William 1 F 12-1
WILMER, Rebecca 1 M 1-1
WILSON, Catherine 1 F 19-1
George H. 1 F, 1 M 20-2
Robert G. 2 F 11-1
WIMES, Richard 1 F 12-1
WINGATE, Thomas 1 F 3-1
WINN, Martha 4 F 20-2
WINTERS, Louis 1 F 19-1
WOLFORD, Edward 3 F 15-2
WOLLETT, John 1 F, 2 M
4-1
WOOLFORD, Samuel 1 F 5-
6-1
WOLFORD, William 1 F 14-
2
WOOD, William 2 F, 3 M
15-1
WOODWARD, Ann 1 F 18-5
C. 1 F 20-2
Mary 1 F 18-5
Rachael 1 F 3-1
William 2 F 14-1

WORRELL, Ann 1 F 5-6-2
WORTHINGTON, Abraham 4
   F, 5 M 7-2
Dr. 1 F 20-3
Samuel 1 F 11-5
WRIGHT, J. 1 F 3-2
Mary R. 4 F, 2 M 15-1
Terpin 1 F 15-1
W. H. D. C. 5 M 11-4

YOUNG, George 1 F 3-1
 James 1 F 3-1
 Jane 1 F 3-1
ZELLOT, Coleman 1 M 12-1
ZIMMERMAN, John W. 1 F
   12-2
ZOE, Mary 3 F 20-2
 Narcissa 1 F 20-2
ZOWELL, Amelia 1 F, 2 M
   2-1

The Dandy Slave
A slave escorts his mistress home from church (Baltimore).

Taken from the *Illustrated London News*, 8 April 1861.

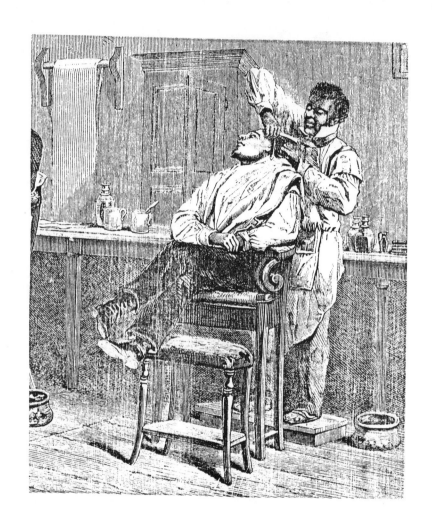

A Barber's Shop At Richmond

The Baltimore City directory of 1870 reflects a number of
Black owned businesses. The number one business in the
community was the barber shop. Taken from the *Illustrated
London News*, 9 March 1861.

THE BLACK FAMILIES OF EAST BALTIMORE - 1870

The following is an index of the census schedule listings of the Black families of East Baltimore (Wards 1-6) for 1870.

Statistics reveal a significant growth in the Black population of Baltimore from 27,898 in 1860 to 39,558 in 1870[1].

This growth was due, in part, to natural increase and the migration from other states and rural areas of Maryland of substantial numbers of Blacks into Baltimore after the Civil War.

Of the total Black population of wards 1-6 in 1870, 799 (8%) were born out of state...540 (5%) from Virginia.

A study of the late 1860's and early 1870's in Baltimore will reveal a number of changes occuring in the Black community.

The educational system opened its' doors to Black children in 1867 with the formation of ten schools city-wide.

The passage of the 15th Amendment resulted in the voter registration of large numbers of Blacks affiliating themselves with the Republican Party.

Black Churches (six in number in East Baltimore) took deeper root as the center of political and social (as well as religious) activity.

Clubs, organizations, and societies were on the rise as well as Black-owned businesses.

Throughout the city, Blacks owned shops dealing in refreshments, carpentry, provisions, hair dye manufacturing and barbering to name a few.

In order to form an accurate analysis of the Black community two documents are of great importance...Baltimore city directories and Federal Census Population Schedules.

City directories reflect churches, societies, businesses, residence and occupation figures along with the names of approximately 45% to 50% of the total overall Black population.

[1] contains both slave and free stats

Census schedules indicate the entire populace in 1870, denoting heads of house, age, occupation, place of birth, education, and property holdings alongside individual names.

While using these records it is crucial to recognize the method of collection, reason for the documents creation, and the historical context in which the collection is made.

Much of the data was recorded as a result of visual and audible interpretation, leading to an abberation of certain classes of information.

As a result caution must be exercised when applying information gleaned from census tracts to sociological, historical, and genealogical studies.

With the proper precautions such an index can reveal a potential wealth of information for all three categories of research.

The index is organized by surname, first name, middle initial (if given), age, ward number (in parenthesis), and page number. An asterisked name represents an individual listed in the records as a head of house.

Page numbers are followed by the letter A or B. The numbering system chosen for this index was the stamped number in the upper right hand corner of every other page of the schedule. The reason for this choice was the consistency of that numbering system throughout the document. The letter A represents the numbered or stamped page, while the letter B represents the following unstamped page.

The following is the interpretation of a sample entry in the index.

Jones, *John J. 23 (1) 27B

(John J. Jones, 23-year-old head of house, resides in the first ward of Baltimore City in 1870 as revealed in the schedules for that ward on page 27B.)

ADAMS, Alice 32 (5) 158B
Amelia 70 (5) 161B
Anna 9 (4) 110A
*Dennis 34 (4) 110A
Eliza 15 (4) 110A
Elizabeth 17 (2) 247B
Estell V. 2 (4) 110A
Frances 98 (3) 411B
*George W. 63 (5) 158B
Hester A. 44 (2) 247B
Howard A. 8 (4) 110A
James 10 (5) 274B
John 3 (23) 523A
John 42 (2) 377A
John W. 22 (2) 247B
Laura 34 (5) 158B
Lewis 14 (4) 110A
Lizzie 18 (3) 480B
Margaret 28 (4) 110A
Margaret G. 4 (2) 247B
Maria 50 (3) 411B
Martha 11 (4) 110A
Mary 23 (2) 300A
Perry 50 (3) 411B
Phillip S. 9 (4) 110A
Rebecca 71 (5) 158B
Sedonia 35 (4) 110A
Sophia 24 (2) 303A
Welford 7/12 303A
Wesley 22 (2) 303A
*William 51 (2) 247B
William W. 13 (2) 247B
ADDISON, Benjamin 24 (3)
563A
Minnie 21 (3) 563A
Rebecca 60 (6) 323A
ADKINSON, *Abraham 63 (6)
311B
Elizabeth 30 (6) 311B
ADLEY, Catharine 42 (4)
102B
Daniel 3 (3) 506A
Mary C. 11 (4) 102B
Thomas 31 (3) 506A

ADLEY (continued)
*William 45 (4) 102B
AFSKIN, Thomas 13 (3) 487A
AHEA, Doleres 28 (6) 388B
AIKENS, Ellen 48 (3) 496A
Maria 15 (3) 496A
AIRES, Amelia 35 (6) 434B
Bretta 15 (6) 434B
Ella F. 2 (6) 434B
John Henry 6/12 (6) 434B
John W. 18 (6) 434B
Louis 30 (6) 434B
AKEN, Susan 40 (1) 57A
AKES, James 8 (4) 109B
Josephine 28 (4) 109B
William 29 (4) 109B
AKINS, Julins 12 (2) 335A
ALBAUGH, John 10 (6) 455B
Leteita 3 (6) 455B
Mary 6 (5) 455B
Mary E. 28 (6) 455B
Willie 8 (6) 455B
Wm 27 (6) 455B
ALBERT, Elemora 6 (5)
203A
Mary 14 (5) 203A
Perry 12 (5) 203A
Peter 16 (3) 480A
William 8 (5) 203A
ALDEN, Bertha 9 (6) 473B
Elenora 7 (6) 473B
Ellen 3 (6) 473B
Hellen 36 (6) 473B
Maria 1 (6) 474A
Mary 13 (6) 473B
Virginia 35 (6) 428A
*William 39 (6) 473B
ALDRIDGE, Singleton 30 (5)
148A
ALECK, Ellen 24 (4) 26A
ALEXANDER, Fanny 30 (1)
3A
John 6/12 (1) 3A
ALLA, Margaret 17 (6) 399A

ALLEN, Adeline 14 (3) 495B
*Alexander 49 (2) 303B
Alfred 40 (4) 110A
Ann M. 20 (6) 346B
Charles 1 (2) 303B
Cornelius 25 (3) 502B
Frank 17 (3) 495B
Hannah 46 (3) 495B
Harriet A 46 (2) 303B
Horace 13 (3) 495B
*John 50 (3) 495B
John F. 18 (3) 495B
John H. 1 (6) 346B
Lucy 15 (3) 495B
*Margaret 23 (2) 247A
Martha 40 (6) 295B
Martha 59 (2) 303B
Mary 18 (3) 535A
Mary 20 (3) 506B
Rebecca 22 (4) 99B
William 27 (2) 339B
AMBER, Hester 45 (1) 25A
Thomas 25 (3) 487A
AMBROSE, Ellen 9 (3) 563B
Emma 11 (3) 563B
Fannie 39 (3) 563B
Georgie 5 (3) 563B
*John 47 (3) 563B
John 13 (3) 563B
Minnie 7 (3) 563B
AMBY, Ann 1 (3) 413B
Camelia 15 (2) 347B
Eliza 91 (2) 298A
Hester 48 (3) 517A
Joseph 25 (3) 413B
AMEN, Barbara 26 (3) 480A
AMOS, Albert 9 (6) 448A
*Benjamin 28 (6) 348B
Cornelia 8 (6) 448A
Mary C. 7 (5) 203B
Mary L. 14 (5) 203B
*Peter 54 (5) 203B
*Peter 56 (6) 448A
Sophia 30 (6) 348B
Treassa M. 13 (6) 448A
Virginia 35 (5) 203B

AMOS (continued)
Virginia 46 (6) 448A
Walter Alex 11 (6) 348B
William A. 8 (5) 203B
ANDERSON, Adaline 62 (2) 228A
Alverta 2 (6) 410B
Amelia J. 13 (4) 18A
Ann L. 37 (5) 134B
Anna 3 (5) 151B
Anna 56 (5) 134B
Ardella 5 (5) 152B
Cecelia 15 (4) 86A
Cecelia 15 (5) 152A
Elenora 19 (5) 274A
Eliza 48 (5) 274A
Eliza 72 (6) 468A
Elizabeth 20 (5) 184A
Elizabeth 45 (5) 212A
*Emanuel 52 (2) 228A
Frederica C. 1 (2) 221B
George 1 (3) 521B
Harison 22 (2) 221B
Isabella 13 (5) 152B
Isabella 22 (5) 274A
Isabella 36 (5) 152A
*Jacob 29 (6) 410B
Jacob C. 4/12 (6) 410B
James 58 (5) 134B
James J. 35 (5) 134B
John 25 (2) 389B
John 29 (5) 268A
John H. 11 (6) 410B
Josephine 2 (5) 152B
Josephine 24 (6) 435A
Julia 50 (1) 5A
Kate 2/12 (5) 274A
Laura 12 (5) 274A
Laura 7 (5) 152B
Margaret 16 (5) 274A
Martha 22 (2) 221B
Martha 26 (5) 157B
Mary 17 (5) 152A
Mary 28 (2) 389B
Mary 3 (2) 389B
Mary 50 (5) 152A

ANDERSON (continued)
Mary 6/12 (5) 157B
Mary F. 5 (5) 154A
Mary O. 22 (5) 134B
Mary T. 29 (6) 410B
Nathaniel 1 (5) 274A
*Rachel 2 (5) 157B
*Robert 38 (2) 389B
Robert 1 (2) 389B
Robert A. 10 (5) 152B
Rosetta 70 (2) 334A
*Samuel 28 (5) 157B
*Stephen 50 (5) 274A
Stephen 21 (5) 274A
Thomas 40 (5) 152A
Thomas E. 6 (6) 410B
*Wilkinson 37 (5) 152A
Wm 5 (6) 435A
ANDREWS, Cecilia 17 (5)
    219A
Louisa 16 (5) 219A
Mary 57 (5) 219A
ANT, Mary 16 (1) 132B
ANTHONY, Adam 16 (5)
    150A
Adeline 5 (5) 150A
Anna M. 42 (5) 150A
Catherine 46 (3) 463A
Columbus 2 (5) 150A
*Daniel 50 (3) 463A
Daniel 8 (3) 463A
Emma J. 14 (5) 220A
*Harriet 52 (5) 166A
Hester 47 (5) 203A
*Hoklese 47 (5) 203A
Jane 50 (6) 293B
*John 45 (5) 150A
John 10 (5) 150A
Kate 3 (3) 463A
Levin 4/12 (5) 150A
Lloyd 8 (5) 150A
Martha 11 (3) 463A
Mary 22 (5) 161A
Mary 6 (3) 463A
Nancy 9/12 (5) 161A
Sarah 69 (5) 150A

ANTONY, Henrietta 17 (6)
    303B
Henrietta 29 (6) 303B
ARMLER, *Alfred 38 (6)
    405A
Harriett C. 5 (6) 405A
Julia 30 (6) 405A
Katie D. 6 (6) 405A
Louis S. 10 (6) 405A
ARMSTED, Florence 5 (5)
    256B
Georgeanne 19 (5) 256B
*Joseph 49 (5) 256B
Martha 30 (5) 256B
ARMSTRONG, Alfred 33 (6)
    310B
Ann 25 (2) 344B
Caroline 35 (6) 306B
Catherine 4 (6) 306B
Clara E. 1 (5) 126B
Georgiana 12 (6) 306B
Harriette 30 (6) 310B
*Henry 36 (3) 479A
Henry 40 (6) 306B
Ishmeal 29 (2) 303A
James H. 3 (2) 303A
Jennie 15 (3) 522A
Johnny 6 (6) 306B
Lizzie 21 (3) 479A
Louis A. 4 (5) 126B
Mary E. 30 (5) 126B
Thomas 10 (6) 306B
William 1 (6) 306B
William W 6 (5) 126B
ASBERRY, Emily 25 (3)
    521B
Emma 1 (3) 521B
George 3 (3) 521B
*James 33 (3) 521B
James 7 (3) 521B
Mary 5 (3) 521B
ASHTON, Anna 32 (5) 147B
Anna 5 (5) 148A
Geneva 48 (6) 415B
George 1 (5) 148A
George 16 (2) 380A

ASHTON (continued)
George F. 8 (6) 415B
Jemima 13 (6) 415B
*John 52 (6) 415B
John C. 16 (6) 415B
Mary E. 11 (6) 415B
Moses 33 (6) 342B
Nathan E. 6 (6) 415B
Robert 24 (5) 203A
Robert H. 24 (6) 415B
*Thomas 36 (5) 147B
ASKENS, Effie 53 (3) 488A
Ellen 25 (3) 488A
George 19 (3) 488A
James 23 (3) 488A
Josephine 21 (3) 488A
Mary 15 (3) 488A
Thomas 25 (3) 488A
ASKINGS, Ann M. 20 (5)
265A
Anna 19 (5) 265A
Harriet 50 (5) 265A
ASKINS, *Charles H. 40 (5)
265A
Diana 17 (4) 95A
Emory 25 (5) 149A
Isabell 25 (6) 331B
Jestin 12 (5) 149A
*John H. 17 (5) 142A
Joseph 30 (6) 331B
Richard 23 (5) 265A
Sarah 15 (5) 265A
Sophia 8 (5) 265A
*Thomas 58 (3) 488A
Tisia 30 (5) 149A
Toy L. 12 (5) 265A
William A. 15 (5) 142A
ASPER, Levin 14 (6) 434B
ATKINSON, Susan 20 (5)
155A
AUGUSTA, *Harriett 69 (5)
165B
Mary 65 (5) 157B
AUGUSTUS, *Abraham 39 (6)
410A
Caroline 30 (6) 410A

AUGUSTUS (continued)
Charles W. 17 (6) 410A
AUSKINS, Samuel 25 (2)
377B
AUTHER, Henry 40 (3) 567A
AVERY, Charles 24 (4) 110B
AYRES, Charles H. 3 (4) 20A
Hannah A. 4 (4) 20A
Hester A. 26 (4) 20A
*James H. 31 (4) 20A
Simon Q 8 (4) 20A
BACKES, *Emeline 40 (3)
567A
BACON, Elizabeth 6 (5) 221A
Harriet 67 (5) 158A
Louisa 38 (5) 220B
Olevia 12 (5) 220B
Richard A. 40 (5) 159B
Samuel 15 (5) 220B
BAGWELL, Harriett 31 (6)
317A
Willie 1 (6) 317A
BAIBES, Charlotta 74 (5)
154B
BAILEY, Alice 5 (1) 133B
Amelia 58 (3) 541A
Ann 3 (1) 40A
Anna 7 (1) 133B
Augusta 12 (1) 40A
Catharine 42 (5) 274B
Charles 15 (5) 284A
*David 40 (1) 39B
Dorah 26 (3) 563A
Eliza 6 (5) 269A
Elizabeth 36 (2) 248A
Flinkey 3 (5) 269A
George 30 (5) 268B
Grace 65 (5) 235B
Harriet 16 (5) 269A
Harriett 23 (1) 40A
*Henry 37 (1) 133B
*Henry 45 (5) 269B
*Henry 60 (3) 541A
Henry 15 (1) 133B
Henry 24 (4) 95A
James 28 (3) 563A

BAILEY (continued)
Jenjins * 50 (5) 283B
John 1 (1) 40A
John 15 (6) 295A
*John A. 55 (5) 274B
Joseph 13 (5) 269A
Joseph 8 (2) 248A
Letitia A. 35 (5) 220A
*Levin 64 (3) 521A
Lucy 21 (5) 207B
Margaret 34 (1) 133B
Mary 2 (1) 133B
Mary 46 (5) 268B
*Mary 48 (2) 226A
Mary 6 (1) 40A
Mary F. 29 (2) 303A
Nicolas 12 (1) 133B
Perry 30 (2) 303A
Peter 70 (5) 235B
Priscilla 57 (3) 485B
Rachel A. 25 (6) 378B
Randolph 6 (6) 378B
Rosanna 7 (2) 248A
Samuel 11 (5) 269A
*Samuel 60 (2) 303A
Sarah 14 (4) 109A
Sarah 40 (3) 521A
Silas 12 (5) 284A
Sophia 24 (5) 284A
Sophia 58 (2) 303A
*Thomas 50 (5) 220A
Virginia 10 (1) 133B
William 17 (1) 133B
Windfield 9 (2) 248A
Wm 21 (5) 268B
Wm H. 6 (2) 226A
BAILY, Elizabeth 85 (5) 220A
BAKER, Bebrah 40 (3) 505A
Maria 17 (3) 450B
Thomas 26 (5) 155B
BALDWIN, Julia 35 (3) 494A
BALL, Daniel 26 (5) 169B
*Jane 24 (5) 169B
Mary 20 (5) 169B
Wm H. 4 (5) 169B

BALTIMORE, Eliza 70 (2) 387A
BANKS, Abraham 13 (3) 506A
Ann 1 (3) 506A
Ann 18 (5) 176A
Ann J. 6 (5) 176A
*Ann M. 41 (2) 225B
Anna 23 (5) 274B
Anna 3/12 (1) 3B
Anna 60 (5) 150A
Basil 22 (5) 157A
Benjamin 2 (5) 171B
Berwell 45 (5) 276B
Charity 28 (5) 276B
Charles 1 (5) 157A
Charles 12 (5) 176A
*Ellen 40 (5) 176A
Emily 1 (5) 275A
Henrietta 38 (5) 275A
Henrietta 8 95) 275A
Henrietta 9 (5) 176A
Hester 18 (5) 275A
Hester 29 (3) 496A
Jerry 29 (5) 153A
John 17 (5) 176A
John 25 (5) 171B
John 33 (5) 157A
Joseph 4 (5) 275A
Julia 3 (3) 496A
Lavina 21 (6) 296B
*Leonard 39 (3) 506A
Louisa 4 (5) 176A
Mary 11 (5) 176A
Mary 22 (1) 3B
Mary 25 (4) 118B
Mary 28 (6) 395B
Mary E. 23 (5) 171B
Matilda 32 (3) 506A
Moses 8 (3) 496A
Nancy 18 (6) 325B
Peter 7 (5) 275A
*Peter 42 (5) 275A
Rachel 20 (3) 583A
*Rebecca 23 (5) 157A
Samuel 20 (5) 176A
Washington 27 (4) 18B

BANKS (continued)
Wesley 48 (5) 176A
*William 24 (1) 3B
Wm 10 (3) 506A
Wm 22 (5) 274B
*Wm 40 (3) 496A
Wm 6 (3) 496A
BANTAM, Charles 20 (5)
206A
Cordelia 55 (5) 206A
Harrison 45 (5) 206A
Horace 37 (5) 206A
John 4 (5) 206A
*John 62 (5) 206A
Lucy 18 (5) 206A
Mary 55 (5) 206A
BANTEM, Cornelia 34 (1)
82B
BANTOM, Mary E. 40 (6)
367B
BANTUM, Charles W. 7 (2)
221B
Charlotte 53 (2) 340B
Daniel 20 (6) 346B
Enols 67 (2) 340B
Harriett A. 27 (6) 410A
Sarah 19 (4) 18B
BANTURN, Edward 27 (4)
18B
Harriet Ann 3/12 (4) 18B
BARBAIR, Amelia 20 (3)
541B
Ann 46 (3) 541B
*Auguste 50 (3) 541B
Ellen 12 (3) 541B
Margaret 17 (3) 541B
BARBER, Cornelius 1 (3)
484A
Emma 8 (3) 484A
*James 60 (3) 484A
Jane 2 (3) 484A
Mary 50 (3) 484A
BARBOUR, Ann 45 (5) 195A
Frances 7 (5) 195A
BARNES, *Abraham 52 (5)
219B

BARNES (continued)
Adeline 7 (5) 219B
Allen 22 (4) 10B
Amelia 20 (3) 496A
Amelia 20 (3) 496A
Andrew 8 (5) 219B
Ann M. 28 (6) 311B
Anna 13 (6) 453B
Annie 24 (3) 477B
Caroline 4 (6) 310A
Caroline 45 (5) 219B
Charles S. 3 (6) 453B
Edward 2 (5) 219B
Elenora 11 (6) 453B
Elenora 48 (5) 268A
Elizabeth 12 (5) 219B
Elizabeth 17 (6) 453B
*Elizabeth 42 (6) 453B
*Francis 47 (6) 311B
George H. 22 (2) 384A
Harriet 14 (5) 219B
Harriett 15 (6) 453B
Henry 12 (6) 453B
Henry 21 (5) 219B
*James 52 (3) 477B
*John 39 (6) 453B
John 22 (3) 540A
John 24 (3) 496A
John 30 (6) 310A
John 40 (6) 311B
Joseph 26 (6) 368A
Joseph 6 (6) 310A
Leonora 25 (2) 221B
Leven 38 (2) 328A
Maggie 5 (6) 453B
Margaret 40 (5) 138A
Maria 24 (6) 310A
Martha 13 (3) 477B
Martha 51 (3) 477B
Mary 22 (4) 44A
*Mary 42 (3) 496A
Mary A. 29 (6) 453B
Noah 30 (5) 203B
Robert 45 (4) 112B
Sarah 19 (3) 477B
*Sarah 40 (4) 112B

BARNES (continued)
*Sophia 66 (3) 540A
Thomas 14 (6) 453B
Thomas 21 (5) 268A
William 20 (3) 477B
William 28 (3) 496A
BARNET, Cora 28 (2) 379A
Emma 5 (3) 496A
BARNETT, Ann M 60 (5)
   165B
Annie 36 (3) 542B
Edward F. 1 (6) 332A
Eliza 22 (3) 599B
Elizabeth 14 (5) 165B
Elizabeth 78 (1) 131B
Ellen 45 (3) 599B
*Ellen 55 (3) 599B
Ellen J. 12 (4) 23B
Henry 45 (3) 599B
Hester A. 37 (6) 332A
John 19 (3) 599B
John W. 13 (4) 6A
Martha A. 5/12 (4) 6A
Mary 11 (3) 542B
Mary 17 (3) 599B
Mary 32 (4) 6A
Rose A. 11 (6) 332A
Rose A. 75 (6) 332A
Steven 32 (4) 6A
Susan 9 (3) 542B
Theadore 16 (4) 8B
Willie 6 (3) 542B
Zacheriah 47 (6) 332A
BARNEY, Albert 3 (3) 496A
*Albert 40 (3) 495B
Augustus 4 (1) 46A
Charles 3 (3) 518B
Eliza J. 39 (5) 235B
George 12 (3) 496A
George 30 (3) 518B
*James 40 (1) 46A
*John 45 (5) 235B
Laura 7 (5) 235B
Louisa 22 (3) 518B
Maditta 35 (1) 46A
Martha 1 (3) 518B

BARNEY (continued)
Mary 20 (5) 235B
Mary 9 (3) 496A
Priscilla 36 (3) 496A
Susan 7 (3) 496A
William 14 (3) 496A
William R 33 (2) 345A
Willie 5 (3) 518B
BARNS, Annie 9 (3) 545A
Emily J. 11 (3) 545A
George W. 7/12 (3) 545A
Harry 3 (3) 564A
Henry 35 (3) 564A
Luvenia 4 (3) 545A
Mary 1 (3) 564A
Mary 29 (3) 545A
Peter 34 (3) 545A
Sallie 26 (3) 564A
BARNY, Adaline 13 (4) 5B
Charlotte 31 (4) 5B
Ellen Jane 12 (4) 5B
*George 39 (4) 5B
BARREL, John H. 8 (5) 166A
BARRELL, *Emeline 28 (5)
   166A
BARRENS, Thomas 13 (6)
   317B
BARRETT, Anna 7 (5) 285A
Anna E. 33 (5) 196A
Edward 5 (5) 196A
Elizabeth 16 (5) 196A
George 13 (5) 285A
Harry 1 (5) 196B
James 9 (5) 285A
*James H. 39 (5) 284B
Lillia 11 (5) 285A
Mary 39 (5) 284B
*Robert 35 (5) 196A
BARRICK, Mary 40 (5) 219B
BARRIT, Ann R. 14 (5) 219B
Emma F. 15 (5) 219B
Howard 10 (5) 219B
James 4 (5) 219B
Lawrence 2 (5) 219B
Samuel 12 (5) 219B
Susan 38 (5) 219B

BARRIT (continued)
Susan 9 (5) 219B
Thomas 42 (5) 219B
BARTEN, *William 70 (3)
423A
BARTON, Alverta 26 (5)
161A
Charles C. 14 (5) 209A
Emily J. 26 (5) 275B
Jane 49 (2) 385A
John 25 (2) 385A
John 35 (5) 161A
John M. 1 (5) 275B
Maria 66 (6) 358A
Rebecca 1 (5) 161A
*William E. 33 (5) 275B
BASSFORD, Cornelius 23 (3)
506B
Mary 18 (3) 506B
BATEMAN, Alverta 13 (5)
162A
Charles 3 (5) 166A
Eliza 25 (5) 166A
John 19 (6) 319A
Joseph 40 (5) 162A
*Julia 58 (5) 162A
Mary C. 10/12 (5) 166A
BATEN, Olivia 10 (4) 9A
BATES, Fannie 14 (3) 577A
BAUCHAMP, Jane 24 (3)
432A
BAXTER, Henrietta 28 (5)
178A
BAYLEY, Alexander 12 (5)
145B
Anna A. 11 (5) 145B
Carrie 3 (5) 170A
Charles 21 (5) 170A
*Elizabeth 28 (5) 159B
Ella S. 18 (5) 170A
Henrietta 24 (5) 150B
Henry 30 (5) 145B
Jane 41 (5) 170A
Julia 7 (5) 159B
Lilla 9 (5) 170A
Lydia 25 (5) 145B

BAYLEY (continued)
Mary C. 11 (5) 159B
Nathan 5 (5) 150B
Samuel 16 (5) 170A
Samuel W 4/12 (5) 145B
*William 50 (5) 170A
Wyssus 1 (5) 170A
BAYLIE, Mary 56 (6) 447B
BAYNARD, Alexander 25 (5)
166B
BEACHAM, Rose 21 (4) 25A
BEAL, Anna 43 (2) 386A
Catharine 19 (4) 16B
*Henry 43 (2) 386A
Nancy 77 (2) 386A
BEAN, Rodney W 7 (4) 94B
BEAR, Julia 17 (5) 168A
BEARD, Clementine 5 (6)
452A
*Joshua 39 (6) 452A
Sarah E. 7/12 (6) 452B
Sarah J. 33 (6)452A
BEARER, Charles 7 (6) 405A
Delia 27 (6) 405A
BELL, Alford 30 (6) 317A
Alfred 35 (6) 312A
Anna 33 (6) 317A
Carrie W. 1 (6) 312A
Catharine 24 (2) 345A
Dora V. 4 (6) 317A
Emma 24 (5) 248B
Fanny 8 (5) 126A
Francis R. 26 (6) 346B
Harriett 25 (6) 312A
*John 27 (6) 346B
John 30 (5) 248B
*Louisa 42 (6) 413A
Mary 22 (3) 585A
Samuel 24 (2) 345A
Samuel 5/12 (2) 345A
Susanna E. 6 (6) 346B
*William 40 (5) 155A
BENEL, Sallie 5 (3) 413B
BENETT, Mary B 13 (3)
476B
BENJAMIN, John 23 (5) 197B

BENJAMIN (continued)
*Virginia 47 (3) 519A
BENNET, Abraham 15 (3)
   541B
 Alexander 34 (2) 401B
 Charlotte 25 (3) 558B
 Eliza 36 (1) 157B
 John 9 (3) 542A
 Mary 1/12 (1) 157B
 Sarah 11 (3) 541B
 Sarah 40 (3) 541B
BENNETT, Anna 29 (6) 372A
 Bebrah 19 (3) 505A
 Charles 2 (5) 149A
 Charles 70 (5) 149A
 Charlott 24 (6) 366A
 Florence 5 (6) 368A
 Georgiana 21 (6) 452B
 Jacob H. 7/12 (6) 368A
*James 30 (6) 372A
 John S. 11 (6) 368A
 Laura 3 (6) 368A
 Mary 10 (6) 368A
 Rachael 20 (4) 14B
 Rachel 65 (5) 149A
 Rosa 2 (2) 251A
*Samuel 23 (6) 366A
 Sarah 58 (6) 452B
 Susan 19 (2) 251A
BENSON, Elizabeth 16 (2)
   400B
 Harriett 31 (6) 405B
 James 24 (2) 377B
 James 9 (6) 362A
 James H. 4/12 (6) 405B
 John 12 (6) 362A
*John A. 38 (6) 362A
 Mary 36 (3) 575B
 Mary C. 6 (6) 362A
 Mary J. 37 (6) 362A
 Rebecca 50 (5) 207A
 Thomas 16 (3) 505A
BENSTON, Clara 9 (6) 449B
BENTLEY, Frisby P. 12 (5)
   204A
 Louis 30 (3) 560A

BENTLEY (continued)
 Sarah A. 30 (4) 94B
 William 25 (4) 94B
BERRETT, Annie 30 (3)
   541B
 Edward 2 (3) 541B
 William 38 (3) 541B
 William 4 (3) 541B
BERRY, Charlotte 50 (5)
   241B
 Clara 6 (1) 5A
 Elijah 7 (5) 180A
 Elisa A. 42 (5) 180A
 Fanny 9/12 (1) 5A
 Francis 45 (1) 5A
 George 18 (5) 180A
*George W. 66 (5) 241B
 Harriett 55 (1) 66A
 Hester 13 (5) 180A
*Jacob 44 (5) 180A
*John 40 (1) 5A
 John E. 1/12 (5) 180A
 Josephine 16 (1) 5A
 Louisa 15 (1) 65B
 Mary 11 (5) 180A
 Mary 2 (1) 5A
 Mary 30 (5) 168A
 Nicholas 2 (5) 180A
 William 30 (5) 168A
BERRYMAN, Caroline 27 (2)
   295B
 Eleanor 10 (2) 303A
 Henry 45 (2) 222A
 John A. 12 (2) 295B
 John C. 45 (2) 295B
 William 20 (2) 295B
BEVANS, Isaac 19 (3) 563B
BIAS, Major 7 (6) 449B
 Sophia 28 (6) 412A
BIAYS, Martha 18 (3) 424B
BILLIPS, Eliza F 24 (4) 9B
 Grace 1 (4) 9B
BIOUS, Shepherd 20 (3) 487A
BIRD, Reuben 60 (4) 19A
BIRDLEY, Alice 37 (3) 524B
 Alice 5 (3) 524B

BIRDLEY (continued)
Laura 3 (3) 524B
Leva 7 (3) 524B
Mary 9 (3) 524B
*William 40 (3) 524B
BISHOP, Elijah 25 (2) 221B
Eliza 19 (2) 221B
*Manuel 40 (6) 331B
Marget 25 (4) 108A
Mary 45 (3) 510A
Mary E. 3/12 (2) 221B
Roseann 85 (5) 146A
Sarah 35 (6) 331B
Sarah 4 (6) 331B
BIVENS, Henrietta 20 (2)
   221B
John T. E. 2 (2) 221B
Joseph P. 1/12 (2) 221B
*William E. 26 (2) 221B
BLACK, *Cornelius 37 (3)
   542A
Lizzie 28 (3) 542A
Maria 8 (3) 542A
Mary 6 (3) 542A
Morris 3 (3) 542A
Thomas 22 (1) 70A
William 4 (3) 542A
BLACKERSON, *Samuel 72
   (6) 405B
Susan 15 (6) 405B
Susan 72 (6) 405B
BLACKSTONE, Martha 14 (5)
   166B
Susan 37 (5) 155B
*William 80 (5) 166B
BLACKWELL, Evander 9 (6)
   409A
Lucinda 25 (6) 409A
Luconda 25 (6) 409A
Royston 37 (6) 409A
Urias 15 (6) 409A
William 10 (6) 409A
BLAKE, Alexander 25 (4)
   102B
Alverta 10 (6) 358A
Alverta 11 (6) 368A

BLAKE (continued)
Anna 32 (6) 368A
Annie 15 (3) 559A
Charles 12 (3) 485B
Charles 177 (3) 559A
*Daniel 31 (6) 412A
Elizabeth 40 (5) 163A
Elizabeth 40 (5) 166B
*Frances 29 (3) 542A
Garrison 40 (3) 559A
George 13 (3) 559A
*George 22 (5) 166B
Georgie 7 (3) 559A
Harriet 37 (3) 559A
*Hester 24 (4) 102B
Hezekiah 21 (6) 368A
Hunsley, 45 (6) 306A
Isabella 36 (6) 412A
James 30 (4) 102B
*James 50 (6) 368A
Jeremiah 1 (4) 102B
*John 50 (3) 505A
Joseph 12 (5) 166B
Julia 21 (5) 166B
Julia 9 (3) 559A
Laura V. 12 (6) 318B
Lizzie 45 (3) 505A
Lydia 20 (5) 149B
Martha 11 (3) 559A
Martha 2 (5) 149B
Martha 21 (6) 306A
Martha T. 8 (6) 306A
Mary 70 (6) 412A
Mary A. 48 (6) 318B
Mary J. 13 (5) 163A
Nettie 13 (5) 138B
Samuel H. 4 (4) 102B
*Susan 35 (5) 166A
Temperance 42 (6) 306A
William 24 (5) 149B
*William 50 (4) 84B
BLAY, Adaline 25 (2) 340A
Charles 19 (2) 340B
*Charles 52 (2) 340A
Charlotte 48 (2) 340A
Charlotte 7 (2) 340B

BLAY (continued)
George 11 (2) 340B
Maria 21 (2) 340B
Martha 13 (2) 340B
Mary 17 (2) 340B
Robert 9 (2) 340B
BLONDIN, Anna 28 (5) 144A
Thomas 30 (5) 144A
BLOUGH, Elizabeth 58 (2)
  247B
*Thomas 60 (2) 247B
BOAND, *Annie 47 (3) 422A
John 20 (3) 422A
BOLEY, Elizabeth 25 (5)
  197B
John 5 (5) 197B
*William 28 (5) 197B
BOLSTON, Betsey 60 (5)
  147B
Frank 8/12 (5) 147B
*George 23 (5) 147B
James 3 (5) 147B
Margaret 26 (5) 147B
Mary E. 5 (5) 147B
BOLTEN, Kate 16 (3) 591B
*Rebecca 40 (3) 591B
BOLTON, Harriet 2 (2) 340A
John S. 29 (2) 340A
Mary C. 1/12 (2) 340A
Mary V. 24 (2) 340A
BOND, Abraham 17 (6) 308B
Alice 22 (1) 47A
*Andrew 39 (3) 576B
Ann R. 30 (5) 148B
Anthony 7 (4) 110A
Charles 13 (5) 212A
Delia 56 (5) 234B
Ellen 28 (4) 110A
Fannie 17 (3) 503A
George 10 (5) 212A
George 20 (6) 431B
*George W. 30 (5) 148B
Hannah 70 (5) 150A
Harrison 11 (6) 308B
Henry F. 3 (6) 308B
James 1 (5) 212A

BOND (continued)
Jane 20 (6) 473A
Jane 35 (5) 212A
John 12 (6) 431B
John 22 (5) 203B
*John 47 (6) 308B
John W. 6/12 (6) 308B
Joshua 28 (6) 409B
Lavinia 28 91) 82B
Lloyd 18 (6) 308B
Louisa 14 (5) 275A
Louisa 39 (6) 308B
Martha E. 32 (3) 576B
Mary 1 (3) 576B
Mary 35 (5) 158A
Mary 8 (6) 308B
*Mary 54 (2) 340A
Minor 25 (5) 172A
Morrison 14 (5) 158A
Naomi 30 (6) 409B
Olivia C. 15 (2) 293B
Rachel 24 (6) 449A
Sallie 5 (2) 340A
Samuel 3 (3) 576B
Samuel 30 (4) 110A
Sarah 40 (4) 102B
Sarah Jane 16 (6) 308B
*Solomon 29 (6) 308B
Sophia 43 (6) 308B
William 9 (6) 308B
BONES, Annie 49 (3) 505A
John 20 (3) 505A
Sarah 19 (3) 562A
Sophia 23 (3) 562A
Willie 1 (3) 562A
BONEYPART, *Josiah 52 (2)
  296A
Nancy 33 (2) 296A
BOOKER, Anna 1 (5) 151A
*James 30 (5) 151A
Josephine 23 (5) 151A
BOOM, Mary 23 (2) 386A
BOON, Besin 28 (4) 110A
Charlotta 28 (5) 197B
*Joshua 33 (5) 197B
Margaret 20 (4) 110A

BOON (continued)
*Richard 49 (5) 155A
Virginia 27 (5) 155A
BOONE, Catharine 10 (5)
186B
*Catharine 68 (5) 186B
*Harriet 65 (3) 544B
Joseph 14 (3) 544B
Joseph 23 (3) 544B
Lucretia 30 (3) 544B
Margaret 56 (4) 5B
Maria 12 (5) 186B
Maria 15 (3) 544B
Martha 6 (3) 544B
Mary 30 (3) 477B
Mary 45 (3) 544A
Mary 8 (5) 186B
*Mary 65 (5) 154A
Philip 17 (3) 544B
*Richard 46 (3) 544A
Stephen 16 (3) 544A
Susan 11 (3) 520A
Susan 39 (3) 544B
Susan 55 (3) 520A
Theadore 19 (3) 544B
William 15 (3) 520A
BOOTH, Mary 18 (1) 36A
BOSLEY, Priscilla 20 (5)
235B
BOSTON, Alice 3 (3) 544B
Charles 19 (3) 544A
Charles 19 (4) 5B
David 33 (3) 477B
Elizabeth 30 (5) 139A
Georgeanna 20 (3) 520A
Jane 33 (5) 187B
John 17 (3) 520A
John 49 (1) 3A
John L. 9 (3) 544B
Sarah 39 (1) 3A
BOULDEN, Charles 9 (5)
205B
Emma 3/12 (3) 564A
*George 30 (3) 564A
James 15 (5) 205B
*Louisa 47 (5) 205B

BOULDEN (continued)
Louisa 29 (3) 564A
Mary 12 (5) 205B
Samuel 17 (5) 204A
Washington 49 (5) 205B
William 12 (5) 205B
BOULDER, Jeremiah 22 (5)
205B
BOULDIN, *Daniel 24 (6)
476A
Fanny 36 (5) 183A
Gracey A. 44 (6) 448A
Joseph 1 (6) 476A
Mary A. 22 (6) 476A
*Merchant 33 (6) 448A
Shadrack 35 (5) 258B
BOUSER, James 29 (2) 335A
Louisa 48 (2) 335A
BOWDEN, Harriet 54 (5)
153A
James 8 (6) 449B
*Richard 40 (6) 449B
Sarah A. 38 (6) 449B
BOWEN, Mary 19 (3) 549B
Richard 75 (5) 145A
BOWLEY, Annie 26 (3) 469A
*George 39 (5) 283A
Millie J. 9 (5) 283A
Rachael 60 (4) 20A
Samuel 19 (4) 20A
Samuel 22 (3) 469A
Sarah A. 35 (5) 283A
*Simon 57 (4) 20A
BOWMAN, Flora (3) 506A
*John 38 (3) 540B
Mary 40 (3) 540B
BOWSER, Anna 54 (5) 144A
Charlotte 49 (5) 235B
Elizebeth 26 (6) 468A
*George 46 (3) 502B
Hannah 78 (3) 503A
Joseph 78 (5) 235B
Maria 50 (4) 106B
Mary 37 (3) 502B
William 18 (3) 599B
BOYD, John W. 2 (5) 166B

BOYD (continued)
Mary J. 4 (5) 166B
*Mary J. 30 (5) 166B
Thomas C. 35 (5) 166B
BOYDAN, Joseph 26 (5) 203B
BOYER, *Andrew 35 (5) 153A
Ellen 25 (5) 153A
Fanny 14 (5) 144A
BRADFORD, Alexander 44
    (2) 339B
Anna 34 (6) 433A
Elizabeth 30 (4) 27B
Elizabeth 32 (5) 172B
George 11 (5) 145A
George T. 1 (2) 339B
Harriet 34 (2) 339B
John 35 (5) 172B
John 5 (5) 145A
John C. 5 (2) 339B
Julia 8 (3) 522B
Maria 29 (3) 522B
Maria 6 (3) 522B
*Richard 36 (5) 145A
Rose 17 (5) 145A
Sarah 2 (5) 145A
Severn 14 (5) 145A
Susan 36 (5) 145A
William 18 (2) 339B
BRADY, *Brice 30 (5) 203A
Julia 36 (5) 203A
BRAGG, Eliza 29 (4) 83A
BRANCH, Richard 29 (3)
    525B
BRAND, Georgeanna 27 (2)
    400B
Georgeanna 28 (5) 169B
Hanibal 9 (2) 400B
Hannibal 9 (5) 169B
William 38 (2) 400B
BRANERICK, *Mary 44 (5)
    275A
BRANNAN, Lindy 29 (6)
    308B
Mary 6/12 (6) 308B
BRANT, Jane 50 (1) 49B
BRAVEN Joseph 7 (3) 487A

BRAVEN (continued)
Margaret 40 (3) 487A
BRAWNER, Catharine 28 (5)
    248B
Harriett 2 (5) 248B
*Joseph 32 (5) 248B
BRAXTON, *Alexander 22 (5)
    157B
Elizabeth 21 (5) 157B
Willie 11/12 (5) 157B
BRAY, Adelaide 21 (3) 441B
BRAYWARD, Louisa 18 (6)
    311A
BRAYWOOD, *Daniel 56 (2)
    339B
Nancy 46 (2) 339B
William 24 (2) 383A
BRIAN, Anna 17 (6) 433B
Anna 26 (4) 106A
Kate 25 (6) 321A
Matilda 30 (6) 317A
*Rose 64 (6) 433B
Rose 9/12 (6) 433B
BRIANT, Lewis 23 (4) 19A
Wade 21 (4) 19A
BRICE, Aaron 29 (5) 122B
Ann E. 25 (5) 122B
Dolly 60 (5) 286A
Elizabeth 17 (5) 215A
Elizabeth 5 (5) 122B
Fanny S. 22 (5) 122B
James 22 (5) 206A
James 58 (5) 248B
*John H. (Rev) 57 (5) 122B
John E. 1 (5) 122B
John H. Jr. 31 (5) 122B
Mary 4 (5) 122B
Mary J 57 (5) 122B
*Rachel 30 (3) 563A
Rebecca 41 (5) 154B
Thomas 6/12 (5) 122B
Victoria 7 (3) 563A
William H 2/12 (5) 122B
BRICK, *John 40 (6) 449B
John H. 19 (6) 449B
Mary V. 13 (6) 362B

BRICK (continued)
Rosetta 23 (6) 362B
Sarah 35 (6) 449B
BRIGGS, *Charles 70 (6) 302B
Mary A. 60 (6) 303A
BRIGHT, Ellen 40 (6) 332A
Emily 21 (6) 332A
James 22 (6) 332A
Susan 26 (2) 386A
*Walter 40 (6) 332A
Walter 18 (6) 332A
William 41 (2) 386A
William 7 (6) 332A
BRINKLEY, John 40 (3) 477B
Lydia 39 (3) 478A
BRINTON, John 21 (3) 560B
Mary 18 (3) 560B
BRISCO, John 53 (4) 110A
BRISCOE, Alverta 16 (6) 348A
Elvena 12 (6) 348A
*Fredrick 60 (6) 348A
George 11 (6) 468A
Harriett A. 17 (6) 348A
Lucy A. 11 (6) 348A
Mary 14 (6) 449A
Rosetta 1 (6) 468A
Sarah 20 (6) 468A
Sarah 40 (6) 348A
*William 53 (6) 468A
William H. 10 (6) 348A
BRITTON, John 20 (6) 408A
*Mary J 38 (6) 408A
Robert 13 (5) 196B
BROADEN, Fanny 22 (6) 314A
BROADWAY, *George 45 (5) 273B
Rachael 42 (5) 273B
BROCK, *Beverly 50 (5) 219B
Charlotte 44 (5) 219B
Mary A. 6 (5) 220A
Perry B. 9 (5) 219B
Sarah 15 (5) 219B

BROKENBERY, Charles N 13 (2) 335A
BROOK, David 22 (6) 431B
Henry A. 1 (6) 431B
Louisa 19 (6) 431B
BROOKINS, Arthur 24 (6) 325B
Daniel 8/12 (6) 325B
Lydia 21 (6) 325B
Matilda 50 (5) 135B
BROOKMAN, Abraham 50 (5) 147A
*Carrol 30 (5) 162A
Jane 22 (5) 162A
BROOKS, Adarilla 56 (3) 502B
Adeline 24 (6) 327A
*Alexander 40 (5) 171B
*Alexander 65 (3) 502B
Alexander 11 (3) 502B
Alexander 13 (6) 447A
Alexander 45 (6) 442B
Alice 20 (3) 505A
Benjamin 9 (3) 502B
Charles 19 (4) 8A
Charles 27 (5) 171B
Dolly 50 (4) 96B
Edwards 34 (5) 144A
*Elizabeth 32 (6) 405A
Elizabeth 11 (5) 171B
Elizabeth 29 (6) 413B
Elizabeth 50 (3) 576B
Ellen 22 (5) 172A
Emily 9 (5) 171B
Emma 7 (3) 502B
Georgiana 6 (6) 413B
Harriet 30 (6) 296B
Harry 16 (6) 447A
Joanna 12 (3) 502B
Lewis 5 (5) 147A
Louisa 2 (5) 171B
Lucy 25 (5) 144A
Margaret 25 (5) 228B
Maria 18 (5) 171B
Maria A. 16 (6) 447A
Martha 19 (6) 447A

BROOKS (continued)
Martha 42 (6) 447A
*Mary 30 (3) 506B
Mary 28 (5) 147A
Mary M. 5/12 (5) 171B
Mary T. 3 (6) 413B
Matilda 15 (3) 502B
Matilda 26 (5) 171B
Richard 15 (4) 93B
Robert 66 (3) 576B
Rosana 7 (6) 413B
Sarah C. 15 (6) 405A
*William 56 (6) 447A
William 15 (6) 447A
William 16 (5) 236A
William 25 (4) 18A
William 4 (3) 506B
*William H. 30 (6) 413B
BROUGHTON, Harriet 23 (5)
   176A
Martha 20 (2) 221B
*Stephen 24 (2) 221B
BROWN, Abraham L. 2 (6)
   451B
Alexander 14 (5) 187A
Alice 28 (5) 148B
Alice 32 (6) 306B
Amelia 1 (4) 20A
Amelia 24 (3) 503B
Ann 35 (3) 466B
Ann E. 49 (5) 274A
Anna 10 (5) 283B
Anna 18 (1) 59B
Anna 25 (4) 95A
Anna 30 (6) 294B
Anna 38 (5) 283B
Anna E. 9 (4) 85A
Annie 27 (3) 424B
Annie 66 (3) 521A
Araminta 41 (2) 380A
Arthur 15 (5) 283B
*Baptist 69 (3) 478A
Bell 6 (6) 311B
Bristow 30 (6) 475B
Caroline 30 (3) 466A
Carrie 2 (1) 39B

BROWN (continued)
Catharine 34 (5) 137A
Catherine 22 (1) 1B
Cecelia 28 (5) 146A
Chalotta 16 (1) 59B
*Charlotte 50 (5) 220A
Charles 14 (3) 424B
Charles 2 (5) 137A
Charles 20 (5) 156B
Charles 24 (5) 150B
Charles 8 (5) 146A
Charles A. 3 (2) 379B
Charley 14 (6) 476A
Daniel 20 (5) 274A
Daniel 70 (3) 484A
Dora 4/12 (6) 306B
Edward 13 96) 306B
Edward 25 (3) 545A
Elisabeth 20 (5) 148A
Eliza 19 (4) 19B
Eliza 30 (4) 85A
Eliza 32 (3) 522B
Elizabeth 50 (5) 165B
Elizebeth 22 (6) 311B
Elizebeth 50 (6) 410B
*Ellen 40 (5) 253A
*Ellen 58 (5) 146A
*Ellen 61 (6) 475B
Ellen 32 (1) 47B
Ellen 7 (6) 475B
Emiline 51 (2) 315B
Emma 4 (6) 475B
Emma 40 (3) 493B
*Ezekiel 41 (2) 226B
Florence 13 (5) 206A
Francis 30 (3) 510A
Francis 6 (6) 305A
Frank 5 (6) 306B
Gennetta 24 (5) 234A
George 10 (6) 451B
George 15 (1) 59B
George 2 (4) 19B
George 22 (5) 204A
George 35 (2) 379B
George 40 (6) 451B
George 5 (3) 522B

BROWN (continued)
*George W. 26 (4) 95A
Georgeanna 11 (3) 524A
Georgella 5 (2) 379B
Dr. H. J. 39 (6) 324A
Harriet 20 (4) 26A
Harriett 10 (6) 470A
Harriett 12 (3) 424B
Harriett 26 (6) 451B
Henrietta 15 (4) 25B
Henrietta 18 (3) 544B
Henry 23 (5) 253A
Henry 3 (6) 324A
Henry 52 (2) 247B
Henryetta 46 (3) 424B
Hester 16 (3) 432B
Hester 18 (5) 203B
Hetta 55 (6) 324B
Ida 4 (6) 451B
Isaac F. 30 (6) 476B
Jacob 52 (3) 412A
James 17 (4) 24A
James 2 (4) 85A
James 20 (4) 18A
James 21 (5) 253A
James W. 2 (2) 379B
Jane 4 (5) 154A
Jane L. 8 (5) 126A
Jennerire 2 (6) 324A
Joanna 9 (3) 522B
John 10 (3) 503B
John 11 (3) 522B
John 2 (6) 475B
John 20 (3) 504B
John 22 (3) 540A
John 25 (3) 447B
John 30 (3) 503B
John 30 (5) 161B
John 8 (6) 311B
John 9 (3) 524A
*John 23 (5) 148A
*John 35 (6) 306B
*John 36 (3) 522B
*John 51 (3) 424B
John F. 26 (5) 145B
John H. 22 (5) 206A

BROWN (continued)
John T. 21 (5) 220A
*John T. 53 (5) 205B
John T. 55 (5) 220A
Jon 9 (6) 324A
Joseph 1 (3) 503B
Joseph 11 (2) 379B
Joseph 22 (6) 295A
Joseph 28 (5) 265A
Julia 15 (3) 524A
Julia A. 40 (6) 318A
Juliet A. 52 (2) 226B
Kate 10 (3) 424B
Kauffman 37 (6) 475B
Lamertine J. 14 (6) 324A
Laura 25 (5) 152B
Layton 13 (5) 283B
Lizzie 16 (3) 536B
Lizzie 19 (3) 521A
Lizzie 21 (1) 59B
Lizzie 21 (3) 569B
Louisa 12 (5) 253A
Louisa 28 (3) 571B
Lucy 23 (5) 147B
*Lucy 40 (5) 235B
Lucy 45 (3) 542A
Lydia 22 (5) 150B
Lydia 50 (5) 156B
Maggie 30 (3) 474A
Maggie 40 (6) 475B
Margaret 15 (5) 131A
Margaret 25 (5) 139A
Margarette 15 (6) 311B
Maria 13 (3) 524A
Maria 31 (3) 542A
Maria 70 (3) 548B
Martha 22 (5) 145B
Martha 41 (5) 205B
Martha 47 (3) 478A
Martha 8 (6) 306B
*Mary 70 (1) 47B
Mary 12 (3) 514B
Mary 15 (6) 451B
Mary 18 (3) 478A
Mary 19 (5) 152B
Mary 19 (5) 197A

94

BROWN (continued)
Mary 2 (3) 506A
Mary 23 (5) 265A
Mary 27 (3) 503B
Mary 33 (2) 379B
Mary 36 (6) 311B
Mary 39 (3) 524A
Mary 44 (3) 412A
Mary 55 (5) 142A
Mary 8 (5) 283B
*Mary 40 (3) 447B
Mary A. 20 (5) 161A
Mary A. 22 (5) 197A
Mary A. 60 (5) 137A
Mary E. 23 (6) 476A
Mary E. 30 (5) 150B
Mary E. 5 (6) 476A
Mary Ellen 22 (4) 20A
Mary J. 18 (6) 356B
Mary J. 30 (6) 475B
Mary Jane 6 (6) 475B
Moses 27 (1) 1B
Nancy 29 (4) 104A
Nancy 52 (3) 422B
Oreanrlia 8 (6) 324A
Pauline 32 (6) 324A
Philip 9 (5) 150A
*Rachel 40 (5) 197A
Rebecca 12 (5) 205B
Rebecca 44 (6) 470A
Rebecca 6 (5) 235B
Rebecca 7 (5) 139A
Richard 75 (4) 48A
Robert 22 (2) 225B
Robert 23 (1) 59B
Robert 3 (5) 283B
Robert 7 (3) 522B
Ruth 25 (1) 59B
Rye 16 (2) 329A
Samuel 8 (3) 504A
*Samuel 35 (6) 470A
Sarah 11 (6) 311B
Sarah 14 (1) 39A
Sarah 15 (5) 253A
Sarah 16 (3) 507B
Sarah 19 (3) 582A

BROWN (continued)
Sarah 5 (3) 424B
Sarah 5 (3) 504A
Sarah J. 7 (5) 137A
Solomon 30 (1) 47B
Sophia 19 (3) 563A
Sophia 20 (3) 580B
Sophia 34 (5) 208A
Sophia 45 (1) 39A
Sophia 8 (1) 39B
Steven 20 (4) 88B
*Susan 55 (1) 59B
Susan 19 (6) 311B
Susan 26 (1) 47B
Susan 3 (6) 306B
*Susan 47 (6) 476A
*Thomas 40 (5) 283B
Thomas 21 (3) 563B
Thomas 36 (5) 139A
Thomas 40 (5) 235B
Thomas 50 (3) 422B
Thomas N. 23 (2) 401B
Verde M. 7 (6) 324A
*Waters 55 (1) 39A
William 26 (6) 470A
William 35 (1) 47B
William 46 (6) 311B
*William 30 (5) 150B
*William 35 (3) 424A
*William 35 (4) 85A
*William H. 42 (5) 283B
William J. 9 (5) 283B
William T. 35 (5) 220A
Willie 3 (3) 504A
Zachariah 22 (4) 20A
BRUMMEL, Sarah 69 (2)
   306B
Sarah E. 10 (2) 306B
BRUMMELL, Charles 29 (5)
   236A
Eliza 27 (5) 236A
Wallace 2 (5) 236A
William H 9 (5) 236A
BRUNT, Catherine 11 (6)
   415B
*Henry 27 (6) 415B

BRUNT (continued)
Ida 27 (6) 415B
John E 6/12 (6) 415B
BRYAN, Annie 9 (3) 591B
Flora 41 (6) 305B
Hannah 27 (3) 591B
Ida 10 (6) 305B
Louis P 41 (6) 411B
Mary 5 (3) 591B
*Nathaniel 42 (6) 305B
Sallie 7 (3) 591B
Susannah 13 (6) 305B
*Thomas 39 (3) 591B
Thomas 2 (3) 591B
BRYAND, Lewis 25 (5) 209B
BRYAS, Amelia 38 (2) 306B
George 8 (2) 306B
Susan B. 3 (2) 306B
William H 14 (2) 306B
BUCHANAN, Harriet 39 (5)
    157A
James H. 21 (5) 157A
*John 35 (5) 157A
BUCK, Isabella 20 (5) 155A
BUCKHANNAN, Allice 10 (4)
    110B
Ann 40 (4) 110B
Martha 18 (4) 110B
Matilda 20 (4) 110B
*Thomas 41 (4) 110B
BUCKLEY, James 28 (6)
    408B
BUCKNER, Isaiah 2 (6) 433A
Martha 4 (6) 433A
Susan J. 13 (6) 433A
BUNDAY, Victoria 23 (5)
    274B
BURAL, *Robert 46 (5) 146A
Catharine A 38 (5) 146A
Eliza 18 (5) 146A
BURGAN, Henry 40 (5) 205A
BURGESS, Abraham 4 (5)
    256A
*Albert J. 30 (5) 256A
Eliza J. 2 (5) 248A
Ellen 4 (5) 248A

BURGESS (continued)
James A. 2 (5) 256A
John T. 10 (5) 248A
Margaret 28 (5) 248A
Mary A. 28 (5) 256A
Rachel 30 (5) 163A
Sarah R. 8 (5) 248A
*William 38 (5) 248A
BURK, Cora 3 (2) 345A
*David 23 (2) 345A
*David 95 (2) 229B
Emily 8 (3) 426A
John F. 21 (3) 563B
Martha 28 (2) 229B
Mary 22 (2) 345A
Nancy 69 (2) 229B
Rachel 26 (5) 146A
Robert John 1 (2) 345A
Sarah 21 (3) 517A
Sarah 35 (3) 422B
William 23 (6) 468A
BURKE, Lucy 10 (5) 154B
Rachel A. 26 (5) 154A
*Thomas 26 (5) 154A
William 3 (5) 154B
BURLEY, Catherine 75 (5)
    171A
BURNELL, James 30 (6)
    309A
Mary F. 29 (6) 309A
BURNES, Abey 12 (2) 345A
Isabella 23 (2) 345A
James A. 10 (2) 345A
*James H. 49 (2) 344B
Julia A. 40 (2) 345A
Martha 25 (2) 345A
Thursday 2 (6) 310B
BURNEY, Mary 2/12 (3)
    520B
BURNS, Abbie 13 (3) 459A
Florence 5 (3) 496A
John 24 (3) 496A
Mary 3 (3) 496A
Mary 7 (3) 496A
Sarah 25 (3) 496A
Willie 1 (3) 496A

96

BURRIS, Eliza 16 (5) 236A
Kate 52 (5) 236A
*Michael 61 (5) 236A
Sarah E 15 (5) 236A
BURTON, Alexander 11 (5)
  153A
Charley 17 (6) 477B
Elias 9 (6) 478A
Emory 13 (5) 153A
Henry 10 (5) 153A
*Hezekiah 48 (6) 477B
Jacoob 19 (6) 477B
John 10 (6) 478A
John 17 (5) 153B
Sarah 11 (5) 153B
BUSH, Elizabeth 30 (4) 8B
Joseph 16 (6) 435A
Lydia 40 (6) 434B
Mary 1 (4) 8B
Mary L 6 (6) 435A
*Richard 51 (6) 434B
Samuel 45 (4) 8B
Sarah 3 (3) 424B
Walter 13 (6) 435A
BUSSEY, Hannah 14 (3) 534B
BUTLER, Ann M 42 (5) 146B
Charles 16 (5) 168A
Eliza 18 (5) 168A
Eliza 27 (5) 273B
Emily 40 (5) 168A
Emily C. 28 (5) 205B
Frances 18 (5)168A
Henrietta 12 (3) 432A
*James 29 (5) 205B
Jesse 13 (5) 168A
Julia 12 (5) 146B
Louvina 17 (4) 88B
*Margaret 52 (5) 168A
Margaret 17 (5) 168A
Margaret 22 (5) 168A
Mary 28 (5) 149A
Mary E. 10 (5) 167B
Mary E. 3 (5) 205B
*Noah 45 (5) 168A
Perry 28 (5) 149A
Rachel 5 (5) 205B

BUTLER (continued)
*Sidney A. 59 (6) 476A
Thomas E. 30 (6) 476A
William H. 23 (5) 168A
William J. 7/12 (5) 205B
BUTT, Ella 18 (5) 226A
BYAS, Thomas 45 (6) 310A
BYNIS, Eliza 18 (6) 310A
Isaac 24 (6) 310A
James 9 (6) 310A
John 10 (6) 310A
Lydia A. 7 (6) 310A
Martha 12 (6) 310A
Mary Jane 39 (6) 310A
CADAY, Alfred T 29 (5) 274B
Ann 66 (5) 274B
*Dennis 46 (5) 274B
Igella 19 (5) 170B
Isabella 18 (5) 274B
James * 65 (3) 426A
Marey 30 (3) 426A
Mary F. 20 (5) 274B
Nelson A. 28 (5) 170B
Rosa 13 (5) 274B
Samuel 17 (5) 274B
CAGER, Ann M 41 (5) 274B
CALDWELL, Ann E. 21 (2)
  247B
Ann M. 14 (6) 408B
*Charles 54 (2) 295A
Charles J. 4 (2) 295A
*Chas 54 (2) 295A
Clemiann 54 (2) 295A
*Daniel 38 (2) 336A
Dinah 29 (6) 408B
Elizabeth 32 (5) 146B
Frances 7 (2) 295A
Mary 81 (2) 295A
Mary E. 11 (5) 154A
Moses 40 (5) 146B
Sophia 43 (2) 247B
CALVIN, Nancy 59 (6) 415B
CAMDEN, Harriet 20 (3)
  460A
CAMERON, Lizzie 22 (6)
  325A

CAMERON (continued)
Moses 62 (6) 325A
Walter 24 (6) 325A
CAMPBELL, Anna 11 (1)
    54A
Charity 70 (5) 213A
*Charlotte 40 (5) 213A
Levi 16 (5) 213A
Mary 25 (5) 217B
William 16 (5) 213A
CAMPER, Andrew 8 (4) 85A
Ann 62 (4) 85A
Charlott 36 (3) 465B
*Dennis 45 (4) 85A
Elvin 12 (4) 85A
George 23 (4) 85A
Mary 11 (2) 380A
Peter 19 (4) 85A
Rachel 30 (6) 291B
Sarah J. 27 (4) 85A
CAMPHER, *John 31 (6)
    413A
Lavenia 28 (6) 413A
Mary E. J. 3 (6) 413A
William J. 1 (6) 413A
CAMPHOR, *Peter 47 (6)
    362A
Adeline 8 (3) 520B
Amelia 2 (6) 362A
Anna 10 (6) 362A
Anna 30 (6) 362A
Caroline 6 (6) 362A
Delia 10 (6) 451A
Eliza 15 (6) 362A
*Emil 29 (5) 167B
Emma J. 8 (6) 362A
George W. 32 (5) 167B
*Henrietta 44 (5) 146A
infant enumerated with Peter
    Camphor 1/12 (6) 451A
*John 45 (3) 520B
John 12 (3) 520B
John H 18 (6) 451A
Josiah 41 (2) 385A
Leah 3 (3) 520B
M. Emily 30 (6) 451A

CAMPHOR (continued)
Peter 4 (6) 362A
Peter 45 (6) 451A
Rachel 30 (3) 509A
Rebecca 10 (3) 520B
Rebecca 32 (3) 520B
Salenia 1/12 (6) 362A
Sarah 14 (6) 451A
Sarah 6 (3) 520B
Saulsbury 7 (6) 451A
William Sprey 22 (6) 451A
CANNON, Anna 27 (6) 473A
Anna 3 (6) 473A
Charity 45 (3) 508A
Elijah 27 (5) 276A
Hannah 21 (6) 473A
Hannah 51 (5) 212A
Joseph 1 (6) 473A
Nathaniel 23 (3) 487A
CAREY, Ann 56 (2) 248A
Ann B 4 (2) 248A
Henrietta 27 (2) 248A
Noah 20 (2) 248A
CARMACK, Francis 24 (1)
    59B
*Lewis 40 (5) 203B
Sarah 42 (5) 203B
Sophia 13 (5) 203B
Stephen 19 (5) 203B
CARMICHAEL, Daniel J. 4
` (5) 145B
Joseph H. 3/12 (5) 145B
Mary 29 (5) 145B
*Simon 35 (5) 145B
Simon 2 (5) 145B
William T. 3 (5) 145B
CARPENTER, Hester 11 (4)
    111B
Hiram 23 (2) 295B
James H. 20 (6) 362B
*Nathaniel 38 (6) 362B
Rachel 95 (3) 542B
Sarah E. 35 (6) 362B
CARR, Alice 19 (1) 82A
Charles 1 (3) 487A
Dortha 19 (6) 292B

CARR (continued)
Emily 26 (2) 344B
Frances 30 (2) 379A
Hannah 12 (3) 521B
Henrietta 30 (5) 167A
Henry 3 (3) 487A
James 29 (2) 344B
John 29 (4) 85A
John 31 (2) 379A
John 44 (5) 167A
John 49 (2) 328A
Maria 35 (3) 487A
Martha 17 (3) 521A
Mary 3 (5) 167A
Mary 40 (3) 521A
*Purnell 75 (3) 521A
Robert 11 (2) 379A
Sarah 30 (4) 85A
Stephen 24 (3) 487A
Susan 89 (2) 345A
CARROL, *Anna 80 (5) 248B
David 26 (5) 258B
Sophia 30 (5) 158B
William 24 (3) 541B
CARROLL, Annie 24 (3)
490A
Charles 20 (3) 541B
Charles 28 (5) 158B
*Daniel 26 (3) 504A
Emily A. 23 (3) 504A
Grace 80 (2) 382B
CARTER, Adelaide V. 27 (6)
474B
Daniel 22 (5) 232B
Ellen 21 (6) 346B
James 25 (3) 505B
Julia 18 (5) 232B
Margaret 16 (5) 263A
Mary 23 (3) 505B
Mary E. 4/12 (6) 346B
Samuel P. 5 (6) 474B
Victoria 21 (1) 216A
William B. 2 (6) 474B
CARY, Louiza 23 (5) 198A
*William 24 (5) 198A
CASTER, Emma 16 (5) 139A

CASTER (continued)
Maria 18 (5) 139A
CAUTION, Hamilton 30 (5)
282A
Hannah 58 (5) 282A
*Samuel 55 (5) 282A
Samuel 29 (5) 282A
William 23 (5) 282A
CEEDOW, Susette 75 (5)
121B
CHALK, Henrietta 34 (1) 59B
Isabella 14 (1) 59B
*Joshua 36 (1) 59B
Mary 16 (1) 59B
CHAMBERS, Amelia 5 (4)
95A
Ann 7/12 (5) 176A
*Anna 29 357B
Charles 40 (5) 175B
Francis 45 (4) 6A
*Horrace 45 (4) 6A
Isaiah 2 (6) 357B
Joseph 28 (5) 156B
Lizzie 5 (6) 357B
Lydia 37 (5) 175B
Maggio 9 (6) 357B
Margaret L. 9 (5) 175B
Mary 9 (4) 95A
Sarah A. 42 (5) 167A
Sarah L. 2 (5) 175B
*Sophia 36 (5) 210B
Wesley 15 (2) 380A
CHAMPHOR, Ann 30 (5)
214B
Laura 25 (5) 198A
CHANCE, Washington 55 (5)
146A
CHANCY, George 15 (3) 545A
George 64 (1) 23B
CHAPLIN, David 23 (3) 520A
*Joseph 47 (3) 520A
Josephine 14 (3) 520A
Mary 18 (3) 520A
Matilda 16 (3) 520A
Matilda 45 (3) 520A
CHAPMAN, *Alicia A. 50 (6)

99

CHAPMAN (continued)
468A
Amanda 16 (6) 468A
Elizebeth 34 (6) 342B
George 14 (6) 342B
*H. 57 (4) 18A
Henrietta 9 (6) 342B
James 5 (5) 141B
Kate 23 (5) 141B
Martha A. 45 (4) 18A
Sarah 10 (4) 18A
Sarah 12 (6) 342B
*Wilson E. 38 (6) 342B
CHAPPEL, Sarah 30 (5) 145A
CHARISTY, Jane R. 5 (5)
234A
Lillie H. 4 (5) 234A
Mary E. 7 (5) 234A
Mary J. 29 (5) 234A
Robert H. 1 (5) 234A
CHARLES, Bennet 24 (5)
167B
Lucy 21 (5) 167B
Theadore 78 (5) 156B
Theodore 27 (3) 562B
CHASE, Agness 7 (5) 151B
*Allen 73 (5) 206A
Amand 19 (6) 306A
Ann 60 (5) 169B
Benjamin 15 (6) 306A
Caroline 37 (5) 275B
*Charles A. 40 (6) 407B
*Daniel 41 (5) 275B
David 22 (5) 151B
Ella 20 (6) 306A
Ellen 23 (6) 321B
*Fuller 49 (6) 306A
George 23 (6) 306A
George W. 16 (5) 136B
Hatte A. 4 (5) 151B
Hattie 14 (6) 390A
*Henry 30 (5) 159A
Ida 15 (5) 275B
Isabella 37 (6) 407B
Jane 12 (1) 63B
Johanna 2 (3) 496A

CHASE (continued)
*John 27 (1) 46A
*John 37 (6) 362B
John 31 (1) 3A
John C. 18 (6) 407B
Joseph 11 (5) 151B
Josephine 37 (5) 136B
Julia 4 (5) 159A
Julia 42 (2) 380B
Lawrence 22 (3) 496A
*Lewis 61 (5) 169B
Martha 30 (5) 159A
Mary 50 (1) 52B
Mary E. 22 (5) 169B
Mary Eliza 17 (6) 306A
Nancy 54 (5) 206A
Owins 4 (6) 306A
Pricilla 42 (5) 151B
Rachel 13 (6) 306A
*Samuel 45 (5) 151B
Sarah 30 (6) 362B
Sarah E. 35 (5) 159A
*William 24 (3) 496A
William H. 15 (6) 407B
CHAULK, Rebecca 20 (1)
47A
CHERRIS, Nancy 70 (5) 178B
CHESNEY, Daniel 22 (6)
448A
Elizebeth 20 (6) 448A
Joseph 26 (6) 448A
CHESTER, Andrew 18 (2)
382B
Clarence 14 (2) 382B
Dorsey 25 (3) 521A
Elizebath 32 (3) 520A
Ida 5 (2) 382B
*Jeremiah 53 (2) 382B
Jeremiah 9 (2) 382B
Laura J. 22 (2) 382B
Lizzie 19 (3) 520A
Margaret 13 (6) 341A
Maria 17 (3) 520A
Mary 22 (3) 521A
Rachael 16 (2) 382B
Rebecca 28 (6) 331A

CHESTER (continued)
Rebecca 50 (2) 382B
Thomas H. 28 (2) 382B
Wilhemina 87 (3) 520A
William 21 (3) 520A
*William H. 29 (6) 331A
William H. 2 (6) 331A
CHEW, Ann E 30 (5) 236B
Charlotte 45 (3) 441B
Hannah 43 (3) 580B
Margaret 11 (5) 241B
Philip 26 (5) 162A
*Sutton 52 (3) 580B
CHISLEY, Henry 1 (5) 160B
Margaret 19 (5) 160B
Rachel 40 (5) 160B
CHRIST, *Phillip 31 (4) 50B
CHRISTIN, William 29 (5)
157B
CHRISTMAS, *James 39 (6)
457B
Mary 37 (6) 457B
CHURCH, Ann M 30 (6) 412A
Georgeanna 5 (5) 269B
*Jonathan 35 (6) 412A
Laura J 3 (6) 412A
CINPHOR, Kate 13 (2) 297A
CIO, Francisca 27 (6) 390B
CISSEL, Jeremiah 22 (2)
335B
Mary 15 (2) 335B
Sarah 45 (2) 335B
CLARK, George 30 (3) 473A
Georgie A. 8/12 (5) 171A
Henry 26 (3) 545A
Hester A. 30 (5) 207A
John 20 (3) 523A
Joseph 24 (5) 154A
*Lydia 50 (5) 154A
Margaret 23 (5) 171A
Maria 16 (3) 508A
Maria 40 (3) 503A
Martha 27 (3) 518B
Mary 12 (3) 503A
Moses 40 (3) 503A
William 15 (3) 503A

CLARK (continued)
William 25 (5) 171A
William 28 (3) 518B
CLASH, John 20 (1) 4A
CLAY, Alice 18 (3) 504A
Caroline 40 (3) 504A
Charles 16 (3) 504A
Edward 12 (3) 504A
George 14 (3) 504A
CLAYTON, Anna 19 (6) 303A
*Chas 36 (2) 295A
Harry 29 (5) 179B
Henrietta 1 (2) 295A
Henrietta 33 (2) 295A
John 7 (5) 179B
Louisa 23 (5) 179B
Mariah 26 (4) 19A
Mary E. 3 (2) 295A
*Mathew 26 (4) 88B
Percilla 39 (6) 303A
Rachael 50 (3) 426A
Robert 5 (2) 295A
*Samuel 39 (4) 19A
Samuel W. 42 (4) 40B
CLEMENTS, Susannah 12 (6)
387A
CLEMMENTS, Walter 19 (5)
170A
CLENDENNAN, James 10 (3)
549A
Joseph 13 (3) 549A
CLESHMAN, *Catherine 45
(5) 153A
Peter 16 (5) 153A
CLINTON, Cynthia 68 (2)
257A
*David 70 (2) 257A
John W. 1 (5) 168B
Mary E. 28 (5) 168B
Thomas 35 (5) 168B
CLOSS, Jenny 16 (6) 368A
COATS, John L 28 (2) 221B
COBURN, Daniel 28 (2) 348B
John 28 (4) 18A
COCKEY, Elizabeth J. 1 (5)
286A

COCKEY (continued)
Jarret 35 (5(286A
Mary C. 4 (5) 286A
Rachael A 22 (5) 286A
COLBERT, Anna E 3 (5)
276A
Edward 4 (5) 150A
Elizabeth 9 (5) 150A
George 18 (5) 150A
Henry 32 (5) 276A
James 4 (5) 150A
Laura 21 (5) 150A
*Louisa 36 (5) 276A
Mary A. 40 (5) 178A
Mary E. 1 (5) 276A
Mary E. 12 (5) 150A
William 28 (5) 170A
William 3 (5) 150A
COLE, Benjamin 21 (5) 162B
Castillea 15 (3) 496A
Charles 12 (4) 18B
David 9 (5) 162B
Elizabeth 11 (3) 496A
Elizebath 45 (3) 496A
Ellen 29 (5) 147A
Ellen 45 (4) 51A
George 19 (5) 151B
George 6 (6) 450A
Harriet 12 (5) 162B
Harriett 50 (5) 162B
*Henry 30 (5) 161A
*Isaac 34 (5) 147A
John H. 12 (5) 147A
John W. 13 (5) 162B
Jusilla 13 (3) 496A
*Maria 50 (5) 275B
Mary 21 (2) 386A
Moses 21 (2(386A
Moses 23 (3(550B
Robert 8 (5) 255B
Saline 5 (5) 162B
Sarah J. 35 (4) 18B
Sophia J. 25 (5) 275B
Thomas 10 (5) 147A
William 17 (5) 162B
William 7 (3) 496A

COLE (continued)
*William H. 49 (4) 18B
COLEMAN, Amanda 22 (6)
392A
Anna 4 (1) 4A
Catharin 25 (4) 12A
*Charles 30 (1) 4A
Charles 9 (1) 4A
Charlott 32 (6) 366A
Elenora 5 (6) 310A
Ella 1 (1) 3A
Emilie 25 (1) 4A
George A. 12 (6) 310A
Georgetta 1 (6) 310A
Georgetta 25 (6) 310A
Handy 30 (5) 168A
Henrta 20 (1) 3A
Hester 28 (5) 168A
*Isaac 29 (6) 366A
Jacob 4 (3) 563A
James 17 (6) 433A
*John A. 49 (6) 310A
Lewis 3 (1) 3A
Littleman 41 (3) 563A
Martha 2 (1) 4A
Mary 8 (3) 563A
Mary Ann 10 (6) 310A
Moses 4 (5) 168A
Philip 2 (3) 563A
Rachel 21 (1) 78A
Rose 6 (3) 563A
Sarah 26 (3) 507A
WIllie T 3 (6) 310A
COLLIER, Alexander 3 (5)
203B
*Hnery 55 (5) 178A
*Isaac 28 (5) 210A
COLLINS, Amelia J 23 (6)
309B
Ann M. 16 (6) 321A
Ann M. 26 (2) 339B
Carrie 8 (6) 311A
Charles 47 (2) 387B
Charles 5 (5) 258B
Elizabeth 20 (5) 148B
Elizabeth 9 (6) 414A

COLLINS (continued)
 Emily J. 15 (6) 311A
 Emmer 2 (6) 414A
 Estelle 8 (6) 449A
 *George 61 (5) 237A
 *George F. 35 (5) 258B
 George F. 12 (5) 258B
 Howard M. 7 (6) 449A
 Ida 6 (6) 414A
 *Idler 49 (6) 414A
 Isabella 19 (6) 414A
 James S. 10 (5) 206A
 *John 47 (6) 311A
 Margaret 41 (2) 387B
 Mary 15 (5) 259A
 Mary 36 (6) 414A
 Mary E. 14 (6) 311A
 Mary E. 2 (2(339B
 Mary L. 2 (5) 258B
 Mathew 15 (6) 414A
 *Noah 37 (6) 449A
 Richard 21 (6) 311A
 Robert 28 (2) 339B
 *Robert 29 (6) 309B
 Robert J. 4 (5) 258B
 Sarah 3 (6) 414A
 Sarah 33 (5) 258B
 Sarah A. 41 (6) 311A
 Sophia 28 (6) 449A
 Sophia 28 (6) 449A
 Susan 25 (5) 237A
 Susan 58 (3) 597A
 Susan 7 (6) 414A
 Susan J. 22 (5) 204B
 WIllie 1 (6) 414A
COLWELL, Anna 21 (1) 52B
 Arminta 40 (3) 561B
 Florence 15 (3) 561B
 Isabella 21 (3) 561B
 Thomas 19 (3) 561B
 William 56 (3) 561B
COMEGERS, Matthew 25 (5)
 255B
COMMINS, Amanda 28 (3)
 503B
 Charles 4 (3) 503B

COMMINS (continued)
 Ham 5 (3) 503B
 Louvinia 2 (3) 503B
 Mary 7 (3) 503B
 Rebecca 9 (3) 503B
 Samuel 14 (3) 503B
 Samuel 36 (3) 503B
CONLEY, Jerry 23 (3(599B
CONNER, Eliza 26 (3) 486A
 Elizabeth 27 (2) 340B
 Isaac 26 (3) 486A
 James 56 (2) 340B
 Lizzie 1 (3) 486A
 Margaret 44 (3) 486A
 Mary 24 (3) 476A
 Mary 66 (1) 4A
 Ralph 3 (3) 486A
 *Ralph 67 (3) 486A
 Thomas 5 (3) 486A
CONNIER, Robert 30 (4) 93B
 Simon 1 (4) 93B
CONOWAY, Alice 11 (3)
 576B
 Edward 36 (6) 334A
 Georgian 1 (6) 334A
 Georgian 25 (6) 334A
 *Joseph 30 (4) 20A
 Lewis 18 (4) 20A
 Louvenia 28 (4) 20A
 Robert 20 (4) 20A
CONWAY, Charlotta 21 (5)
 149B
 Clementine 46 (4) 18B
 Frances 26 (2) 295A
 Henry 23 (5) 149B
 Janes 15 (4) 18B
 John S. 37 (2) 295A
 John T 1 (2) 295A
 Susan 13 (4) 19A
COOK, Anna 26 (6) 342A
 Annie 7/12 (3) 505A
 *Charles E. 45 (5) 150A
 Clara 14 (5) 237A
 Clara E. 5 (5) 160A
 *Columbus 38 (3) 561A
 Eliza 26 (5) 160A

COOK (continued)
Eliza Jane 17 (3) 505A
Frank 12 (5) 150A
Frank 9 (3) 560B
George 6 (6) 342A
Harriett 42 (6) 316B
Henrietta 1 (5) 237A
Henrietta 30 (5) 237A
James 4 (5) 150A
James 4 (6) 342A
James F. 17 (6) 316B
John 28 (5) 160A
John 30 (6) 451A
John 6 (3) 560B
*Lucy 25 (6) 317A
Maria 30 (3) 561A
Mary E. 28 (5) 150A
Mary J. 3 (5) 160A
Mollie 38 (3) 560B
Nathaniel 43 (6) 308B
Ophelia 11 (5) 150A
Penrose 4 (3) 560B
Stephen 40 (3) 560B
Thomas 36 (5) 237A
Valestine 6 (5) 237A
William 4 (5) 237A
*William 29 (6)342A
William E. 9 (5) 150A
William H. 21 (6) 317A
COOPER, *Aaron 40 (2) 303A
Aaron 6 (2) 303A
Alexander 2 (2) 303B
Alexena 15 (6) 448A
Alice 19 (5) 149B
Anna 6 (2) 252A
Annie 24 (3) 525A
Annie 6 (3) 422B
Caroline 38 (5) 209A
Caroline E. 17 (2) 241B
Catherine 36 (1) 2A
Catherine 36 (1) 2A
Charles 2 (3) 479A
Charles 2 (3) 528A
Charles 22 (2) 251B
Charles A. 6 (2) 219A
Clara 19 (3) 563B

COOPER (continued)
Cora 4 (2) 303B
Cornelius 12 (2) 251B
Davis 20 (2) 251B
Dawson 30 (1) 131B
Delia 25 (3) 477B
Edward 8 (3) 422A
Eliza 26 (2) 303A
Eliza 3 (3) 477B
*Eliza 60 (5) 219B
Ellerzenia 14 (6) 431A
*Elsbury 57 (3) 422A
Frances 12 (3) 563B
George 22 (2(251B
George 40 (3) 479A
George 49 (6) 347B
George F. 13 (2) 219A
Gurtenia 5 (5) 205A
Hammond 4 (2) 251B
Hariet 23 (3) 477B
Harriet 20 (5) 148A
Harriet 39 (2) 251B
Helen 13 (1) 131B
Henrietta 4 (5) 205A
Henry 19 (2) 384A
Henry 21 (5) 205A
Henry 23 (5) 148A
Henry 40 (3) 524B
Ida 14 (1) 131B
Isabella 24 (4) 20B
*Isaiah 31 (5) 149B
*Jacob 25 (3) 424B
*James 30 (3) 525A
*James 60 (2) 251B
James 14 (1) 110B
James 22 (4) 20A
James 32 (5) 205A
James L. 2 (5) 205A
John 22 (3) 521A
John 32 (2) 300A
*John 40 (4) 94B
John H. 28 (5) 166B
Joseph 18 (6) 448A
*Joseph 48 (2) 251B
Joseph H. 30 (2) 334A
Josephine 13 (6) 330B

COOPER (continued)
Josephine 20 (1) 131B
Josephine 22 (3) 424B
Josephine 31 (5) 166B
Kate 13 (3) 446B
Laura 6 (2) 252A
*Levin 38 (5) 205A
Lydia 59 (3) 477B
Maggie 4 (3) 528A
Margaret 20 (3) 524B
Margaret 56 (3) 422A
Margaret 7 (3) 422A
Maria 1 (3) 563B
Maria 7 (6) 451B
Martha 4 (3) 477B
Mary 16 (2) 251B
Mary 19 (3) 422A
Mary 27 (2) 334A
Mary 37 (3) 479A
Mary 4 (3) 479A
Mary 53 (4) 94B
Mary 56 (1) 131B
*Mary 69 (2) 251B
Mary A. 1 (5) 205A
Mary C. 33 (2) 219A
Mary E. 24 (5) 205A
Nancy A. 63 (2) 251B
Oclalin 23 (3) 528A
*Oliver 43 (5) 209A
Orlando 6 (3) 479A
Penny 23 (3) 563B
*Robert 39 (1) 2A
*Robert 61 (1) 131B
Rosanna 9 (2) 334A
Samuel 17 (4) 94A
Sarah 16 (1) 131B
Sarah 25 (6) 451B
Sarah 38 (2) 251B
Solomon 15 (3) 477B
Sophia 31 (5) 205A
Sophia 8 (2) 303A
Stewart 4 (5) 205A
Tabertha 16 (6) 448A
Thomas 1 (3) 477B
*Thomas 40 (2) 384A
William 10 (3) 496B

COOPER (continued)
William 9 (1) 2A
*William 30 (3) 528A
COOTS, *Thomas 27 (5) 157A
COPPER, Hannah 36 (3)
537B
CORDERAY, John 57 (2)
339A
Matilda 69 (2) 339A
CORNEL, *Enos 57 (1) 47A
Isaac 22 (1) 47A
Mathew 31 (1) 47A
Sarah 66 (1) 47A
CORNELIUS, Anna E 20 (6)
475A
*Ellen 64 (6) 475A
George 18 (6) 475A
Martin 23 (6) 475A
Susan 32 (6) 475A
Virginia 28 (6) 475A
CORNER, Albert 17 (3) 544B
CORNISH, Ann 69 (5) 220B
Annie 3 (3) 591A
Betsey 19 (3) 424B
Bridget 60 (3) 525A
Charles 4 (3) 561A
David 33 (3) 503B
David 5 (3) 591A
*David 27 (3) 591A
Dortha 5 (5) 157B
Eliza 31 (3) 561A
Elizabeth 64 (4) 88B
Emily 34 (6) 309A
Francis 23 (6) 451B
Harrison 18 (4) 18A
Hester 1/12 (5) 166B
Isabella 37 (6) 475A
*James 68 (4) 88B
Jane 19 (4) 99A
John 25 (6) 475A
John 35 (3) 561A
*John 56 (3) 525A
Joseph Mooney 15 (6) 309A
*Josiah 26 (4) 6A
Josiah 36 (3) 487B
Lizzie 27 (1) 22B

CORNISH (continued)
Louis 1 (3) 561A
Louisa 20 (4) 111B
Lucinda 35 (5) 147A
Mahalia 27 (6) 447B
Margaret 11 (5) 147A
Margaret 16 (5) 257A
Mary 12 (6) 451B
Mary 29 (5) 157B
Mary 8 (3) 561A
*Mary 39 (6) 447B
Mary A. 30 (4) 6B
Rachel 29 (6) 447B
Robert F. 32 (6) 309A
Rose 26 (3) 591A
Rosetta 18 (6) 292A
*Samuel 35 (5) 157B
Sarah 36 (3) 487B
Sophia 17 (5) 166B
Sophia 6 (3) 561A
William 1 (3) 591A
*William P. 32 (6) 309A
CORNTNEY, *Mary 55 (5)
    149A
CORPELL, Joseph 23 (5)
    151A
CORPERAL, Edward 4 (5)
    198A
Jane 40 (5) 198A
CORSEY, Margaret 11 (3)
    562B
COSTEN, *Hnery 35 (3) 503A
Martha 18 (5) 194B
Purnell 23 (5) 194B
COSTER, Francis 18 (5)
    205B
COSTIN, Henrietta 10 (3)
    503A
COULTER, Abraham 4 (5)
    166A
*Andrew 55 (5) 166A
Deborah 50 (5) 166A
Edward 11 (5) 166A
Gennet 2 (5) 166A
William 12 (5) 166A

COUNTESS, *Benjamin 30 (6)
    414A
Mary H. 29 (6) 414A
Rachel A. 8 (6) 414A
COVINGTON, Alexander 30
    (1) 200A
Armstead 60 (5) 234B
Armstead Jr. 27 (5) 234B
John M. 14 (5) 234B
*Joseph 72 (5) 170B
COX, Elizabeth 35 (4) 94B
Harriett 21 (5) 208A
CRAWFORD, Elizabeth 50
    (2) 389A
George 35 (5) 153B
Harriet 62 (2) 389A
Henry 39 (2) 389A
*Henry 41 (2) 251B
Mary 49 (2) 251B
CRAWLEY, Ely 26 (2) 295B
London 21 (2) 295B
CRAYTON, Charlotte 40 (3)
    504B
John 12 (3) 520B
Margaret 17 (3) 504B
*William 50 (3) 504B
CREEK, Malinda 30 (6) 474B
Samuel 38 (6) 474B
CREEKS, Mary 39 (5) 151B
William 26 (5) 151B
CREIGHTON, *Daniel 48 (1)
    40A
*Sophia 25 (1) 40A
CROMWELL, William 37 (5)
    214A
CRONEL, Estelle 6/12 (6)
    415B
James 41 (6) 415B
Jane 37 (6) 415B
CRONNELL, Charity 27 (6)
    416A
CROSBY, *Caroline 26 (5)
    275A
Samuel 35 (5) 149B
Viginia 30 (5) 149A

CROSLEY, Caroline 26 (5) 281B
Catharine A. 1 (5) 275A
Joseph 31 (5) 275A
Mary A. 4 (5) 275A
Moses 3 (5) 275A
CROW, Elenora 40 (5) 196A
Mary 13 (6) 414B
CRUMMEL, Julia 20 (6) 377B
CUGER, Adda C 11 (6) 310A
Carrie 29 (6) 453B
Elizabeth 16 (6) 310A
Georgiana 14 (6) 310A
Henry 3 (6) 453B
Henry J. 47 (6) 453B
*John Henry 45 (6) 310A
Margaret 30 (6) 310A
CULLINS, *Enoch 56 (3) 488A
Margaret 57 (3) 488A
CUMBACH , John D. 6/12 (6) 409A
George E. 4 (6) 409A
Sarah J. 25 (6) 409A
CUMMING, Julia 60 (4) 6A
CUMMINGS, Benjamin 40 (5) 162B
Caroline 16 (5) 160B
Charlott A. 3 (6) 408B
Cordelia 28 (6) 408B
Eliza 35 (5) 160B
*Fanny 37 (5) 162B
*George 24 (6) 306A
*Harris 42 (6) 305B
*Horace 38 (5) 160B
*James 40 (6) 408B
James 35 (5) 160B
James H. 10/12 (6) 408B
Laura J. 8 (6) 408B
Lizza 5 (6) 408B
Lucy 12 (5) 204B
Margaret 13 (5) 161A
Mary E. 10 (6) 408B
Sarah 27 (6) 305B
William 20 (6) 306A

CUNNINGHAM, George 34 (5) 273B
George A. 36 (4) 118A
*Mary J. 38 (5) 273B
CURLEY, Matilda 45 (5) 149A
CURRAN, Elizabeth 1 (5) 161A
*Henry 27 (5) 161A
Mary E. 3 (5) 161A
Roseanna 23 (5) 161A
CURREY, Wilby 21 (6) 324A
CURRY, *Kendal 33 (5) 168A
Martha 28 (5) 168A
Rosa 9 (5) 168A
CURTIN, William 24 (1) 35B
CURTIS, *Abendego 67 (5) 157B
Betsey 60 (5) 194B
Elizabeth 60 (5) 157B
Francis 30 (3) 476B
Hester 80 (3) 542A
Ida 1 (5) 194B
Isaac 26 (5) 194B
James 4 (2) 388A
John 18 (5) 157B
Lydia 15 (5) 120A
Margaret 17 (4) 104B
Mary E. 10 (2) 300B
Pricilla 20 (5) 194B
Sarah 9 (5) 126A
Sarah E. 2 (5) 194B
CUSTUS, George H. 5 (5) 148A
John 40 (5) 148A
Sarah 35 (5) 148A
DAIRY, Rosetta 49 (6) 415B
DAKINS, Catharine 28 (2) 380A
*William 27 (2) 380A
DAMBY, William 37 (3) 412A
DAMMOND, *Robert 24 (2) 295B
Selena 25 (2) 295B
DANBY, Bell 11 (3) 543B

DANBY (continued)
 Charlotte 27 (3) 483B
 Emma 5/12 (3) 543B
 Henry 15 (3) 543B
 *James 40 (3) 543B
 Julia 41 (3) 483B
 Julia 7 (3) 543B
 Laura 9 (3) 543B
 Mary 13 (3) 543B
 Mary 38 (3) 543B
 Mary 62 (3) 483B
 Phillip 3 (3) 543B
 William 37 (3) 483B
 William 5 (3) 543B
DANE, Julia 12 (6) 327A
DANGSTON, Harriett 28 (1)
 23B
DANIEL, Ann M. 3/12 (6)
 318B
 Edward M. 1 (2) 225B
 Georgiana 30 (6) 318B
 *Henry 29 (6) 318B
 *Lewis 29 (2) 225B
 Robert J. 12 (2) 225B
 Ruth A. 35 (2) 225B
 Samuel C. 7 (2) 225B
 William H. 10 (2) 225B
DANNIELS, *David 18 (4) 6A
DANSBURY, *Eliz 69 (6)
 309B
 James W. 2 (6) 309A
 Lucinda 28 (6) 309A
 *Thomas 24 (6) 309A
DARBEY, George H 29 (5)
 145B
DARBY, Isaiah 25 (5) 287A
 *Major 62 (5) 287A
 Sarah A. 61 (5) 287A
DARD, David T. 13 (6) 469B
 Margarett 48 (6) 469B
 *Thomas 58 (6) 469B
DAREY, Amanda 28 (6) 413A
 George W. 10 (6) 413A
DARKEY, Hester 16 (3) 574B
 Mary 12 (3) 574B
DARKINS, Albert 3 (1) 4A

DARKINS (continued)
 Amanda 5 (1) 4A
 Barn 30 (1) 3B
 Bush 15 (1) 4A
 Catherine 28 (1) 3B
 Charles 19 (1) 3B
 Harriett 23 (1) 3B
 Hebrew 9/12 (1) 4A
 Hester 25 (1) 4A
 Hester 26 (1) 3B
 James 17 (1) 3B
 James 8 (1) 4A
 John 7 (1) 4A
 *Levin 50 (1) 3B
 Milly 12 (1) 4A
 Milly 55 (1) 3B
 William 10 (1) 4A
DARLING, Caroline 40 (6)
 465B
 Hannah 15 (6) 465B
 Harriett 20 (6) 465B
 John 12 (6) 465B
 Rose 3 (6) 465B
 Thomas 9 (6) 465B
 *William 40 (6) 465B
 William 19 (6) 465B
DASHIELL, Caroline 7 (2)
 335B
 Estelle 4/12 (2) 335B
 Eugiene 12 (2) 335B
 Frederick 9 (2) 335B
 *Henry R. 42 (2) 335B
 Josephine 36 (2) 335B
 Mary A. 5 (2) 335B
DAUUGHERTY, Eliz. 53 (6)
 309B
DAVAGE, Elizabeth 32 (5)
 174B
DAVENPORT, Charles H 4
 (5) 205B
 Cornelius 10 (6) 395B
 Frances 40 (5) 205B
 Margaret 5 (5) 205B
 Martha A. 9/12 (5) 205B
 Mary J. 9/12 (5) 205B
 *William 46 (5) 205B

DAVIS, Aaron 35 (4) 110B
Adaline E. 15 (4) 94B
Adell 27 (4) 9B
Ann M. 18 (6) 348B
Ann M. 26 (5) 161B
Carrie C. 27 (6) 477B
Catharine 35 (4) 94B
Charlott 17 (6) 477B
D. H. 23 (4) 19B
Daniel 25 (3) 484A
Ellen 24 (5) 150B
*Fanny 80 (5) 151A
Hanna 23 (4) 28B
Harry 11 (4) 94B
*Henrietta 72 (4) 113A
Henry 2 (5) 150B
Henry 21 (6) 477B
Israel 18 (5) 176A
*Jacob 31 (5) 171B
Jefferson 32 (5) 161B
*John 30 (5) 264A
John 26 (3) 560A
John 30 (5) 204A
John H. 26 (5) 162A
Josephine 10 (5) 264A
*Julia 35 (6) 408B
Kate 40 (3) 494B
Katie A. L. 23 (6) 477B
Laura V. 13 (6) 408B
Maria 47 (3) 559B
Martha 30 (4) 110B
Mary 27 (3) 484A
Mary 28 (5) 204A
Mary J. 30 (5) 171B
*Pinkney 49 (6) 477B
Rachael 23 (2) 303A
Rachael 30 (5) 264A
*Richard 28 (5) 155A
Richard 28 (5) 169B
Richard 6 (5) 150B
Robinson 13 (4) 94B
Samuel 10 (5) 195A
Samuel K. 8 (5) 154A
Sarah 10 (3) 559B
Sarah 18 (6) 296A
Sarah E. 18 (5) 169B

DAVIS (continued)
Susan 55 (5) 264A
*Walker 24 (1) 44B
*William 35 (2) 303A
William 2 (2) 303A
William 20 (3) 522A
William 4 (5) 154A
William 8 (3) 559B
DAWSON, Charles A. 25 (2)
219A
George F. 29 (2) 219A
*Mary L. 66 (2) 219A
DAY, Aaron 35 (3) 488A
Cato 23 (2) 383A
Charlotte 3 (3) 488A
Della 36 (3) 505B
Della 9 (3) 505B
Frances 30 (3) 488A
Francis 5 (3) 488A
Hester 38 (2) 389A
Joseph 18 (3) 505B
Mary 7 (3) 488A
Rebecca 5 (3) 505B
Stephen 13 (3) 505B
Susan 18 (1) 18A
Susan 3 (3) 505B
*Welford 46 (3) 505B
DEAL, Catherine 28 (6) 476A
DEANS, Anna 10 (4) 18A
DEAVER, Emily A. 34 (5)
204B
Gertrude 3 (5) 248B
*James C. 35 (5) 204B
Mary 29 (5) 248B
Oliver 12 (5) 204B
Robert 10 (5) 204B
DEAVERS, Caledonia 5 (5)
248B
*Charles 55 (5) 282A
Harriet A. 28 (5) 282A
Maggie E. 18 (5) 282A
Mary A. 52 (5) 282A
*Robert 30 (5) 248B
Sarah E. 20 (5) 282A
DEBOISE, Margaret 21 (3)
569B

DEBOUIS, Josephine 32 (2) 335B
  Josephine P. 5 (2) 335B
  *Larme 45 (2) 335B
DEBOY, Ambrose 18 (1) 133B
  Ambrose 40 (1) 133B
  Anna 7 (1) 133B
  Hannah 12 (1) 133B
  Hannah 36 (1) 133B
  John 16 (1) 133B
  Margaret 4 (1) 133B
  Mary 9 (1) 133B
  Nellie 2 (1) 133B
  Obediah 14 (1) 133B
  William 21 (1) 133B
DEBRITS, *Miles 53 (4) 94B
  Sarah 50 (4) 94B
DeCOMA, Fortunia 92 (5) 157B
DECORSEY, Hariet 18 (4) 117A
  John 46 (5) 209A
  Margaret 33 (5) 209A
DEITS, Jacob 4 (1) 200A
  *John 30 (1) 200A
  Margaret 2 (1) 200A
  Mary 26 (1) 200A
  Mary 9 (1) 200A
DEMBY, Alexander 9/12 (5) 152B
  Varena 25 (5) 152B
DENBY, Ann Eliz 12 (6) 395B
  Anna 43 (6) 395B
  *Austin 54 (6) 395B
  Catharine 30 (3) 467A
  Charles E. 9 (6) 395B
  Dinah 57 (6) 314A
  Elenora 4 (6) 395B
  Henry 19 (6) 395B
  James A. 12 (6) 314A
DENISON, James M. 18 (5) 147A
  Lydia 45 (5) 147A
DENNIN, Lizzie 23 (3) 571A

DENNIS, Bennett 15 (5) 236A
  Charles 38 (2) 384B
  Corra 1 (6) 416A
  George 21 (5) 236A
  Henrietta 26 (3) 564A
  Isaac 7 (3) 564A
  Israel 7 (5) 236A
  Josephine 10 (6) 416A
  *Josiah 42 (6) 416A
  Julia 23 (6) 416A
  Julia 90 (3) 561B
  Margarett J. 2 (6) 416A
  Maria 30 (2) 384B
  Maria 50 (5) 236A
  Mary 32 (3) 560A
  Mary L. 4 (6) 416A
  *Stephen 27 (3) 521A
  Stephen 22 (3) 564A
  Stephen 5 (3) 564A
  Virginia 6 (6) 366A
DENTIST, Hannah 30 (6) 294B
DERVZIE, *Carl 41 (6) 457A
  Caroline 32 (6) 457A
  Lucreatia 14 (6) 457A
DESHIELDS, Charles 7 (3) 540B
  Emma 5 (3) 540B
  George 11 (3) 540A
  Henrietta 38 (3) 540B
  Henry 40 (3) 540A
  *James 40 (3) 540B
  James 9 (3) 540B
  Martha 36 (3) 540A
  Mary 11 (3) 540B
  Mary 9 (3) 540A
  Samuel 15 (3) 540B
  William 16 (3) 540B
DEVERETZ, *Myers 50 (4) 95A
  Sarah 55 (4) 95A
DEXTER, George 22 (5) 157B
DICKERSON, Anna 80 (5) 166B
  *Charles 56 (5) 157A
  Charles 12 (5) 157A

DICKERSON (continued)
David 8 (5) 157A
Eliza 9 (5) 126A
Elizabeth 36 (5) 157A
*James 65 (5) 170A
James 48 (4) 19A
John W. 14 (4) 19A
Josephine 16 (5) 157A
Mary 15 (5) 231A
Mary 24 (4) 31A
Mary 56 (6) 303B
Mary A. 6 (5) 157A
Mary E. 16 (4) 19A
Sophia 65 (5) 170A
DICKINSON, Alick 24 (3)
    485B
Anna 20 (4) 85A
Charles 21 (3) 485B
Emaline 30 (4) 23A
George 8 (4) 6A
Lewis 41 (4) 6A
Lori 28 (3) 485B
Margarett 39 (4) 6A
Victorine F. 23 (4) 6A
DICKSON, Catherine 24 (2)
    379A
James 26 (2) 379A
Joseph 29 (2) 389A
Mary E. 29 (2) 389A
Mathilda 4 (5) 274B
DIGGS, *Benjamin 49 (6)
    412A
Benjamin 14 (6) 412A
Charles H. 10 (6) 412A
George 8 (6) 412A
Harriett 45 (6) 412A
Hezekiah 25 (1) 200A
James A. 19 (6) 412A
Josephine 10 (6) 412A
Josiah 5 (6) 412A
Julia 29 (6) 412A
Martha S. 3 (6) 412A
William 12 (1) 168A
DILLER, Charles W. 11 (5)
    178A
*Eliza 40 (3) 541B

DILLER (continued)
Ida 5 (5) 178A
James H. 8 (5) 178A
John W. 35 (5) 178A
Mary A. 28 (5) 178A
William L. 3 (5) 178A
DILLIN, Frank 23 (3) 567A
DILLION, Ellen 4 (3) 560A
Joseph 7 (3) 560A
Lucy 9 (3) 560A
Maria 58 (3) 560A
William 37 (3) 560A
DISTANT, Joseph 21 (4)
    111B
DIVENS, *Michael 40 (3)
    558B
DIXON, Albert P. 7 (4) 1B
Alexander 2 (4) 1B
Ann 24 (3) 543A
Ann Eliza 11 (4) 1B
Anna 34 (4) 1B
Benjamin 18 (4) 110A
Benjamin 23 (3) 543A
Charles F. 9 (4) 1B
Daniel 33 (6) 325B
Emily 50 (5) 198A
Francis Ann 9 (4) 102A
George W. 24 (4) 1B
Harriet 20 (3) 541B
Hester 34 (3) 541B
Isaiah 26 (5) 198A
James 19 (4) 110A
James H. 13 (4) 1B
Jane 9 (3) 541B
John 26 (3) 560A
Julia 19 (3) 552A
Julia A. 1 (4) 1B
*Levi 46 (4) 1B
Louisa 50 (6) 431B
*Marcella 45 (4) 102A
Maria 10 (3) 541B
Mary Ann 40 (4) 102A
Merrzenia 20 (6) 350B
*Robert 40 (3) 541B
*Sophia 80 (6) 350B
Sophia 65 (4) 111B

DIXON (continued)
Susana 26 (6) 325B
Whitmina 2/12 (3) 543A
Willie 7 (3) 541B
DOBSON, *Perry 65 (4) 94B
Prisella 62 (4) 94B
Sarah J. 23 (5) 236A
William 45 (5) 166A
DOCKINS, Hester 14 (6) 325B
James 25 (6) 308B
James S. 3 (6) 308B
Mary A. 13 (6) 325B
Rhoda A. 21 (6) 308B
Sarah E. 9/12 (6) 308B
DODD, Anna 20 (5) 203A
Harriet 2 (5) 203B
Mary L. 5/12 (5) 203B
Robert 24 (5) 203A
DONE, Emma 3 (3) 567A
John 5 (3) 567A
Lizzie 27 (3) 567A
DOOR, *Henrietta 59 (6) 458A
DORAM, Abey 67 (5) 153A
DORIS, Francis 49 (2) 387B
DORMAN, Harriet 30 (3)
563A
John 14 (3) 563A
DORMON, Mollie 19 (3) 561B
DORRETY, *Samuels 59 (2)
334A
DORRITERY, Ann 59 (2)
340A
DORRITY, Margaret A. 12 (2)
344B
DORSEY, Alice 20 (6) 304B
Amanda 6 (5) 154B
*Amelia 70 (5) 167B
Ann 49 (6) 412A
*Benjamin 35 (6) 412A
Caroline 22 (6) 309B
Caroline 44 (5) 154B
Caroline 50 (3) 558B
Catharine 39 (2) 339A
Catherine 60 (6) 310B
Charles 11 (5) 150B
Charles 12 (5) 204A

DORSEY (continued)
Della 1 (5) 154B
Eli 30 (1) 5A
*Elias 25 (6) 309B
*Eliza 32 (5) 153B
Elizabeth 20 (5) 219B
Ellen 22 (1) 5A
Ellen 40 (5) 171A
Frances 18 (5) 149A
George 6/12 (5) 204A
George 7 (6) 412B
Harriet 68 (5) 223B
Ignatius 16 (2) 339A
Jane 40 (5) 223B
*John 48 (5) 154B
John 9/12 (1) 5A
Joseph 39 (5) 153B
Lizzie 8 (1) 101B
Lydia 25 (6) 412A
M. Ann 1 (6) 412A
Maria 54 (5) 150B
Martha 35 (5) 204A
Martha 9 (5) 153B
*Mary J. 31 (6) 408B
Mary 20 (4) 106B
Mary 25 (4) 18A
Mary C. 13 (5) 126B
Mary E. 6 (6) 412A
Matilda J. 10 (2) 339A
Nora T. 18 (6) 412A
Peter H. 7 (5) 153B
Robert H. 5 (6) 408B
Sallie 17 (3) 561B
Sophia 17 (6) 305A
Susan 20 (3) 567A
William 1 (5) 219B
William 22 (3) 567A
William H. 1 (6) 408B
*Zacharia 40 (2) 339A
DOTTS, *Cassie 36 (3) 559A
Frank 11 (3) 559A
George 9 (3) 559A
Margaret 14 (3) 559A
Mary 5 (3) 559A
William 7 (3) 559A
DOUDVILLE, Caroline 68 (2)

DOUDVILLE (continued)
219A
DOUGLAS, William 40 (5)
172B
DOWDEN, Caroline 56 (6)
470A
Charity 58 (5) 156B
DOWELL, Anna 34 (6) 433A
Hopper 8 (6) 433A
DOWLING, Caroline 50 (5)
217B
DOWNING, Daniel 27 (5)
169B
James 1 (3) 522A
*Jerry 25 (3) 522A
Joseph 35 (6) 348B
Lizzie 19 (3) 522A
Mary 21 (3) 551B
DOWNS, Alice C 12 (3) 483B
Allen 43 (3) 483B
Andrew 23 (3) 483B
Charlott 19 (6) 312A
*Ewing 28 (5) 160B
*Harrison 49 (6) 415B
Hester 43 (5) 147B
Isaac 2 (5) 147B
Isaiah 49 (5) 147B
John C. 5 (5) 147B
John W. 3 (3) 483B
Louiza 26 (5) 160B
Margaret 45 (2) 305B
Maria 24 (3) 483B
Mary 40 (3) 483B
Mary A. 37 (2) 306B
Paris 8 (5) 160B
Richard 6 (5) 160B
*Sarah 30 (5) 147A
Sarah E. 10 (5) 160B
Sarah J. 40 (6) 415B
*Thomas 38 (2) 306B
William 12 (5) 147A
William H. 8 (5) 147B
DOWRY, Louisa 8 (5) 170A
Margaret 31 (5) 170A
Mary 12 (5) 170A
*Robert 46 (5) 170A

DOZIER, Charles 35 (3) 518B
Edward 11 (3) 518B
John 2 (3) 518B
Martha 30 (3) 518B
Mary P. 1/12 (3) 518B
William 12 (3) 518B
DREWSBURY, Eliza 50 (5)
153B
John 30 (5) 153B
DRITY, Mary 28 92) 339A
DRUMMER, Francis 18 (4)
27A
DUCKEY, James M. 22 (5)
275B
Mary F. 19 (5) 275B
DUDLEY, Eliza Jane 5 (4)
5B
John 45 (6) 306A
Phillip 8 (4) 5B
Rachall 46 (4) 5B
*Samuel 56 (4) 5B
Samuel 12 (4) 5B
Sarah 45 (6) 306A
Sarah Rebecca 12 (6) 306A
DUDLY, Mary 19 (4) 69B
DUFF, Eliza J 4 (5) 234A
Gertrude 1 (5) 234A
*Josephine 29 (5) 234A
Josephine 3 (5) 234A
Mary A. 10 (5) 234A
Rachall 60 (2) 383A
Thomas 32 (5) 234A
Thomas A. 8 (5) 234A
DUFFIN, *John T. 34 (5)
168B
John T. 9 (5) 168B
Mary E. 2 (5) 168B
Mary E. 23 (5) 168B
William F. 8/12 (5) 168B
DUFFY, Daniel 1 (6) 347B
*Edward 28 (6) 347B
Elizebeth 25 (6) 347B
Emma 4 (6) 347B
Mary 19 (4) 19B
DUMPSON, Jane 19 (5) 253A
DUNCAN, Richard 31 (3)

113

DUNCAN (continued)
426B
DUNGAN, Hester 16 (4) 101B
DUNGER, Cecelia 31 (5)
171A
 Daniel 18 (5) 156B
 *Edward 36 (5) 171A
 Martha A. 36(5) 156B
 William 8 (5) 171A
 *William M. 50 (5) 156B
DUNGY, Charles E. 8 (5)
158B
 *John 41 (5) 158B
 John H. 14 (5) 158B
 Joseph C. 6 (5) 158B
 Mary 1 (5) 158B
 Sophia 35 (5) 158B
 William D. 11 (5) 158B
DUNLAP, Eliza 18 (5) 221A
DUNN, *Amelia F. 25 (5)
265A
DUNNING, Martha 18 (6)
437B
DURHAM, *Mathilda 40 (5)
283B
DUTTON, *Charles 44 (3)
543B
 Charles 14 (3) 543B
 Elenora 3 (5) 248B
 Emily 17 (4) 6A
 Emily J. 5 (5) 248B
 Hester 46 (4) 110A
 John F. 8/12 (5) 248B
 Julia 11 (3) 543B
 Julian 42 (4) 6A
 *Levi 37 (5) 248B
 Lewis E. 8 (5) 248B
 Louisa 33 (5) 248B
 Mary 15 (3) 543B
 Mary E. 12 (5) 248B
 Rachael 4 (4) 6A
 Sarah 40 (3) 543B
 Sarah E. 19 (4) 6A
 William H. 10 (5) 248B
 William H. 20 (4) 19A

DYSON, *Amanda 23 (3) 561A
 Benard 17 (5) 148A
 John 30 (3) 561A
 Lucinda 24 (5) 148A
 Nathaniel 22 (5) 148A
 Rose 2 (5) 148A
EARLE, Georgeanna 1 (5)
139A
 James 10 (5) 139A
 *Jane 30 (5) 138B
 *John 30 (5) 138B
 Sarah E. 15 (5) 138B
 William H. 14 (5) 138B
EASTEP, Lama 10 (1) 21B
EBBS, Selia 8 (5) 126B
EDLER, Amelia 2 (3) 521A
 Margaret 4 (3) 521A
 Mary 5 (3) 521A
 Peter 29 (3) 521A
 Rachel 24 (3) 521A
EDWARD, Augusta 22 (3)
521A
 Emily Jane 30 (4) 1B
 Jacob 36 (4) 1B
 James 20 (3) 521A
 John 1 (3) 562A
 Mary 23 (3) 562A
 *Walter 25 (3) 562A
EDWARDS, Amelia 14 (3)
591A
 David 14 (5) 143B
 Edward 20 (5) 172B
 Elizebeth C. 28 (6) 452A
 Emily 41 (3) 591A
 Emma 6 (3) 591A
 George W. 3 (6) 452A
 Harriet 24 (3) 462A
 Harriett 26 (1) 28A
 *Hezekiah 36 (5) 162A
 Ida Estell 10 96) 452A
 *Isaac 32 (5) 151B
 John 4 (3) 462A
 John 9 (3) 591A
 John E. 214 (5) 219A
 Lewis 26 (5) 144A

EDWARDS (continued)
Lucy 26 (5) 162A
Lydia 24 (3) 525B
Martha 30 (5) 144A
*Mary 50 (5) 172B
Mary 60 (3) 413B
Mary E. 1 (5) 219A
Mary J. 34 (5) 152A
Rebecca 19 (3) 591A
Robert 11 (3) 591A
Samuel 60 (3) 545A
*Samuel A. 30 (6) 452A
*Sarah 22 (5) 219A
Sarah T. 2/12 (6) 452A
*Thomas 45 (3) 591A
Thomas 16 (3) 591A
William 11 (2) 335B
William 38 (6) 297A
EDY, Joseph 50 (3) 544B
Mary 56 (3) 544B
ELESIA, Amelia 70 (5) 146B
ELGERT, John 2 (3) 521A
Lizzie 25 (3) 521A
William 29 (3) 521A
ELLIOT, Anthony 40 (4) 19B
Harriett 31 (4) 19B
ELLIOTT, Emma 2 (3) 559A
*John 30 (3) 559A
John 6 (3) 559A
Lucinda 26 (3) 559A
Mary 4 (3) 559A
Washington 30 (3) 559A
William 1/12 (3) 559A
ELLIS, George 23 (5) 204A
Harriet C. 24 (5) 212A
Harrison 30 (2) 339B
Jane 40 (3) 474B
John T. 4 (5) 212A
Mary 14 (5) 126A
Mary C. 3/12 (5) 212A
Milly A. 5 (4) 95A
Robert 9 (4) 18B
William H. 6 (5) 212A
ELLISON, Maria 55 (5) 158A
ELSEY, Amalia 18 (1) 50A

EMERSON, Cordelia 50 (2)
379A
James 6/12 (1) 59B
Owen M 13 (2) 379A
Sophia 22 (1) 59B
*William 28 (1) 59B
EMILS, Augusta 3 (3) 563A
Catharine 24 (3) 541A
Francis 25 (3) 541A
Patience 27 (3) 563A
Robert 1 (3) 563A
Sarah 5 (3) 563A
EMORY, James 27 (5) 160A
Mary 13 (5) 160A
Matilda 26 (5) 160A
ENNALS, Murry 20 (4) 20A
ENNELLS, Mary E 30 (6)
309A
ENNELS, John 22 (3) 496B
ENNIS, *Anna 20 (5) 147A
Ephriam 24 (5) 147A
ENNOLDS, Amanda 13 (2)
344B
Charles 40 (1) 3A
*Eliza 63 (1) 46A
*Emilie 24 (1) 46A
Maria 32 (2) 344B
*Mary 30 (1) 46A
Mary A. 3 (2) 344B
*Sarah 27 (1) 46A
*Stephen 49 (2) 344B
William H. 3/365 (2) 344B
ENOS, Cary Sophia 25 (2)
248A
Charles 30 (2) 248A
ERME, *Alonzo 29 (5) 285A
Celestina 5 (5) 285A
Eugenia 7 (5) 285A
Mary A. 28 (5) 285A
Mary V. 3 (5) 285A
Virginia 2/12 (5) 285A
ERRING, John 40 (3) 560A
EUSTON, *Amanda 22 (1)
46B
Edward 35 (1) 46B

EUSTON (continued)
John 5 (1) 46B
EVANS, Amanda 35 (2) 384B
*Ann E. 32 (5) 210A
Augusta 20 (3) 545A
*Charles 36 (3) 472B
Emily 11 (3) 549B
Isaac 24 (3) 545A
Jenny 3 (3) 545A
John 10 (3) 472B
*Joseph 26 (2) 384B
*Martha 40 (5) 283A
Martha 11 (3) 545A
Martha 2 (6) 409B
Mary 21 (6) 409B
Mary F. 1 (5) 210A
Mathew N. 33 (5) 210A
Sarah 26 (3) 472B
Sarah 30 (6) 303B
*Thomas 24 (2) 385A
Thomas 30 (6) 303B
Washington 25 (6) 409B
EVES, Rebecca 12 (2) 252A
FALLS, Alice H. 6 (6) 331A
Charles H. 11 (6) 331A
*Edward 30 (6) 331A
Mary V. 25 (6) 331A
FAUKLIN, Rachael 36 (2) 377B
FAUSTER, Rebecca 12 (2) 328A
Sarah 40 (2) 328A
William 38 (2) 328A
FERGUSON, Anna 17 (6) 325A
David 23 (6) 325A
Mary E. 1/12 (6) 325A
FERNANDIS, Catharine 2 (2) 298A
*John A. 42 (2) 298A
John A. 5 (2) 298A
Maria 16 (2) 298A
Moore 12 (2) 298A
Rebecca 35 (2) 298A
Walter 18 (2) 298A
Wells 14 (2) 298A

FERNANDIZ, Alonzi 10 (2) 247B
Caroline 26 (2) 247B
FEROON, Eliza 50 (3) 458A
FERRY, John 10 (4) 87A
FICKEL, *Eli 50 (5) 158B
FIELD, Matilda 14 (4) 10B
FIELDS, Albert 3 (3) 544B
Allen 21 (4) 110A
Angeline 45 (4) 19B
Ann 5 (3) 544B
Ellenora 21 (4) 18B
Frederick 9 (3) 544B
Isaac 30 (4) 18B
James 24 (4) 110A
James 58 (4) 109B
Jesse 17 (4) 19B
John 15 (4) 110A
John 4 (3) 496B
John 40 (2) 391B
Lucy 26 (1) 56A
Maria 38 (3) 544B
Mary 32 (4) 6A
Matilda 15 (4) 19B
Richard 50 (4) 19B
Rose 19 (4) 110A
Solomon 7 (3) 544B
Thomas 28 (4) 109B
FINLEY, Caroline 35 (5) 212A
Marion 20 (5) 212A
FINNICK, Anna 15 (4) 118B
FISHER, Adelade 4 (5) 149A
Benjamin 12 (3) 576B
Bertha 7 (5) 149A
Cary 30 (5) 156B
*Charles 40 (3) 576B
Charles 25 (2) 303A
Charlott 30 (6) 303B
Charlotta 19 (5) 158B
Daniel 16 (3) 576B
Gaddie 42 (3) 576B
*George 51 (6) 303B
George 19 (5) 158B
Georgiana 3 (6) 346B
Isabella 7 (6) 306B

FISHER (continued)
*Jacob 50 (6) 346B
Jacob 1/2 (6) 346B
Jane 79 (6) 457A
John H. 3 (6) 306B
*Joseph 40 (2) 344B
Joseph 1/12 (6) 303B
Joseph 22 (2) 339B
Louisa 18 (3) 576B
Lucy 31 (2) 344B
Margaret 53 (6) 395B
Mary 35 (6) 346B
Mary E. 8 (5) 149A
Percilla 29 (6) 306B
Philip 2 (5) 149A
*Richard 61 (6) 306B
Richard 6 (6) 306B
Sarah A. 5 (6) 346B
William 60 (5) 169A
FLEMMING, Eliza 26 (5)
   286B
Elizabeth 25 (1) 47A
George 7 (5) 286B
*John 25 (1) 47A
Josiah 6/12 (1) 47A
*William 23 (5) 286B
William 8 (5) 286B
FLOOD, Cornelius 24 (2)
   387A
Emma 1 (2) 387A
Mary J. 27 (2) 387A
FOLKS, Thomas 17 (3) 507A
FOOLER, Thomas 21 (3)
   504B
FOOT, Laura D 16 (6) 413B
FOOTS, James 21 (4) 110A
FORD, Anna 20 (4) 80B
Georgeanna 18 (3) 574A
Lewis 70 (5) 146B
Mary A. 35 (5) 146B
Richard 30 (5) 179A
Sarah 15 (3) 412A
Susan 23 (5) 179A
FOREMAN, *Charles 32 (4)
   89A
*George H. 50 (6) 469B

FOREMAN (continued)
George H. 20 (6) 469B
Hannah 17 (6) 469B
Hannah 48 96) 469B
Harriett 28 (6) 469B
Lucinda 10 (6) 469B
Martha 30 (4) 89A
Virginia 1 (4) 89A
William 12 (6) 469B
FORSTER, Ellen 35 (5) 237A
FORTIE, Ellen 47 (5) 158A
Ellen 9 (5) 158A
Harriet 11 (5) 158A
Henry 60 (5) 158A
John 5 (5) 158A
*Lewis 52 (5) 158A
Lewis 8 (5) 158A
FORTUNE, Joseph 14 (5)
   187A
FOSTER, Ann 15 (6) 455B
Ann 40 (5) 156A
George W. 6 (6) 455B
Hester 17 (6) 455B
Hester 41 (6) 455B
Jennie 18 (4) 24B
*Lewis 38 (5) 156A
Robert 12 (6) 455B
Robert 26 (5) 155A
Susan 7 (5) 160A
Tommy 10 (6) 455B
William 5 10 (5) 156A
FOWLER, Emma 3 (3) 540A
George 1 (3) 540A
*Izaih 35 (3) 539B
James H. 50 (6) 417A
John 12 (3) 539B
Joseph 10 (3) 540A
Julia 6 (3) 540A
Mary 33 (3) 539B
Mary 8 (3) 540A
Sarah 14 (3) 539B
FRAINE, John 20 (3) 525A
Julia 40 (3) 525A
Lizzie 16 (3) 525A
William 45 (3) 525A

FRANCIS, Elizabeth 40 (5) 144A
*John 72 (2) 340B
John 27 (2) 340B
John J. 35 (5) 144A
Julia A. 60 (2) 340B
Lewis 29 (2) 340B
Mary 13 (1) 36A
Nicholas 26 (2) 340B
William 8 (5) 144A
FRANK, Anthony 21 (3) 567A
Anthony 24 (3) 567A
FRANKLIN, Abraham 32 (5) 160A
Alexander 25 (6) 469B
Fannie 14 (3) 564A
George 35 (5) 144A
*Hannah 29 (5) 159B
Henrietta 2 (5) 160A
Henrietta 30 (6) 325B
John W. 6 (5) 160A
Julia 17 (3) 564A
Julia 39 (3) 564A
Maria 10 (3) 564A
Mary 24 (6) 469B
Mary F. 3 (5) 160A
Rebecca 2/12 (5) 160A
Sarah 4 (5) 160A
Thomas 12 (3) 564A
FRASIER, Mary 22 (5) 147B
FRAZIER, Agness 45 (6) 305B
*Ann 26 (5) 154B
*Benj 32 (6) 305B
Benjamin F 8 (6) 305B
Caroline 22 (6) 305B
Chas. W. 23 (2) 221B
*Eliza J. 47 (2) 221B
Elizer A. 10 (6) 305B
Ellen J. 3 (2) 221B
Frances 35 (2) 221B
Georgianna 25 (2) 221B
John W. 8 (5) 154B
Louisa 1 (6) 305B
Margaret 10/12 (2) 221B
Mary T. 4 (6) 305B

FRAZIER (continued)
Nelson 22 (4) 85A
Virginia 12 (6) 305B
FREELAND, Fanny 24 (4) 51B
FREEMAN, Benjamin 35 (5) 264B
Catharine 35 (5) 264B
Charles E. 4 (5) 274B
Clara 10/12 (5) 268A
David 8 (5) 264B
Deborah 55 (5) 264B
Elizabeth 30 (5) 252B
Eveline 30 (5) 268A
Harry A. 8 (5) 274B
James 14 (5) 253A
James H. 36 (5) 274B
Mary A. 31 (5) 274B
Mary E. 10 (5) 274B
*Solomon 23 (5) 252B
William 25 (5) 268A
William 71 (5) 264A
FREMAN, John 21 (3) 422A
Rebecca 41 (4) 109A
FRENCH, Ann 40 (3) 496A
Ann 9 (3) 496A
Anna 55 (4) 81B
Charles 7 (3) 496A
James 25 (6) 434B
Jerry 21 (3) 496A
William 11 (3) 496A
FREY, Mary 23 (5) 194B
FRISBY, Anna 50 (5) 131A
Charity 59 (5) 166B
Frances 40 (5) 274B
*Richara 50 (5) 274B
FRISBY, Richard 21 (5) 274B
FULLER, Caroline 50 (5) 166B
FURGESON, Charlotte 84 (5) 285A
FURGUSON , Eliza 28 (5) 286B
GAIL, Caroline 40 (6) 309A
*George H. 40 (6) 309A
GAILOR, Caroline 70 (1) 44B

GAINES, Causman 30 (3) 484B
Edward 30 (3) 541B
Elizabeth 11 (5) 237A
Ella 4 (3) 484B
Emily 23 (5) 146B
George 22 (2) 339B
Hester 60 (1) 23B
John 25 (5) 146B
John 37 (3) 543A
Joseph 2 (3) 485A
Levin W. 32 (3) 485A
Lucy 13 (3) 543A
Lydia 28 (5) 237A
Margaret 15 (3) 543A
Maria 59 (3) 485A
Mary 11 (3) 543A
Moses 16 (5) 237A
Olevia 2 (5) 146B
Rebecca 28 (3) 484B
Sophia 11 (5) 133A
Susan 60 (5) 236B
Thomas K. 21 (5) 236B
William 16 (3) 485A
*William R. 72 (5) 236B
Henry 27 (2) 379A
GALAGHER, *Sarah 60 (5) 197B
GALAMISON, Charlotte 50 (2) 379A
GALE, Alice 2 (5) 154B
Anna M. 22 (5) 154B
Charles 24 (5) 154B
Charles 6/12 (5) 150B
David 3 (5) 154B
Elizabeth 45 (5) 150B
Jane 20 (3) 572A
*John 56 (5) 150B
John 5 (5) 150B
Martha 33 (5) 150B
Robert 3/12 (5) 154B
GALES, *Annie 26 (3) 542B
Betzy 50 (4) 6B
Harrison 45 (4) 6B
GALLOWAY, Ellen 12 (5) 236A

GALLOWAY (continued)
Harriet 30 (5) 236A
James 25 (5) 236A
William 4 (5) 236A
GAMSEY, Hester 40 (5) 160B
GANSEY, Agness 7 (5) 160B
Anna 9 (5) 160B
Arabella 8/12 (5) 160B
Henrietta 21 (5) 160B
*Joseph 52 (5) 160B
Joseph A. 4 (5) 160B
GANT, Jane 20 (3) 509A
GARDINER, Elizabeth 66 (5) 139A
Jerry 30 (5) 162A
GARDNER, Alexina 35 (6) 413B
Charles 35 (6) 413B
George W. 10 96) 414A
Solomon 33 (6) 413B
GARMAN, *Charles 37 (3) 560A
John 7 (3) 560B
Julia 9 (3) 560B
Maria 36 (3) 560B
Mary 5 (3) 560B
Sallie 3 (3) 560B
GARNER, Ann 29 (5) 274A
John 30 (3) 505A
Thomas 23 (3) 475A
GARNES, Ann 29 (5) 274A
GARRETT, Mary 23 (5) 284B
GARRISON, Annie 40 (3) 446B
Emily 19 (3) 446B
Laura 6/12 (3) 446B
Mary 3 (3) 446B
*Sarah 58 (5) 150B
GARRITT, *Hesikiah 40 (3) 544B
John 21 (3) 544B
Lydia 19 (3) 544B
Sarah 38 (3) 544B
GASCON, Eliza 35 (6) 342A
Fredrick 31 (6) 342A
Lamden 14 (6) 342A

GASCON (continued)
Nancy 11 (6) 342A
GASH, Elijah 56 (3) 543A
Eliza 10 (3) 543A
George 17 (3) 543A
Henrietta 15 (3) 543A
John 21 (3) 543A
Maggie 13 (3) 543A
William 19 (3) 543A
GASKINS, Hannah 25 (4) 18B
Lavenia 9 (4) 18B
*Solomon 35 (4) 18B
Walter 1 (4) 18B
GASSOWAY, Andrew 7 (5) 236B
John T. 13 (5) 236B
*Maria 44 (5) 236B
Sarah 15 (5) 236B
GATCH, *Edward 49 (6) 334A
Edward 1 (6) 334A
Maranda 36 (6) 334A
Martin J. 16 (6) 334A
Thomas H. 19 (6) 334A
William T. 21 (6) 334A
GATES, Eliza 18 (4) 106B
GAULT, Fannie 59 (2) 393B
GAUNT, Joseph 2 (6) 347A
Mary 28 (6) 347A
Mary P. 12 (6) 347A
Rose 6 (6) 347A
*William 33 (6) 347A
William V. 10 (6) 347A
GAY, Henrietta 19 (6) 297B
GAYLOR, *James 35 (5) 207A
James 2 (5) 207A
Joseph 6/12 (5) 207A
Martha 28 (5) 207A
Samuel A. 12 (5) 207A
Thomas 14 (5) 207A
GAYNES, Adeline 38 (5) 274B
*Orlando 55 (5) 274B
GEORGE, Caroline 25 (3) 467B
Maria 47 (3) 504B

GEORGE (continued)
Priscilla 25 (3) 510A
*Samuel 60 (3) 504B
Samuel 20 (3) 504B
William 17 (3) 504B
GIBBS, Alexandria 22 (3) 576B
Anna S. 4 (5) 134B
Caroline 23 (4) 18A
Charles H. 1 (5) 134B
Ebenezer 45 (5) 144A
Emma 10 (3) 576B
Frances 8 (3) 576B
Henry 14 (5) 205B
Henry 36 (5) 160B
James 23 (3) 576B
Jane 20 (3) 576B
*John L. 57 (5) 155B
Julia 25 (5) 160B
Louiza 38 (5) 155B
Maray 28 (3) 576B
Maria 44 (3) 476A
*Mary 54 (3) 576B
Mary E. 8 (5) 134B
Melvina 24 (3) 576B
Rachel 39 (5) 144A
Rebecca 12 (3) 576B
Robert H. 41 (5) 134B
Robert R. 6 (5) 134B
Susan 55 (4) 85B
William 14 (3) 576B
GIBSON, Alfred 16 (3) 542B
Benjamin 12 (6) 410B
Criscinda 2 (2) 393B
Ellen 23 (2) 335A
Emily 33 (6) 308B
Frances 26 (2) 393B
Ida 5 (3) 542B
*Jacob 25 (5) 253A
James 20 (6) 412A
Louisa 56 (5) 136B
Mary C. 19 (5) 253A
Mary E. 11 (5) 154A
Sarah 55 (3) 542B
Susan 46 (6) 410B
*William 44 (3) 542B

GIBSON (continued)
 *William 50 (6) 410B
GIDDINGS, Kitty 15 (3) 508A
GIDDINS, James 40 (5) 235A
 Kitty 50 (3) 508A
GILBERT, Mary J 7 (6) 306A
 Millinda 35 (4) 106A
 Sarah 13 (4) 94B
 Sarah J. 30 (6) 306A
 Valinda 26 (5) 144A
GILES, Alice 7 (6) 311A
 Barbara 36 (6) 311A
 Debey 45 (5) 212B
 Harriette 14 (6) 309B
 *Henry S. 57 (6) 309B
 Jeffunice 13 (6) 311A
 Joseph 5 (6) 311A
 Julia 10 (6) 309B
 Rachel 45 96) 309B
 Samuel 13 (6) 309B
 Stephens 10 (6) 311A
 *Uriah 51 (6) 311A
 Uriah 6 (6) 311A
 William 6 (6) 309B
GILLEN, Isabella 24 (4) 19B
GILLEY, William 29 (5)
  155A
GILLIARD, Charles 13 (3)
  487B
 Emma 5 (3) 487B
 Fannie 40 (3) 487B
 Fannie 7 (3) 487B
 *George 55 (3) 487B
 George 17 (3) 487B
 James 16 (3) 487B
 Jesse 2 (3) 487B
 Julia A. 1 (6) 347B
 Lydia 9 (3) 487B
 Mary L. 28 (6) 347B
 *Nicholas 24 (6) 347B
GILLIS, Christiana 7 (1)
  217A
GILLMORE, Caroline 61 (3)
  542B
 Isaiah 12 (3) 542B
 *Isaih 60 (3) 542B

GILLMORE (continued)
 John 15 (3) 542B
 Mary 20 (3) 542B
GITTINGS, Caroline 35 (5)
  137A
 Charles E. 1/12 (5) 166B
 Edward 33 (5) 166B
 Francis 16 (2) 222A
GLAMISON, Alden 7/12 (2)
  340B
 Charles 7 (2) 340B
 *Charles O. 33 (2) 340B
 Ella 3 (2) 340B
 Joseph 8 (2) 340B
 Mary F. 30 (2) 340B
GLASCOE, Henrietta 54 (1)
  47A
 John 21 (1) 47A
 *Stephan 55 (1) 47A
GLASGOW, Emeline 38 (5)
  146A
 Howard 2 (5) 146A
 *John S. 35 (5) 146A
GLASSGOW, Catherine * 65
  (5) 168A
GLEASON, Bell 12 (3) 461B
GLEAVES, Ann M. 11 (5)
  161B
GLEAVES, John A. 6 (5)
  161B
 Margaret 25 (5) 161B
 Margaret 26 (5) 124A
GLOVE, Ruth 19 (3) 540A
GLOVER, *John 26 (3) 542B
 Mary 27 (3) 542B
 Sarah 2 (3) 542B
GODFREY, *Ann 25 (5) 209A
 Mary E. 3/12 (5) 209A
 William 25 (5) 209A
 William L. 10 (5) 209A
GOLDEN, Elizabeth 35 (5)
  169A
 Hannah 49 (2) 338A
 John R. 17 (2) 340A
 *William 33 (5) 169A
GOLDMAN, Jane 102 (6)

GOLDMAN (continued)
303B
GOLDSBOROUGH, Alexander
30 (5) 150A
Henrietta 30 (5) 150A
Laura 1 (5) 150A
William 11 (5) 150A
William 13 (6) 478A
GOLDSBURRY, Eliza 50 (3)
545A
Lizzie 8 (3) 545A
Maggie 6 (3) 545A
Sophia 4 (3) 545A
GOOD, Amelia 2 (3) 524B
*Charles 35 (3) 524B
Lavinia 22 (3) 524B
*Lena 59 (3) 522B
Mary 18 (3) 524B
Sarah 30 (3) 522B
Susan 1/12 (3) 524B
GOODMAN, *Henry 30 (5)
264B
Isaiah 6/12 (5) 264B
Mary 25 (5) 264B
GOOSBERG, Annette 42 (2)
379A
Thomas 45 (2) 379A
GORDMAN, John 14 (5) 212A
GORDON, Ellen 15 (6) 326B
George 22 (3) 446B
George 29 (2) 306A
Henrietta 33 (2) 306A
Marcia 47 (5) 153A
GORE, William 12 (6) 306A
William 14 (6) 410A
GORKMAN, Harriet 28 (3)
525A
Isaac 23 (3) 525A
Samuel 12 (3) 525A
William 19 (3) 525A
GORSUCH, *Aquilla 45 (5)
203B
Eliza 21 (6) 345B
Mary 16 (6) 341A
GOUGH, Henrietta 60 (3)
462A

GOUGH (continued)
Henry 17 (3) 462A
Mary 65 (1) 35B
Sarah 20 (5) 272B
GOULD, Harriet A. 14 (5)
145A
Jane 38 (5) 145A
*Joseph 40 (5) 145A
Mary E. 16 (5) 145A
Rachel 36 (5) 154A
Samuel J. 23 (5) 154A
GOVA, David 7/12 (4) 19A
Eliza 22 (4) 19A
Joshua 39 (4) 19A
GOVAN, George 45 (4) 18A
GOVENS, Charity 50 (5) 276B
GOWN, Mary 15 (6) 289A
GRACE, Adam 33 (2) 345A
Caroline 10 (5) 156A
George 9 (5) 126A
Harriet 35 (5) 156A
James 35 (5) 156A
James 4 (5) 156A
John E. 31 (3) 517A
Josephine 2 (2) 345A
Sarah J. 23 (2) 345A
Thomas 6 (5) 156A
GRAFF, Ophelia 28 (5) 166A
GRAHAM, Anna 17 (6) 346B
Hester 25 (5) 282B
*Percella 46 (6) 346B
GRAINS, John 1 (3) 496B
John P. 48 (3) 496B
Lewis 8 (3) 496B
Mary M. 15 (3) 496B
Robert D. 3 (3) 496B
Sevy Ann 38 (3) 496B
William H. 5 (3) 496B
GRANDERSON, Charles 70
(5) 168A
GRANGER, Georgeanna 45
(3) 506B
Georgeanna 9 (3) 506B
*Phillip 40 (3) 506B
GRANT, Ambrosia 24 (5)
148B

GRANT (continued)
Charles H. 21 (6) 410A
Frances 9 (6) 410A
George H. 23 (5) 148B
Josephine 7 (6) 410A
Josephus 8 (5) 126B
Laura V. 17 (6) 410A
Louis R. 16 (6) 410A
Margaret 14 (4) 24A
Margarett 13 (6) 410A
Sandra 25 (1) 216A
GRASSON, *Eliza 35 (6) 437B
John R. 14 (6) 437B
Pilot A. 17 (6) 437B
GRAY, Alice 23 (5) 199A
Amanda 32 (5) 147A
Charlotte E. 13 (3) 410B
Chester 100 (5) 147A
Eliza 80 (3) 506B
Eliza R. 2/12 (5) 169A
Elizabeth 35 (1) 51B
Elizabeth 35 (5) 210A
Emeline 48 (5) 199A
Emily 27 (5) 275B
Emily E. 7 (5) 275B
Emma 9 (5) 199B
Henrietta 22 (5) 169A
Isabella 20 (3) 476A
*James 74 (4) 88B
James 33 (5) 210A
Joseph 7 (5) 199B
Joshua N. 8 (5) 275B
Lucy 27 (3) 501A
Marcilene 1 (5) 156A
Martha H. 8 (5) 180A
Mary A. 25 (5) 199A
Mary E. 14 (5) 180A
Nathan 2 (5) 156A
Nathan 30 (5) 156A
*Nelson 35 (5) 275B
Precilla 28 (4) 88B
Rachel 12 (5) 199B
Richard 19 (5) 199B
Sarah 30 (5) 156A
Shadrack 21 (5) 169A
Shedrick 27 (2) 395B

GRAY (continued)
Susanah 55 (5) 147A
*Thomas 52 (5) 199A
Thomas 17 (5) 199B
GRAYSON, Amelia 3 (5) 170B
Cecelia 30 (5) 170B
GREEN, Albert 19 (5) 206B
Alice V. 11 (2) 383A
Ann 41 (1) 59B
Ann 50 (4) 71A
Ann A. 35 (4) 19B
Ann M. 49 (5) 166B
Annie 50 (3) 520B
Cassey 40 (5) 206B
*Charles 37 (3) 426B
Charles 11 (3) 426B
Charles 9 (1) 131B
Clarissa 44 (4) 19A
Elizabeth 76 (4) 19B
Elizebeth 32 (6) 412B
Ella F. 8/12 (2) 383A
Ellen 22 (5) 153A
Emily 13 (1) 131B
Emily 49 (2) 248A
*George 45 (1) 131B
*George 78 (2) 248A
George 16 (1) 131B
George W. 9 (2) 383A
Georgeanna 19 (1) 59B
Hannah 80 (5) 234A
Harriett Ann 7/12 (4) 19A
Henrietta 31 (3) 426B
*Henry 38 (2) 383A
Henry 3 (3) 520A
*Hooper 50 (3) 520B
*James 40 (3) 484A
*James 50 (5) 206B
James 47 (4) 19A
James 49 (1) 59B
James H. 8 (2) 345B
Janet 39 (3) 484A
Jerome 3 (1) 131B
*John 33 (5) 264A
John 10 (4) 102A
John 9 (3) 484A

GREEN (continued)
John W. 4 (2) 383A
*Joseph 49 (5) 166B
Joseph 33 (2) 345B
Joseph 35 (5) 178A
Julia 35 (2) 383A
Lucy 36 (3) 520A
Marcella 6 (2) 383A
Margaret 13 (3) 426B
Martha 23 (6) 294B
Martha 29 (3) 577B
Martha 3 (3) 484A
Martha 6/12 (5) 167A
Mary 18 (5) 206B
Mary 25 (5) 167A
Mary 38 (1) 131B
Mary 5 (1) 131B
Mary 5/12 (3) 484A
Mary 9 (3) 520A
Philip 1 (1) 131B
*Richard 50 (4) 19A
Samuel 3 (3) 426B
Samuel 48 (5) 167A
Sarah 32 (5) 178A
Sherman 3 (4) 19A
Sophia 55 (3) 520A
Sophia 7 (3) 520A
Susan 18 (4) 108A
Susan 6 (3) 484A
Thomas 12 (2) 383A
Walter 19 (1) 131B
Westley 35 (3) 520B
Wilhemina 27 (2) 345B
*William 39 (3) 520A
William 10 (5) 206B
William 12 (3) 520A
William 50 (4) 112B
William N. 28 (2) 345A
GREENWOOD, Ann 12 (6)
  415A
Charlott 10 (6) 367B
*Henry 40 (6) 367B
James 12 (6) 367B
Mary 18 (6) 367B
Susan 42 (6) 367B
William 15 (6) 367B

GREENWOOD (continued)
William 18 (4) 97A
GREY, Ann 50 (6) 325B
Anna 36 (6) 347A
Anna M. 26 (2) 228A
Elijah 29 (2) 228A
*George 35 (6) 347A
George 2 (6) 347A
George E. 9 (2) 228A
Henrietta 12 (6) 347A
Mary V. 16 (6) 347A
*Steven 44 (6) 325B
GRIESS, Lucy 4 (4) 18A
GRIFFEN, Ann M. 16 (2)
  303A
Henrietta 60 (2) 377B
GRIFFIN, Alexander 20 (5)
  274B
Amelia 35 (5) 134B
Catherine 22 (3) 487A
Charles 23 (3) 496A
Charles W. 2 (6) 350B
Francis A. 4 (6) 350B
Frank 10 (4) 112B
*George 30 (3) 487A
George Ann 35 (6) 350B
Harriet 34 (5) 274B
Hester A. 14 (2) 378B
Isiah 5 (6) 350B
James 19 (5) 274B
James 27 (5) 160B
*James E. 45 (2) 378B
James H. 16 (6) 350B
Jane 30 (6) 431B
John 28 (5) 156A
*John H. 46 (6) 431B
Josephine 20 (5) 160B
Mary A. 36 (2) 378B
Mary E. 10 (2) 378B
*Mathilda 47 (5) 274B
Robert 38 (6) 350B
Robert 8 (6) 350B
Rosanna 16 (5) 274B
Sarah E. 6 (6) 431B
Susan 65 (4) 112B
Susan A. 18 (2) 378B

GRIFFIN (continued)
William E. 11 (6) 350B
GRIFFITH, *Harriett 30 (4)
  19B
GRIMES, Harry 1 (6) 303A
Ida 3 (6) 303A
Ida F. 12 (5) 162B
John 13 (6) 303A
Lizzie 22 (6) 303A
*Louisa 25 (4) 48A
McDonald 40 (4) 48A
Sarah O. 10 (5) 162B
*Thomas 32 (6) 303A
GRIRRICH, Charity 26 (6)
  438A
Elijah 39 (6) 438A
Frank 9 (6) 438A
Jesse 5 (6) 438A
Nathaniel 3 (6) 438A
GRONAU, Willie 4 (3) 480A
GROOMS, Eliza 65 (5) 219A
Frank 45 (5) 219A
George W. 19 (4) 106A
Jane L. 45 (5) 220A
John E. 53 (5) 220A
Nancy B. 12 (5) 220A
GROOVES, Jinnie 23 (5)
  232B
McTerrice 20 (5) 232B
GROSS, *Adelaide 42 (5)
  169A
Alice 18 (6) 408A
Barbara 13 (5) 169A
Benjamin 39 (5) 159A
Caroline 12 (1) 49B
Carrol 21 (5) 147B
Charity 21 (5) 166B
Charles 1 (5) 159A
Charles 23 (6) 415B
Charles K. 15 (6) 408A
Clara 22 (5) 214B
Deborah 46 (5) 172A
Dorsey 30 (5) 153B
Elizabeth 41 (2) 384A
Hester Ann 8 (6) 408A
Hugh J. 13 (6) 408A

GROSS (continued)
Isabella 8 (5) 147B
James 47 (2) 384A
Jane 47 (2) 297B
Jane 70 (6) 408A
Lewis 11 (5) 169A
*Martha 22 (5) 166B
Mary 30 (5) 153B
*Mary A. 36 (5) 159A
Moah 55 (5) 147A
Quince C. 17 (6) 408A
*Quince Edd 36 (6) 408A
*Robert 42 (5) 203A
Samuel 26 (5) 166B
Samuel 9/12 (5) 166B
Sarah 40 (5) 147A
Sarah J. 16 (5) 147A
Sophia 41 (6) 408A
Susan 18 (5) 147A
*Thomas 20 (5) 196B
GUEST, George 5 (3) 517A
Henrietta 10 (3) 516B
Josephine 7 (3) 517A
GUILFORD, William 24 (5)
  204B
GUY, Ann 55 (4) 100B
*Anna 45 (5) 156A
Laura 20 (5) 156A
Lavinia 5/12 (5) 156A
GWYNN, Elizabeth 1 (5)
  131A
John T. 24 (5) 131A
Rachel 19 (5) 131A
HACKET, Alfred 15 (1) 97B
Elizabeth 12 (1) 98A
Francis 35 (1) 97B
*Samuel 43 (1) 97B
Samuel 7 (1) 98A
HACKETT, Amanda 47 (6)
  411B
Amelia 22 (6) 411B
Caroline 18 (6) 411B
Henrietta D. 11 (5) 171B
Mary 60 (5) 149B
*Mary A. 28 (5) 171B
Moses 20 (6) 325A

HACKETT (continued)
Susan J. 32 (6) 411B
*William 48 (6) 411B
William 16 (6) 412A
HALES, Araminta 8 (5) 153B
*Isaac 46 (5) 153B
Louiza 15 (5) 153B
Matilda 45 (5) 153B
Sally 19 (5) 153B
HALEY, *Alexander 74 (2)
 379A
Anna 19 (2) 379A
Elizabeth 23 (2) 379A
Elizabeth 59 (2) 379A
HALL, Alexander 3 (6) 477B
Amanda 18 (5) 144A
*Andrew 24 (6) 306B
*Andrew 25 (6) 309A
Andrew 6/12 (6) 306B
Ann M. 31 (5) 160A
Anna 50 (1) 28B
Catharine 10/12 (5) 155A
Cenn M. 31 (5) 160A
Charles 12 (3) 521A
*Charlotte 38 (5) 160A
Dorcas 50 (5) 209A
Edward 16 (3) 521A
Edward 5 (5) 160A
*Edward 40 (3) 521A
Edward L. 26 (5) 157B
Elizabeth 12 (5) 160A
Elizabeth 25 (5) 157A
Elizabeth 26 (5) 209A
Ellen 9 (5) 160A
Emma 18 (5) 209A
*George 39 (5) 157A
George E. 2 (5) 157B
Gertrude 15 (5) 160A
Ida 11 (4) 106B
Ida H. 20 (6) 477B
Isaac 7 (5) 148A
*Isaih 29 (6) 477B
Israel 40 (3) 522B
James H. 16 (6) 413B
Jane 3 (5) 160A
*John 38 (5) 160A

HALL (continued)
*John 65 (5) 144A
John 6/12 (5) 160A
Joseph 10 (3) 521A
Joseph 2 (5) 144A
Judy 65 (4) 86B
Julia 16 (3) 581A
Lewis 40 (5) 160A
Lizzie 2 (3) 521A
Lucy 11 (1) 57A
Margaret 23 (5) 195A
Maria 41 (3) 521A
Martha 24 (6) 450B
Mary 17 (5) 160A
Mary 25 (5) 157B
Mary E. 19 (5) 144A
Mordecia 23 (6) 309A
Peter 32 (4) 1B
Rachel 3 (5) 157A
Rachel F. 35 (5) 144A
Richard 4 (3) 521A
*Sarah 40 (5) 133A
*Sarah 60 (6) 309A
Sarah 21 (6) 306B
Sarah 34 (5) 149A
Sarah E. 3 (6) 309A
Susanna 21 (6) 306B
Susn F. W. 2 (6) 413B
Thomas 8 (3) 521A
William H. 25 (4) 1 B
William H. 47 (6) 434B
HAMER, Amelia 13 (5) 206B
Harriett 14 (5) 206B
Harriett 44 (5) 206A
Henry 18 (5) 206A
*Joseph C. 49 (5) 206A
Joseph C. 16 (5) 206B
*Mary A. 91 (2) 269A
Mary J. 20 (5) 206A
Rachel 9 (5) 206B
William 6 (5) 206B
HAMILTON, Eliza 36 (5)
 204B
Francis 22 (3) 459A
Harritt 13 (6) 301B
James B. 54 (2) 220A

HAMILTON (continued)
*Murray 52 (5) 204B
Nancy J. 3 (5) 204B
Perry 6/12 (5) 204B
Pricilla 5 (5) 204B
Richard 14 (5) 204B
HAMMON, Matilda 34 (5) 156A
George A. 12 (5) 156A
*James H. 50 (5) 156A
Henrietta 19 (6) 347A
*Henry F. 38 (6) 395B
HAMMOND, Hinson 36 (6) 347A
John 38 (6) 347A
Maria 40 (6) 347A
Mary A. 48 (6) 395B
Rachel 25 (6) 317A
Rachel 65 (5) 143A
W. A. 19 (6) 343A
HAMMONDS, Alfred 30 (5) 155B
HANDY, *Alexander 30 (6) 325A
Amanda 12 (6) 447A
Anna 3 (6) 446B
Anna 45 (6) 331A
Eliza 44 (2) 380B
*Isaac 36 (6) 306B
John 13 (2) 380B
Margaret 31 (6) 447A
Maria 27 (6) 446B
Mary 31 (6) 306B
Mary 46 (6) 297A
Matilda 32 (6) 325A
Sarah 15 (2) 380B
Thadeus S. 3 (6) 447A
Timothy 9 (6) 447A
Washington 5 (6) 447A
HANSEN, Mary 25 (3) 472B
HANSON, Caroline A. 34 (6) 438A
Clara 30 (5) 155A
*Enoch F. 38 (6) 438A
Florence 12 (6) 438A
Francis A. 11 (6) 438A

HANSON (continued)
John 19 (3) 441B
Mary 1 (3) 488B
Sarah J. 30 (4) 14B
Thenie 14 (5) 155A
HAPKINS, Anna J. 2 (6) 347B
HARA, Nancy 14 (2) 251A
HARDCASTLE, Leah 33 (5) 222A
HARDEN, Ann E. M. 15 (6) 412B
Elenora 20 (6) 412B
Ellen R. 25 (4) 40B
Emmer 2 (6) 412B
Harrietta 18 (6) 412B
*Joseph 46 (6) 412B
*Josiah 40 (5) 145B
Martha 22 (5) 145B
Rachel 22 (5) 215A
Rebecca 12 (6) 412B
Rebecca 32 (5) 212A
Rebecca 9 (5) 145B
Rosa 70 (5) 212A
Susan 36 (6) 412B
William 3 (5) 145B
HARDESTER, Ann 61 (6) 447B
HARDING, Anna 23 (5) 204A
*Charles 28 (5) 122B
HARDING, Edward 7/12 (5) 204A
Frances 23 (5) 122B
Lewis 24 (5) 204A
HARDY, *Elenora 45 (5) 236A
Emiline 11 (5) 236A
John 24 (5) 157B
John 40 (5) 236A
Mary F. 9 (5) 236A
HARGRAVES, Ann M. 20 (5) 205A
Catharine 45 (5) 205A
Sarah F. 10 (5) 205A
*Stewart 49 (5) 205A
HARGROVE, Hestella 5 (6) 402B
Lucy 33 (6) 402B

HARGROVE (continued)
McKendry 38 (6) 402B
HARMAN, August 33 (6) 412A
Henrietta 1 (6) 366A
Isaiah 4 (6) 366A
Laura 18 (5) 144B
Louisa 16 (5) 144B
Mary E. 28 (6) 366A
Sarah J. 22 (6) 366A
HARP, Hannah 6 (5) 197A
HARRIETT, Robinson 20 (6) 386A
HARRIS, Adeline 40 (5) 171B
Alexander 40 (5) 167B
Alice 12 (6) 310B
Alice 14 (2) 299B
*Angeline 60 (5) 169B
*Ann 70 (2) 330A
Ann 32 (2) 329A
Ann 52 (6) 413B
Ann 59 (2) 345B
Anna 18 (3) 521A
Annie 27 (3) 505B
Annie 56 (3) 471A
Austen 40 (5) 204B
Bernard 4 (5) 153A
Caroline 35 (5) 204B
*Catharine 24 (5) 155A
Catharine 48 (2) 330A
*Charles 47 (3) 544B
Charles 12 (3) 521A
Charles 45 (5) 206B
*Charles 47 (3) 544B
Cynthia 13 (5) 126B
Daniel 22 (2) 330A
Daniel 50 (2) 330A
Daniel 6 (2) 299B
Daniel 65 (5) 170A
*Edward 40 (3) 521A
*Edward 74 (6) 310B
Edward 16 (3) 521A
*Elisa 40 (5) 151B
*Elisabeth 101 (5) 137A
Eliza 46 (3) 544B
Elizabeth 14 (2) 330A

HARRIS (continued)
Fredrick 60 (5) 170A
George 6 (3) 544B
George A. 9 (2) 330A
George T. 19 (5) 151B
Henry 24 (6) 362B
Henry 27 (3) 542A
Israel 40 (3) 522B
Jackson 18 (6) 382A
*James 36 (3) 540B
*Jane 48 (5) 167B
Jane 36 (5) 153A
Jobe 18 (6) 310B
John 17 (2) 330A
John 31 (5) 153A
*John P. 35 (2) 299A
*John P. 35 (2) 329A
John W. 17 (6) 413B
Joseph 10 (3) 521A
Joseph 35 (5) 171B
Julia 2 (3) 540B
Julia 50 (5) 167B
Lavinia 1 (5) 153A
*Leeds 55 (6) 413B
Letta 16 (5) 182A
Louisa 3 (2) 299B
Luvenia 24 (3) 540B
Margaret 14 (5) 188A
Margaret 24 (3) 540B
Maria 15 (3) 521A
Maria 41 (3) 521A
Maria 80 (3) 521A
Martha 20 (3) 570B
Mary 15 (6) 310B
Mary 17 (6) 322A
Mary 20 (6) 413B
Mary 24 (3) 485B
Mary 32 (5) 206B
Mary 60 (5) 170A
Mary E. 3/12 (5) 206B
Mintie 39 (3) 560A
Phillip A. 19 (6) 413B
Pricilla 50 (5) 204B
Ranson 3 (5) 206B
Richard A. 16 (2) 330A
Robert 11 (2) 299B

HARRIS (continued)
Ruth 9 (2) 330A
Sarah 50 (6) 310B
Sarah L. 9 (5) 204B
Susan 25 (3) 422B
Susan 60 (5) 232B
Theodore 19 (5) 259B
*Thomas 42 (3) 422B
Thomas 1 (2) 299B
Thomas 11 (5) 206B
Thomas J. 45 (2) 330A
William 25 (3) 505B
William S. 15 (5) 151B
HARRISON, George 9 (6)
   410A
Henry 30 (6) 405A
James 24 (5) 161A
*John 34 (6) 410A
Mary 10 (6) 410A
Mary E. 22 (6) 410A
William 24 (1) 69B
HARRY, Albert 32 (3) 525A
Albert 6 (3) 525A
George 2 (3) 525A
Henry 4 (3) 525A
Jane 30 (3) 525A
John 8 (3) 525A
HARTSHORN, Alice 4 (3)
   560B
Annie 10 (3) 560B
Charles 8 (3) 560B
David 6 (3) 560B
Edward 40 (3) 560B
Florence 12 (3) 560B
Susie 37 (3) 560B
Willie 3/12 (3) 560B
HARVEY, Anna R. 20 (4) 87A
Catharine P. 22 (4) 87A
James H. 27 (4) 87A
*Malinda 50 (4) 87A
HATTON, Dennis 40 (5) 145B
Josephine 12 (5) 145B
*Mary 30 (5) 145B
Mary E. 13 (5) 145B
HAWKINS, *Aguila 62 (5)
   145A

HAWKINS (continued)
Andrew 6 (3) 591A
Catharine 20 (5) 145A
Daniel 15 (3) 422B
Emma 3 (5) 149B
George 30 (5) 156B
George 7 (5) 126A
Isabella 3 (5) 145A
James 22 (1) 57A
Jennett 10/12 (5) 145A
John 22 (5) 167B
*Louisa 26 (5) 149B
Martha 40 (5) 145A
*Mary 60 (5) 156B
Mary 25 (5) 190B
*Moses 60 (3) 422B
Moses 21 (5) 145A
Ruth A. 10 (5) 145A
Susan 14 (5) 145A
Thomas 22 (3) 547B
HAWSER, Sarah E. 16 (6)
   408B
HAYDEN, Alexander 7 (6)
   350A
*Basil 49 (6) 350A
Charlott 47 (6) 350A
Clara 20 (6) 350A
*Elizabeth 60 (5) 209A
Ella A. 2 (5) 167A
Emma 4 (5) 126A
Frank 12 (6) 350A
*Isaac 68 (5) 167A
John S. 21 (5) 167A
Joshua 25 (5) 209A
Julia 30 (5) 209A
Logan 10 (6) 350A
Martha A. 23 (5) 167A
Nicholas 15 (6) 350A
Rebecca 47 (5) 167A
Virginia 28 (6) 350A
HAYMAN, Abraham 15 (4)
   102A
*Alexander 48 (4) 102A
Harriet A. E. 42 (4) 102A
HAYNES, Louisa 2 (4) 103B
HAYS, Hannah 6 (5) 197A

129

HAYWARD, Almira 4 (5) 197B
Amanda 10 (5) 126A
Elizabeth 25 (5) 197B
Marcellis 35 (5) 197B
Mary 30 (2) 330A
Robert 8 (5) 126A
HAZELTON, Anna 2 (6) 476B
*Mary J. 27 (6) 476B
Samuel 22 (6) 476B
Solomon 24 (6) 476B
HAZZELTON, *James 60 (6) 438A
Samuel 26 (6) 438A
Solomon 24 (6) 438A
HEATH, Abbey 6 (5) 157A
*Edward 46 (5) 157A
Edward 18 (5) 157A
Maggie 8 (2) 380A
Mary 40 (5) 157A
Sophia 10 (5) 157A
HEBREW, Ann M 43 (5) 197B
*Elijah 49 (5) 197B
Emily M. 12 (5) 197B
William E. 4 (5) 197B
HEIGHT, *James 38 (4) 84B
Louisa 58 (2) 382B
Mary 26 (4) 84B
HEINER, Alverta 9 (5) 205A
Emily 28 (5) 205A
*George 40 (5) 285B
George 15 (5) 285B
Harriet M. 46 (5) 282A
Harry 3 (5) 285B
*Jacob 48 (5) 282A
James 5/12 (5) 285B
Martha 34 (5) 285B
HEITH, David 6 (6) 450B
Elenora 5 (6) 450B
Emma J. 10 (6) 450B
Gabel 54 (6) 450B
Mary A. 45 (6) 450B
Sarah E. 7 (6) 450B
HELDER, Martha 19 (6) 293B

HEMSLEY, Henry 24 (2) 389A
William 65 (4) 95A
HENDERSON, Amelia 31 (3) 544B
Francis 18 (6) 297A
James 21 (3) 599B
James 24 (4) 20A
James 60 (3) 473B
HENMAN, *Eliza 62 (6) 417A
HENRY, Annie 16 (3) 591B
Daniel 17 (3) 591A
Elizabeth 11 (5) 162B
Ellen 7 (3) 591B
Emilie 12 (1) 18A
Harriett 25 (1) 39B
*James 45 (6) 410A
Jane 22 (1) 133B
Jane 35 (6) 410A
Jane 36 (3) 591A
John 12 (3) 591B
Malvina 50 (4) 8A
Martha Ann 8 (6) 305A
Mary Ann 34 (6) 305A
Matild 23 (4) 12B
Patrick 22 (3) 484A
Riley 9 (5) 162B
Robert 3 (6) 305A
Sarah 5 (3) 591B
Sheridan 10 (3) 591B
Stephen 19 (3) 591A
*Thadeus 56 (6) 305A
Thadeus 12 (6) 305A
HENSLEY, Lucretia 50 (6) 474A
HENSON, *Amos 45 (6) 333A
Francis 8 (6) 333A
*George 51 (5) 157B
*Henrietta 30 (5) 253A
Irene 2/12 (5) 253A
James 30 (5) 253A
Jane 30 (6) 333A
John 12 (3) 479A
John 2 (3) 483B
John 35 (3) 479A

HENSON (continued)
John 36 (3) 483B
John 40 (1) 23B
Julia 35 (3) 483B
Laurel 5 (3) 483B
Lizzie 7 (3) 479A
Mary 10 (3) 479A
Mary 22 (3) 493B
Mary 30 (3) 479A
Mary 51 (5) 157B
Mary 7 (3) 483B
Mary 8 (5) 253A
Mary E. 16 (6) 333A
*Rebecca 40 (3) 483B
Samuel J. 4/12 (6) 333A
Thomas 13 (3) 479A
HESTER, Ann 9/12 (4) 110A
HEUSTER, Caroline 5 (6) 410B
*John F. 39 (6) 410B
John T. 9/12 (6) 410B
Joseph E. 12 (6) 410B
Mary A. 38 (6) 410B
Mary T. 10 (6) 410B
Virginia 3 (6) 410B
HEWS, Ann R 47 (2) 345B
HICKMAN, Emeline 25 (5) 138A
HICKS, *Anna 65 95) 181A
*Charles 28 (2) 389A
*Charles 29 (5) 149A
*Charles 46 (5) 203B
Daniel 9 (5) 203B
Eliza 24 (5) 149A
Eliza 33 (5) 203B
Eliza J. 6 (5) 181A
Elizabeth 21 (5) 161B
Ellen 3 (3) 590B
Georgeanna 22 (2) 389A
James H. 4 (5) 149A
John E. 5 (5) 149A
John H. 3 (5) 181A
Josiah 24 (5) 161B
Lewis (Reverend) 60 (4) 18A
Lizzie 1 (3) 591A
Martha J. 1 (5) 161B

HICKS (continued)
Mary 28 (5) 248B
Mary 30 (3) 514B
Nancy C. 44 (4) 18A
Nathaniel 14 (5) 203B
Susan 21 (3) 590B
Susan 22 (5) 181A
Thomas 33 (3) 590B
HIGH, *Emily 36 (6) 416A
Estelle 3 (6) 416A
Harriet 20 (4) 82B
James 23 (6) 416A
Leah 30 (6) 416A
Leah 30 (6) 416A
HILGARD, *Sophia 35 (5) 160A
Thomas 22 (6) 412B
HILL, Abraham 35 (1) 46A
Arrinett 37 (4) 112A
Caroline 21 (5) 175B
Catherine 11 (6) 448A
*Charles 56 (6) 448A
Charles 19 (6) 317A
Charles 22 (6) 448A
Delia 14 (4) 19B
Eben 50 (3) 485A
Ebenezer 23 (3) 485A
Elijah 25 (5) 165B
Eliza 50 (4) 97A
*Ellen 48 (5) 175B
Emmeline 7/12 (1) 46B
Harriett 8 (1) 46A
Henrietta 6 (5) 165B
*John 35 (4) 19B
*Joshua 72 (5) 165B
Laura 21 (4) 81B
*Lorenzo 47 (6) 317A
Lorenzo 5 (6) 317A
*Louisa 28 (1) 46A
*Louisa 28 (1) 46A
Louisa 23 (5) 165B
Maria 35 (6) 319A
Maria 48 (5) 274A
Martha 14 92) 389A
Martha 24 (6) 352B
*Martha E. 25 (6) 378B

HILL (continued)
Mary 16 (2) 389A
Mary E. 22 (6) 317A
Maryetta 12 (4) 94B
Matilda 45 (3) 485A
Pippen 60 (4) 94B
Rosetta 30 (2) 389A
Rosetta 30 (4) 19B
Sarah 18 (6) 448A
Sarah 49 (5) 165B
Sarah 50 (6) 317A
Sarah 55 (4) 19B
Sarah A. 13 (6) 317A
Sarah R. 10 (4) 19B
Sarah T. 21 (4) 19B
Susan 49 (6) 448A
Susan R. 4 (4) 19B
HILLEN, Caroline 16 (5)
    179B
*Mary 36 (5) 179B
HINDES, *Arthur 28 (6) 346B
Arthur 64 (6) 346B
*Catherine 25 (1) 46A
Charlotte 27 (6) 346B
Emily 30 (5) 234A
Henrietta 35 (5) 236B
*Isaac 40 (5) 234A
Joshua 1 (5) 236B
Lizzie 9/12 (1) 46A
Maggie 10 (1) 46A
Maggie 10 (1) 46A
Nettie 9 (5) 236B
*Samuel 42 (5) 236B
Samuel 10 (5) 236B
Sophia 12 (5) 236B
HINDS, Isaac 39 (1) 46A
HINSON, Alice 2 (6) 458A
Emily 4/12 (6) 458A
*James 55 (6) 457B
Johanna 11 (6) 457B
Leucreatin 35 (6) 457B
Margarett A. 9 (6) 458A
Rebecca 5 (6) 458A
HINTON, Elizabeth 25 (5)
    151B
Louisa 1 (5) 151B

HINTON (continued)
Perry 23 (5) 151B
*Richard 24 (5) 151B
HITCHEN, Earnest 7 (6)
    344A
Steven 8 (6) 344A
HITCHENS, Augustus 6 (2)
    342B
Catherine 15 (6) 343B
Clara 13 (5) 204B
Edward 4 (2) 342B
Elizebeth 40 (6) 343B
Ellen 40 (5) 153B
Emma 3 (5) 153B
Hester 8 (2) 342B
James 13 (5) 153B
James 19 (6) 343B
Jane 52 (5) 204B
*John 57 (5) 204B
John 1 (5) 207A
John C. 15 (5) 204B
John M. 23 (6) 343B
John W. 22 (5) 206B
Joseph 11 (6) 343B
Laura 19 (5) 206B
*Samuel 50 (6) 343B
Samuel 17 (6) 343B
*William 49 (5) 153B
William 16 (5) 153B
HOFFMAN, Amelia 52 (3)
    487A
Annie 21 (3) 487A
George 10 (3) 487A
George 18 (3) 487A
Henry 16 (3) 487A
Mary 8 (3) 487A
HOLLAM, Nellie 16 (1) 49B
HOLLAND, Catharine 30 (5)
    274A
Elizabeth 7 (5) 274A
Robert 10 (5) 274A
Anna 3 (5) 274A
Annie 35 (3) 544B
*David 27 (3) 469A
Eldridge 1 (5) 274A
Ellen 50 (5) 274B

HOLLAND (continued)
Emiline 5 (5) 274B
Fanny 8 (3) 414A
Frisby 45 (3) 414A
Harriet 31 (3) 414A
Harriet 8 (3) 544B
*Henry 50 (5) 274B
Jacob 8/12 (3) 414A
James 5 (3) 414A
James H. 13 (5) 274B
*Jonah 38 (3) 544B
Joseph 29 (5) 285A
Joseph 5 (3) 544B
Julia 3 (3) 544B
Lewis 11 (4) 20B
Maggie 1 (3) 544B
Mary 30 (3) 469A
Mary 45 (4) 14B
Mary 7 (3) 469A
Rebecca 5 (5) 274A
*Robert J. 35 (5) 274A
Sarah 11 (5) 274B
Sarah 7 (3) 544B
Solomon 46 (3) 413B
Susan 18 (5) 133A
Susan 38 (5) 133A
William 8/12 (3) 414A
HOLLEY, Eliza 29 (2) 384A
Manor 22 (3) 503B
Mary 22 (3) 503B
William 24 (3) 503A
HOLLIDAY, *Anna 16 (1) 44B
Caroline 23 (5) 137B
*Codilia (1) 44B
Ella 5 (5) 236A
Georgeanna 8 (5) 236A
Harriett 26 (5) 159B
*Henry 45 (1) 44B
Henry 12 (1) 44B
Ida 3 (5) 282A
James 28 (5) 282A
Louisa 26 (5) 282A
Nelson 6 (1) 44B
Rebecca 35 (5) 236A
Samuel 5 (5) 282A

HOLLIN, Elizebeth 5 (6)
309B
Frances 28 (6) 309B
HOLLINGSWORTH, *Abra-
ham 37 (3) 463A
Annie 41 (3) 463A
Catherine 14 (3) 463A
Charles 19 (5) 179A
Fanny 25 (5) 154B
HOLLINS, *Charles 30 (5)
171B
Eliza J. 6/12 (5) 171B
Hester A. 5 (5) 171B
James W. 6 (5) 171B
Jane 30 (5) 171B
HOLLINSWORTH, *Archibald
75 (6) 470A
Caroline 50 (6) 470A
HOLLIS, Edward 22 (5) 170B
Edward 25 (4) 109A
Francis V. 11 (6) 324B
Martha A. 19 (5) 170B
Rose 25 (6) 324B
*William 52 (3) 543A
HOLLY, Agustus 18 (5) 121B
HOLMIRS, Emma 14 (3)
528A
Maria 17 (3) 528A
HOMER, Carrie 3 (3) 542B
Emma 1 (3) 542B
Rebecca 25 (3) 542B
William 24 (3) 542B
HOOD, Georgiana 40 (6) 446B
Thomas 21 (6) 446B
Tommy 5 (6) 446B
Winson 27 (6) 446B
HOOK, Ellen 30 (6) 408B
George 21 (6) 408B
HOOPER, Amelia 26 (2)
222A
Bejamin 38 (2) 222A
Ellen C. 9 (2) 222A
Harriet 36 (3) 505A
Isaac J. 5 (2) 222A
Lizzie 23 (3) 427A
Mary 48 (2) 222A

HOOPER (continued)
Mela 18 (1) 78B
*Philip 29 (3) 505A
HOPE, Randel 23 (2) 221B
HOPEWELL, Mary 26 (3)
413A
HOPKINS, Ann 40 (5) 242B
Bridget 75 (6) 411B
Charles 6 (6) 433A
Elizabeth 32 (5) 232A
Harriette 8 (6) 433A
Henrietta 3/12 (5) 147B
*Henry 39 (6) 411B
Ida V. 6 (6) 347B
Isaac 12 (5) 203A
*James 40 (3) 543B
*Jane 40 (5) 203A
*Joseph 40 (6) 433A
Josephine 12 (6) 433A
Kate 35 (3) 543B
Louisa 22 (5) 203A
Lucy A. 7 (5) 242B
Martha A. 2 (5) 242B
Mary 17 (6) 433A
Mary A. 9 (5) 242B
Mary E. 18 (5) 147B
Thomas D. 8 (6) 411B
William H. 11 (6) 411B
HORN, Agusta 34 (5) 197B
*Henry 57 (5) 197B
HORNEY, John 49 (2) 389A
HORSEY, Alverta 2 (5) 145A
Ann 40 (6) 453B
Benjamin 29 (6) 366A
Frances 19 (5) 145A
Thomas F. 26 (5) 145A
HOUSTON, Eliza 72 (2) 386A
HOW, Catharine 45 (2) 251B
*Henry 42 (2) 251B
HOWARD, Ann M. 58 (5)
204A
Anna 26 (2) 383A
Anna 32 (4) 1B
Caroline 30 (5) 153A
Charles 4 (6) 346B
Charles 6 (5) 126A

HOWARD (continued)
Charles 71 (5) 157A
Edith 20 (4) 84A
Elizabeth 61 (5) 151A
Elizabeth 9 (4) 18B
Elizabeth A. 27 (4) 18B
Emma 22 (3) 424B
Emory 2 (4) 18B
George 44 94) 1B
Georgianna 28 (4) 18B
Harriet A. 28 (5) 275B
Harriett 21 (3) 424B
*Henrietta 45 (4) 18B
*Jacob 64 (5) 204A
John 34 (3) 424B
Joseph 1 (5) 153A
Joseph 4 (3) 424B
*Joshua 37 (2) 383A
Margaret 1/12 (4) 88B
Margaret 17 (3) 500A
Martha J. 11 (6) 346B
Mary Ann 14 (4) 88B
*Nicholas 75 (5) 151A
Phebe 42 (6) 346B
Rachel 14 (5) 141A
Rachel 35 (5) 223B
Rebecca 20 (3) 424B
*Samuel 48 (6) 437B
Samuel 26 (4) 18B
Simon 4 (4) 88B
Susanah 25 (6) 437B
Teressa 35 (4) 88B
*Wesley 28 (6) 449A
*William 23 (3) 424B
HOWE, *Elizabeth 50 (5)
153A
Elizabeth 12 (2) 340B
Elizabeth 45 (2) 340B
Elizebeth 40 (6) 346B
Emily J. 16 (2) 340B
*Robert 51 (2) 340B
HOWELL, Maleci 33 (5)
273B
HUBB, Ariana 18 (6) 446B
Georgiana 30 (6) 446B
Harry 14 (6) 446B

HUBB (continued)
Martha J 20 (6) 446B
Nancy 26 (6) 446B
Nancy 56 (6) 446B
*William 54 (6) 446B
William 16 (6) 446B
HUBBARD, Emma 14 (5)
  205A
James 12 (5) 205A
Margaret 3 (5) 149A
Mary A. 6 (5) 204B
Robert 35 (5) 159A
Sarah 15 (5) 204B
Sarah 15 (5) 205A
Sophia 5/12 (5) 149A
Virginia 23 (5) 159A
HUDGINS, Simon 40 (4) 112B
HUDSON, Lewis 60 (6) 311A
HUGAS, Elizabeth 8 (3) 477B
George 2 (3) 477B
George 35 (3) 477B
Henrietta 35 (3) 477B
John 4 (3) 477B
HUGHES, *Alexander 30 (5)
  162A
Anna 11 (5) 192A
*Asbury 39 (6) 451B
*Benjamin 38 (3) 560A
*Benjamin 43 (6) 411A
Charles 10 (6) 474A
Charles 15 (5) 145B
Christopher 5 (3) 560A
Elizabeth 35 (3) 524A
Emma 11 (3) 544A
Emma 18 (5) 145B
Florince 14 (3) 544A
Frances 21 (3) 544A
Francis 11/12 (5) 162A
Francis 35 (6) 451B
Frederick 8 (3) 524A
George 16 (3) 544A
George 7 (6) 411A
Henrietta 39 (3) 560A
Hester J. 20 (5) 162A
Ida 12 (3) 560A
James 21 (4) 108A

HUGHES (continued)
James 25 (6) 450B
*Jane 42 (5) 145B
*John 42 (3) 544A
John 35 (3) 523B
Joseph 7 (3) 560A
Kate 26 (6) 450B
Lewis 4 (6) 450B
Lizzie 6 (3) 524A
Margaret 19 (3) 544A
Maria 4 (3) 524A
Maria 45 (3) 544A
Mary 10 (3) 524A
Mollie 10 (3) 560A
Rachel A. 38 (6) 411A
Rebecca 30 (6) 411A
Rosa 12 (5) 145B
Rosa 50 (4) 82B
Sarah 17 (5) 145B
Thomas 6 (3) 544A
Walter 9 (3) 544A
William 22 (5) 145B
HUGHS, William 22 (1) 47A
HULL, Laura 11 (5) 186B
HUNTER, Charles 1 (5) 122B
*John 33 (5) 122B
Lucy 18 (5) 122B
Sarah 13 (1) 25B
HURSON, Mary A 33 (6) 291B
HURST, Elenora 26 (5) 236B
*John 35 (5) 236B
John 3 (5) 236B
Josephine 9 (5) 236B
Mary 7 (5) 236B
Victoria 6 (5) 236B
HUSTON, Ellen 20 (5) 274B
*Jacob 47 (3) 542A
John 15 (3) 542A
Mary 18 (3) 542A
Mary 40 (3) 542A
Noah 8 93) 542A
Richard 17 93) 542A
HUTCHENS, Henry 22 (2)
  377B
HUTCHINS, *Alexander 31 (5)
  155B

HUTCHINS (continued)
Alexander 75 (5) 155B
Eliza 10 (5) 155B
Emma 23 95) 160A
Lavinia 28 (5) 155B
Louisa 18 (5) 204B
Mary 21 (6) 433A
Mary 24 (5) 220B
Mary 45 (6) 443B
Ophelia 1 (5) 155B
Richard 27 (5) 160A
HUTSON, Charles 1/12 (3)
544A
Eliza 17 (3) 544A
Virginia 2 (3) 544A
HUTT, Gaddy 64 (2) 339B
HUTTY, Alphonis 10 (6))
433A
Elizebeth 38 (6) 433A
*John T. 36 (6) 433A
Sumner J. 1/12 (6) 433A
Thomas E. 4 (6) 433A
Treaser 15 (6) 433A
HYDE, Ann 30 (6) 431B
Elizebeth 51 (6) 447A
Rachel 27 (6) 431B
HYER, George W 7 (5) 179B
John A. 12 (5) 179B
Lucretia 39 (5) 179B
Lurena 3 (5) 179B
*Samuel 40 (5) 179B
Thomas 14 (5) 179B
HYNSON, Edwards 30 (5)
146B
Israel 22 (5) 139B
James 78 (5) 283A
Mary 17 (5) 121B
IGLEHART, James B 17 (5)
148A
INSPEY, Amanda 53 (6) 476A
Harriett A. 14 (6) 476A
IRONS, Dina 80 (5) 141B
IRVINS, Deborah E 75 (6)
409B
Harriett W. 4 (6) 409B
John T. 7 (6) 409B

IRVINS (continued)
Mary E. 11 (6) 409B
*William P. 40 (6) 409B
ISAAC, Mary 29 (3) 506A
*William 40 (3) 506A
William 15 (3) 506A
ISAACK, Charlott 22 (6) 409B
Tobias 40 (6) 409B
ISAACKS, *Henry 21 (6) 412B
Harriet 50 (3) 506A
Emma 18 (3) 506A
Joseph 27 (5) 153A
IVES, John 24 (2) 306A
JACKSON, Agnes 18 (4) 99B
Alfred 21 (5) 172B
Alice 5 (5) 172B
Alvetta 2 (2) 330A
Amanda 17 (3) 597A
Ann 22 (5) 120A
Ann 7 (6) 455A
Anna 21 (5) 144B
*Anna 50 (1) 4A
Anna A. 65 (6) 411B
Benjamin 24 (3) 520A
*Benjamin 46 (2) 303A
*Benjamin 50 (5) 170A
Betsey 60 (4) 111B
Betty 25 (5) 154A
Caroline 20 (1) 4A
Caroline 21 (1) 31B
Caroline 25 (2) 303A
Caroline 45 (5) 248A
Catharine 23 (2) 296A
Charles E. 12 (5) 248A
Charles E. 2 (2) 296B
Charles J. 29 (5) 207A
Charlott 10 (6) 368A
Daniel R. 17 (2) 220A
David 30 (5) 154A
Edward 14 (6) 367B
*Edward 31 (6) 455A
*Elemuel 48 (6) 474B
Eliza J. 1 (6) 474B
Eliza J. 24 (5) 142A
Elizabeth 35 (5) 170A
Ella 2 (5) 170A

JACKSON (continued)
Ellen 23 (4) 82A
Ellen 25 (5) 147B
Ellen 4 (5) 196B
Ellen 46 (3) 506B
Emory 24 (5) 144B
Fannie 13 (3) 487B
*Fanny 31 (5) 196B
*George 58 (3) 523B
George 17 (3) 487B
George E. 22 (6) 474B
George F. 21 (2) 220A
George W. 1/12 (6) 455A
Gertrude 7/12 (5) 170A
Hannah 29 (6) 455A
Harriet 3 (5) 142A
*Harriet 35 (5) 161B
Harriet 39 (2) 389B
Harriet 60 (5) 172B
Harriett 17 (1) 4A
Henrietta 14 (2) 220A
Henrietta 50 (5) 155A
Henry 10 (2) 303A
Henry 16 (3) 487B
Henry 2 (6) 368A
Henry 29 (6) 334A
Hester A. 11 (2) 222A
Hester A. 39 (2) 303A
Hester J. 9 (6) 474B
Isaac 10 (2) 220A
James 30 (5) 203B
James 35 (5) 196B
*James 42 (5) 170A
James 50 (2) 377B
*James B. 56 (2) 220A
Jane 50 (6) 295A
Jane 20 (3) 523B
Jane 27 (3) 413B
John 2 (6) 455A
John 22 (1) 22A
John 23 (3) 413B
John 52 (3) 506B
Joseph 12 (6) 367B
Joshua 10 (2) 222A
Julia 18 (5) 248A
Julia 65 (5) 169B

JACKSON (continued)
Letecia 35 (5) 170A
Levia 5/12 (2) 389B
Lillie 30 (3) 520A
Louisa 19 (2) 389B
Lucy 17 (5) 242B
Lucy 32 (1) 57A
Lydia 38 (6) 367B
Margaret 38 (6) 347B
Margaret 47 (2) 220A
Maria 22 (5) 172B
Maria 8 (5) 196B
Martha 22 (3) 454A
Martha 22 (4) 15A
Martha 9 (5) 170A
Mary 11 (6) 455A
Mary 17 (1) 37B
Mary 17 (2) 389B
Mary 20 (3) 452B
*Mary 36 (5) 186B
Mary A. 56 (6) 474B
Mary A. 88 (6) 409B
Mary B. 6 (5) 147B
Mary E. 30 (5) 146A
Mary E. 4 (5) 146A
*Matilda 19 (6) 356A
Matilda 50 (5) 148A
Maulsby 65 (6) 310A
Noah 27 (1) 4A
Olevia 16 (5) 248A
Phoebe 37 (3) 487B
Pricilla 4 (5) 170A
Rachel 2 (5) 172B
Rachel 42 (3) 523B
Rebecca 40 (4) 82A
Richard 2 (5) 186B
Richard 30 (5) 186B
Robert 43 (2) 387A
Samuel 10/12 (5) 142A
Samuel 34 (5) 146A
Samuel 8 (2) 303A
*Samuel 60 (3) 520A
Samuel J. 24 (5) 142A
Samuel J. 8 (5) 146A
Sarah 16 (1) 24A
Sarah 16 (1) 4A

JACKSON (continued)
Sarah J. 15 (2) 220A
Solomon 10 (1) 4A
Sophia 17 (5) 190A
*Stephen 28 (2) 296A
Susan 2 (5) 186B
Susan 20 (3) 583B
Susan 51 (5) 206A
Susan 75 (5) 204B
Theodore 25 (3) 520A
Whitington 52 (5) 206A
Willia 4 (6) 455A
William 8 (2) 220A
Willis 4 (2) 220A
Wm. 16 (2) 303A
Wm. 25 (4) 82A
Wm. 30 (5) 147B
*Wm. 36 (2) 389B
Wm. 40 (2) 303A
Wm. 45 (5) 167B
Wm. J. 1 (5) 146A
*Wm. H. 50 (5) 248A
JACOBS, Daniel 52 (5) 283B
Susan 50 (5) 283B
JAMES, Charlotta 19 (5) 166B
Daniel 90 (3) 424B
Edward 5 (3) 540A
Eliza 15 (3) 540A
Eliza 9 (3) 540A
Elizabeth 25 (2) 384B
Elizabeth 26 (5) 253A
Elizabeth 50 (5) 158B
Ellen 37 (3) 422B
John 12 (3) 540A
John W. 23 (5) 166B
Lizzie 28 (3) 563A
Louisa 65 (4) 99A
Margaret 3 (3) 540A
Martin 25 (5) 158A
Mary 15 (3) 550A
Mary 33 (3) 540A
Nicely 13 (4) 9B
Samuel 22 (4) 95A
Wm 7 (3) 540A

JANEROUSE, Milla 90 (6) 323A
JARRETT, Julia 6 (3) 544A
Maria 4 (3) 544A
Sidney 27 (3) 544A
*Zachariah 26 (3) 544A
JEFFERSON, *Henry 60 (6) 413A
Lidia 50 (4) 98B
Martha 24 (3) 508A
Nancy 50 (6) 413A
Nathaniel 39 (5) 156A
Thomas 14 (5) 156A
Thomas 16 (6) 413A
Thomas 36 (3) 544A
Zaccariah 35 (5) 156A
JEFFRIES, James 16 (6) 309B
JEMINSON, John 18 (3) 561A
JENKENS, *Ann 55 (2) 345B
JENKINS, Adenline 35 (1) 24A
Albert 2 (3) 520A
*Alexander 36 (5) 206B
Ann 60 (5) 167B
Ann M. 19 (6) 312A
Anna 10/12 (5) 206B
Anna 25 (6) 300B
Anna 26 (5) 206B
Augustus 16 (6) 454A
Caroline 29 (4) 6A
Caroline 9 (3) 525B
*Charles 66 (5) 178A
Charles 3 (3) 525B
Charlotta 60 (5) 150A
Clem 1 (4) 6A
*Eliza 32 (6) 454A
Eliza A. 47 (6) 387A
Elizabeth 34 (6) 311B
Ellen 15 (6) 454A
Fanny 58 (5) 165B
*George 65 (5) 150A
George H. 3 (2) 221B
*Harriet 49 (4) 110A
*James H. 40 (6) 311B

JENKINS (continued)
Jennie 29 (3) 525B
*John 24 (2) 221B
John 1 (3) 525B
John C. 32 (4) 6A
John W. 12 (6) 312A
John W. 6 (2) 221B
Joseph 12 (6) 454A
Joseph P. G. 2 (2) 221B
Joshua 35 (3) 508A
Joshua 66 (5) 165B
Laura E. 12 (6) 415B
Maria 56 (5) 178A
Martha 21 (3) 520A
Mary 26 (2) 221B
Mary 7 (3) 525B
Mary R. 3 (5) 206B
Susan A. 7/12 (2) 221B
Thomas H. 15 (6) 311B
Westly 5 (3) 525B
*Westly 37 (3) 525B
Willie 4 (6) 454A
JENKS, Ella 14 (6) 387A
Sallie 17 (6) 367A
JENNINGS, Martha 38 (4)
  94B
*Thomas 38 (4) 94B
JERETT, Matilda 73 (2)
  348B
JESSOP, Alice 7 (5) 122B
JEWET, Sarah 66 (3) 517A
JOBES, Jane 38 (3) 505A
JOHNS, Abraham 15 (4) 93B
Elisha 22 (4) 93B
Eliza 32 (2) 335A
Elizabeth 30 (4) 93B
George 7 (3) 478A
Harry 3 (3) 478A
Henry 32 (3) 478A
Horrace 26 (4) 93B
*Jones 43 (3) 462A
Julia 10 (3) 478A
Lizzie 33 (3) 478A
Lizzie 40 (3) 462A
Louisa 36 (6) 310A
Lydia 5 (3) 478A

JOHNS (continued)
*Margaret 54 (4) 93B
Mary 17 (3) 508A
Servena 14 (4) 93B
Violet 22 (4) 93B
*Wilson 45 (2) 335A
JOHNSON, Abraham 14 (6)
  367B
*Abraham 30 (5) 234B
Adaline 56 (2) 382B
Agness 21 (6) 197B
*Alexander 65 (2) 384A
Alice 12 (2) 384B
Alice 13 (2) 318A
Alice 15 (6) 408B
Amelia 12 (5) 170B
Amelia 2 (5) 283A
Amelia 38 (5) 283A
Amey 20 (3) 494B
Andrew 15 (1) 78A
Ann 10 (3) 462A
Ann 20 (5) 158A
Ann 40 (6) 366B
Ann 45 (3) 426B
Ann E. 1 (6) 325A
Ann Eliz 19 (6) 303A
Ann M. 11 (5) 147B
Ann M. 13 (5) 283A
Ann M. 18 (2) 340B
Anna 1 (6) 325A
Anna 19 (6) 292A
Anna 41 (3) 462A
Anna 45 (5) 178B
Anna 55 (6) 341A
*Anna 20 (5) 171B
*Anna 55 (5) 158A
Annie 53 (3) 506B
Araminta 4 (5) 147B
Benjamin 10 (5) 264B
Benjamin 4/12 (6) 437B
Betsey 40 (5) 139A
Caroline 1 (5) 133A
Caroline 9 (5) 130B
Carra 19 (4) 85A
Catherine 30 (5) 220A
Catherine A. 38 (5) 241B

JOHNSON (continued)
Catherine E. 9 (5) 241B
Charity 22 (2) 339B
Charity 50 (1) 5A
Charity 60 (5) 171B
Charles 17 (2) 225B
Charles 17 (2) 225B
Charles 24 (5) 144A
Charles 25 (5) 199B
Charles 27 (2) 339B
Charles 30 (5) 153A
Charles 4 (3) 478A
Charles 48 (5) 234A
Charles 54 (5) 264A
Charles 57 (6) 325A
Charles 6 (3) 484A
Charles J. 3 (5) 171B
Charles S. 7 (5) 241B
Charlotta 19 (5) 205B
Charlotta 3 (5) 180A
Charlotta 38 (5) 282B
*Charlotta 42 (5) 275B
Christiana A. 28 (6) 411B
Claracy 40 (5) 171A
Claricy 28 (3) 602B
*Collins 27 (4) 6B
Daniel 1/12 (4) 6B
Daniel 4 (3) 484A
Darius 13 (5) 209B
*Darius 37 (5) 209B
*David 30 (6) 325A
David 24 (3) 560A
David 24 (3) 560B
David 52 (1) 200A
David 6 (6) 325A
*Dennis 24 (5) 167B
Edward 25 (2) 339B
Edward 6 (5) 178B
Elijah 18 (5) 147B
*Eliza 58 (5) 286B
Eliza 11 (5) 180A
Eliza 47 (3) 520A
Eliza 50 (1) 200A
Eliza 60 (5) 125A
Eliza A. 32 (6) 309B
Eliza A. 50 (2) 400A

JOHNSON (continued)
Eliza J. 8 (5) 283A
Eliza M. 60 (5) 271A
Elizabeth 3 (6) 362A
Elizabeth 35 (5) 281B
Elizabeth 48 (2) 225B
Elizabeth 48 (2) 225B
*Elizabeth 73 (5) 170A
Elizabeth 55 (2) 384A
Elizabeth 6 (5) 167A
Elizabeth E. 7 (5) 264B
Ellen 25 (5) 286B
*Ellen 69 (2) 339B
*Ellery 60 (3) 545A
Emaline 24 (2) 339B
Emeline 55 (5) 158A
Emily 17 (3) 440A
Emily 18 (3) 424B
Emily 28 (5) 160A
Emily 30 (2) 335A
Emma 20 (3) 462A
Emma 4 (5) 234A
Emma 6 (5) 180A
Emma J. 4 (5) 162B
Ereline 20 (3) 561A
Eugene 11 (5) 264B
Eugene 4/12 (2) 339B
Fanny 10 (1) 60B
Fanny 39 (5) 158B
Fanny 60 (5) 137B
Febie 36 (5) 268A
Frances 37 (5) 209B
Frances 42 (5) 167A
*Frances 50 (5) 264A
Frances J. 12 95) 241B
Francis 11 (3) 462A
Frank 24 (4) 110A
Frank 86 (6) 470A
Fredrick 26 (5) 199B
George 11 (5) 178B
George 17 (6) 413B
George 2 (3) 484A
George 2 (3) 503A
George 26 (4) 19B
George 30 (3) 484A
George 30 (3) 524B

JOHNSON (continued)
*George 38 (5) 283A
George A. 5/12 (5) 205B
George H. 1 (6) 448B
George H. 15 (5) 209B
George W. 1 (5) 283A
George W. 13 (6) 367B
Georgeanna 10 (5) 219B
Gertrude 3 (5) 264B
Gerturde 18 (5) 196B
*Grafton 49 (6) 411B
Hannah 10 (4) 84B
Hannibal 30 (5) 286B
Harriet 11 (3) 464B
Harriet 3 (3) 477B
*Harriet 24 (5) 166B
*Harriet 75 (5) 282A
Harriet 30 (2) 380B
Harriet A. 1/12 (5) 167B
Harriet A. 4 (6) 309B
Harry 12 (6) 437B
Harry H. 4 (5) 241B
Henrietta 20 (2) 251A
Henry 10 (2) 384B
Henry 3 (6) 325A
Henry 39 (5) 158B
Henry 4 (6) 325A
*Henry 40 (3) 462A
*Henry 43 (5) 283A
*Henry 60 (5) 147B
Hester A. 14 (5) 148B
Hester A. 35 (5) 133A
Horns 35 (3) 558B
Ida 13 5) 264B
Ida 3 (5) 205B
Isaac 9 (1) 110B
Isabella 17 (6) 437B
Isadore 20 (3) 525A
Isaiah 6 (5) 148B
*Isaiah 49 (5) 160A
Izah 21 (3) 508A
Jacob 15 (6) 437B
Jacob 45 (4) 112B
Jacob 55 (5) 219B
James 13 (5) 166A
James 17 (6) 413A

JOHNSON (continued)
James 23 (6) 413B
James 24 (5) 286B
James 24 (6) 437B
James 26 (3) 543B
James 3 (5) 209B
*James 33 (5) 220A
*James 40 (5) 180A
*James 44 (5) 153A
*James 51 (3) 520A
James 35 (5) 167A
James P. 50 (5) 162B
Jane 32 (6) 362A
Jane 35 (6) 306A
*Jefferson 50 (5) 178B
Jenny 16 (5) 139A
Job 7 (5) 283A
John 1 (3) 561A
John 1 (4) 6B
*John 26 (4) 6A
*John 29 (3) 564A
*John 40 (2) 335A
*John 40 (6) 408B
John 17 (5) 166A
John 2 (6) 409B
John 3 (3) 543B
John 30 (3) 524B
John 35 (6) 413A
John 50 (5) 158A
John 7 (1) 200A
John H. 11 (6) 309B
John H. 44 (5) 205B
John J. 2 (5) 199B
*John P. 64 (4) 85A
*John W. 54 (5) 271A
John W. 8 (5) 271A
Joseph 17 (3) 411B
Joseph 19 (5) 178B
Joseph 30 (6) 306A
Joseph 35 (5) 133A
Joseph 5 (5) 205B
Joseph J. 19 (4) 94A
Josephine 15 (1) 102B
Joshua 21 (6) 410B
Joshua 22 (6) 437B
Julia 16 (5) 224B

JOHNSON (continued)
Julia 18 (2) 384B
Julia 18 (5) 139A
Julia 22 (3) 462A
Julia 23 (1) 35A
Julia 24 (4) 84B
Julia 34 (2) 318A
Julia 35 (6) 413A
Julia 37 (5) 180A
Julia 40 (5) 248B
Katie 4 (2) 384B
Laura 8 (2) 384A
Laura 8 (2) 384B
Lavenia 19 (6) 416B
*Leah 45 (4) 94A
Lenora 12 (5) 180A
Lewis 8 (5) 178B
Lizzie 10 (1) 200A
Lizzie 28 (3) 478A
Lizzie 35 (6) 408B
Louisa 11 (5) 148B
Louisa 17 (6) 372A
Louisa 19 (2) 306A
Louisa 23 (5) 205B
Louisa 25 (5) 153A
Louisa 5 (5) 209B
*Louisa 47 (5) 264B
Loyde 23 (2) 251A
Lucinda 14 (5) 219B
Lucy 25 (6) 303B
Lucy 51 (1) 36A
Lucy L. 19 (5) 187A
Luvenia 45 (3) 543B
Lydia 65 (5) 205A
Maggy 16 (5) 126B
*Mahalia 38 (6) 367B
Marcelus 22 (5) 274B
Margaret 14 (5) 178B
Margaret 20 (6) 437B
Margaret 55 (3) 422B
Maria 16 (5) 147B
Maria 31 (3) 524B
Martha 12 (5) 139A
Martha 14 (5) 271A
Martha 18 (5) 248B
Martha 24 (2) 295B

JOHNSON (continued)
Martha 24 (2) 339B
*Martha 46 (5) 234A
Martha 25 (5) 162B
Martha 25 (5) 205B
Martha 27 (4) 6B
Martha 30 (5) 186B
*Mary 42 (5) 204B
*Mary 45 (5) 219B
*Mary 45 (6) 372A
*Mary 50 (3) 448B
Mary 1 (3) 477B
Mary 1 (3) 564B
Mary 14 (4) 92A
Mary 16 (1) 200A
Mary 17 (1) 7A
Mary 17 (5) 160A
Mary 17 (6) 352B
Mary 19 (5) 228A
Mary 19 (6) 389A
Mary 20 (3) 442A
Mary 20 (3) 448B
Mary 20 (3) 473B
Mary 20 (5) 248B
Mary 22 (3) 477B
Mary 23 (6) 437B
Mary 25 (3) 524B
Mary 25 (3) 564B
Mary 26 (5) 160B
Mary 27 (3) 484A
Mary 27 (3) 503A
Mary 29 (2) 400A
Mary 3 (2) 384B
Mary 35 (5) 283A
Mary 35 (6) 323A
Mary 39 (4) 112B
Mary 40 (3) 502B
Mary 40 (5) 234B
Mary 6 (3) 478A
Mary E. 12 (2) 332A
Mary E. 16 (5) 170B
Mary E. 19 (2) 391A
Mary E. 19 (5) 153A
Mary E. 22 (5) 271A
Mary E. 25 (6) 325A
Mary E. 28 (3) 560B

JOHNSON (continued)
Mary E. 3 (5) 234B
Mary Eliz 26 (6) 325A
Mary Ellen 7 (6) 303B
Mary F. 11 (5) 283A
Mary F. 12 (5) 162B
Mary J. 50 (95) 162B
Mary L. 31 (5) 220A
Mary L. 6 (6) 372A
Mathews 86 (1) 23B
Nancy 18 (5) 264B
Nancy J. 15 (5) 283A
Nancy S. 10 (6) 309B
Nancy W. 3 (5) 219B
Nicholas 35 (5) 220A
Patty 75 (5) 179B
Perry 30 (5) 205A
Perry 31 (5) 264B
Perry 54 (5) 170A
Peter L. 21 (6) 303A
Philip 17 (5) 264A
*Primus 37 (6) 303B
*R. 70 (6) 338B
Rachel 59 (5) 153A
Rebecca 23 (5) 153A
Rebecca 5 (5) 162B
Rebecca 54 (4) 85A
*Richard 32 (6) 448A
Richard 1 (5) 281B
Richard 10 (5) 171B
Richard 23 (3) 414A
Richard 24 (2) 339B
Richard 25 (2) 389A
Richard 26 (5) 205B
Richard 71 (5) 160A
*Robert 43 (6) 309B
Robert 5 (3) 543B
Robert 53 (5) 204B
Rosa 4 (4) 6B
Sally 3 (4) 6B
Samuel 33 (5) 236B
Samuel 35 (5) 286B
*Sarah 42 (5) 166A
Sarah 20 (4) 10B
Sarah 22 (6) 452A
Sarah 23 (5) 234B

JOHNSON (continued)
Sarah 24 (5) 236B
Sarah 25 (5) 185A
Sarah 27 (5) 167B
Sarah 33 (4) 6A
Sarah 58 (3) 411B
Sarah 7/12 (5) 199B
Sarah 9 (3) 484A
Sarah 9 (5) 283A
Sarah E. 4 (5) 271A
Sarah F. 12 (5) 153A
Sarah J. 14 (5) 139A
Sarah J. 25 (5) 264B
Sarah J. 35 (5) 148B
Sina 61 (5) 147B
Sophia 11/12 (5) 209B
Spencer 28 (2) 391A
Stephen 39 (5) 268A
*Steven 35 (6) 452A
*Steven 40 (6) 366B
Susan 13 (4) 94A
Susan 30 (3) 473B
Susan 41 (5) 127B
Susan 60 (5) 179B
Susan 65 (6) 413B
Sydney 11 (5) 219B
*Theodore 48 (2) 225B
*Thomas 29 (3) 477B
Thomas 15 (5) 264B
Thomas 23 (3) 503B
Thomas 23 (3) 542A
Thomas 23 (5) 178B
Thomas 25 (3) 448B
Thomas 4 (5) 283A
Thomas 46 (6) 362A
Thomas 49 (2) 339B
Thomas H. 25 (5) 234B
*Tilla 20 (1) 21A
Virginia 12 (5) 283A
Virginia 25 (6) 448A
Virginia 39 (6) 305B
Walter D. 11 (5) 241B
*Walter L. 39 (5) 241B
Wilhelmina 32 (2) 332A
*William 25 (5) 153A
*William 26 (2) 295B

JOHNSON (continued)
*William 32 (3) 478A
*William 36 (3) 503A
*William 40 (5) 282B
*William 69 (6) 413B
William 1 (3) 462A
William 11 (5) 209B
William 17 (2) 384A
William 19 (3) 411B
William 2 (6) 303B
William 35 (2) 380B
William 5 (3) 477B
William 5 (6) 452A
William 6 (3) 503A
William 7/12 (5) 199B
William 9 (5) 153A
William C. 17 (5) 178B
William E. 1 (5) 171B
William H. 38 (5) 148B
William Henry 27 (6) 309B
William J. 4/12 (4) 85A
William J. 19 (4) 85A
Willie 40 (3) 459B
Zacariah 42 (5) 171A
Zena 17 (4) 86A
JOHNSTON, Hester B. 35 (6) 293B
JOLLY, *George W. 39 (6) 437B
Joseph H. 15 (6) 437B
Joseph H. 15 (6) 437B
Louivina 26 (4) 95A
Nancy A. 33 (6) 437B
*Nicholas J. 32 (4) 95A
Daniel 4 (5) 170B
JONES, Adell 24 (3) 561A
*Alexander 38 (4) 95A
Alexander 7 (5) 147B
Alice 13 (5) 276A
Amanda 19 (5) 263B
Amelia 20 (1) 138A
Amelia 22 (5) 161B
Amelia Ann 40 (4) 19A
Andrew 1/12 (5) 197A
Andrew 21 (5) 197A
Andrew 7 (5) 158A

JONES (continued)
*Andrew D. 70 (5) 159A
Ann 60 (3) 484A
Ann M. 16 (6) 405A
Ann M. 48 (5) 197A
*Anna 30 (5) 203B
*Anna 80 (6) 405A
Anna 15 (5) 147B
Anna 15 (5) 276A
Anna 24 (5) 232A
Anna 27 (1) 4A
Anna 43 (1) 47A
Anna 60 (5) 148B
Anna M. 28 (5) 158A
Ardella 9 (5) 159A
August 6 (1) 47A
Bell 35 (3) 474A
Benjamin 1/52 (2) 339A
Benjamin 18 (3) 503B
Caroline 20 (5) 139A
Caroline 58 (5) 283A
Carrie 4 (6) 309B
*Catharine 43 (5) 170B
Catherine 4 (1) 4A
Catherine 45 (5) 147B
Cathirine 3 (6) 328B
Cecelia 15 (6) 405A
Cecelia 2 (5) 171A
Cecelia 24 (5) 170B
Cecelia 35 (5) 150B
Cecilia 36 (1) 138A
Charles 15 (5) 197A
Charles 16 (5) 170B
Charles 20 (3) 488A
Charles 20 (6) 405A
Charles 21 (5) 155A
Charles 6 (5) 217B
Charles H. 17 (5) 171A
Charlotte 22 (6) 309B
Codey 6 (5) 170B
Cornelius 12 (6) 411B
Daniel 17 (3) 523B
Daniel J. 13 (5) 171A
David 40 (5) 168B
Debby 21 (6) 295A
*Edward 28 (6) 449B

JONES (continued)
Edward 13 (1) 47A
Edward 13 (6) 405A
Edward 24 (3) 488A
Elenora 18 (5) 197A
*Eli 39 (3) 485B
Eliza 13 (4) 21A
Eliza 60 (5) 155A
Eliza 60 (5) 217B
Elizabaeth 40 (3) 424B
Elizabeth 1 (4) 95A
Elizabeth 25 (5) 139A
Elizabeth 4 (3) 485B
Elizabeth 40 (3) 424B
Elizebath 57 (3) 488A
Ella 31 (5) 276A
Ellen 29 (5) 168B
Emma 40 (3) 549A
Emma E. 22 (5) 171A
Frances 53 (5) 159A
*Francis 58 (3) 541B
Francis 11 (4) 19A
Francis 28 (4) 18A
Francis E. 22 (4) 83A
*George 42 (2) 339A
George 14 (3) 503B
George 15 (3) 485B
George 18 (3) 540B
George 3 (6) 310B
George 4 (5) 171B
George 7 (5) 197A
George A. 2 (5) 158A
Georgeanna 1 (1) 34B
*Hannah 60 (5) 276A
Harriet 12 (2) 339A
Harriet 9 (5) 158A
Harriet A. 12 (5) 197A
Harriett 26 (4) 111B
Hellen 26 (6) 477B
Henrietta 25 (2) 296A
Henry 15 (3) 543B
Henry 23 (3) 560A
*Henry 45 (6) 411B
Hesekiah 22 (5) 197A
Hester 40 (6) 405A
Isabella 25 (3) 506B

JONES (continued)
Isarel 22 (5) 171A
*Israel 50 (1) 47A
*James 25 (5) 253A
James 15 (2) 384B
James 24 (5) 139A
James 24 (5) 237A
James 26 (5) 171A
James 29 (5) 150B
James 35 (4) 94A
James H. 18 (5) 160B
*John 24 (6) 477B
*John 44 (1) 138A
John 16 (3) 503B
John 17 (1) 138A
John 2 (6) 477B
John 21 (3) 504B
John 22 (3) 561A
John 30 (3) 561A
John 8/12 (5) 237A
John 9 (5) 179B
*John W. 46 (4) 19A
Joseph 11 (2) 296A
Joseph J. 19 (5) 171A
Josephine 25 (6) 325A
Joshua 24 (5) 236B
Joshua 25 (5) 171A
*Joshua 50 (5) 169A
Julia 30 (3) 520A
Laura J. 19 (5) 197A
Lavina 17 (4) 18A
Lewis 14 (2) 329A
Lizzie 30 (3) 523A
Louisa 18 (6) 303B
Louisa 27 (3) 424B
Louisa 40 (5) 217B
*Louisa 45 (2) 384B
Louisa 50 (4) 103B
Lucinda 55 (3) 520A
Lucy 11 (3) 540B
Lucy 20 (3) 542A
*Lydia 28 (5) 145B
Madison 28 (2) 379A
Malissa 2 (6) 309B
Margaret 20 (5) 237A
Margaret 28 (5) 151A

JONES (continued)
*Margaret 30 (5) 170B
Margaret 40 (3) 541B
Maria 12 (3) 577B
Maria 19 (3) 561B
Maria 26 (1) 47A
Maria 28 (3) 520A
Maria 30 (4) 95A
Maria 40 (3) 540B
Martha 19 (5) 236B
Marty 33 (3) 485B
Mary 10 (1) 138A
Mary 10 (3) 474A
Mary 12 (5) 170B
Mary 12 (5) 179B
Mary 14 (3) 540B
Mary 18 (3) 439B
Mary 18 (3) 547B
Mary 20 (1) 24B
Mary 21 (1) 34B
Mary 27 (6) 364B
Mary 30 (5) 169B
Mary 37 (3) 543A
Mary 7 (3) 485B
Mary 9 (5) 237A
Mary A. 22 (6) 449B
Mary A. 24 (5) 171A
Mary C. 11 (5) 168B
Mary Cath. 13 (6) 347B
Mary E. 1 (5) 171A
Mary E. 22 (5) 171A
Nathaniel 30 (4) 94A
Nelley 9 (5) 147B
Nelson 14 (5) 139A
Orenia 5 (5) 159A
Phebe 37 (5) 286B
Phebe 58 (5) 286B
Rachel 35 (6) 411B
*Rachel A. 60 (5) 171A
Raul 13 (4) 9B
Rebecca 11 (6) 455A
Rebecca 5 (5) 197A
Rebecca 50 (5) 171B
Richard 14 (5) 170B
Richard 20 (2) 339A
Richard F. 33 (5) 158A

JONES (continued)
*Richard Sr. 67 (5) 171B
Robert 30 (6) 325A
*Roberts 45 (3) 424B
*Royston 35 (5) 169B
Sarah 36 (6) 431B
Sarah 39 (2) 339A
Sarah 45 (5) 159A
Sarah 50 (3) 503B
Sarah E. 38 (6) 405A
Sarah J. 2 (5) 256A
Sarah J. 40 (5) 169A
Sidney 13 (6) 386B
Stephen 12 (3) 485B
Susan 15 (5) 161A
*Susan 39 (5) 179B
Susan 46 (4) 108A
Susan 6 (5) 179B
Susanna 11 (2) 339A
Theresa 10 (3) 506B
Thomas 17 (6) 405A
Thomas 18 (5) 215A
Thomas 18 (5) 224A
Thomas 19 (4) 88B
Thomas 21 (3) 488A
*Thomas 26 (6) 309B
Thomas 42 (3) 523B
Thomas 5 (2) 339A
*Thomas 60 (3) 488A
Thomas H. 25 (5) 197A
Thomas H. 43 (6) 431B
*Thomas J. 56 (5) 197A
Walker 10 (3) 485B
Walter 10 (5) 171A
Wesley 23 (1) 47A
*William 27 (1) 4A
William 16 (3) 540B
William 20 (3) 506B
William 25 (3) 485B
William 26 (1) 34B
William 26 (3) 506B
*William 40 (6) 346B
William H. 16 (5) 169A
Zacariah 9/12 (5) 171A
JONSON, *George 40 (3) 524A
George 13 (3) 524A

JONSON (continued)
Julia 38 (3) 524A
Lizzie 11 (3) 524A
Maria 16 (3) 524A
William 8 (3) 524A
JORDAN, *Alexander 50 (5)
204B
Caroline 37 (5) 203B
Catherine 22 (5) 234B
Edward 53 (2) 378B
Estella 2 (5) 234B
*Ferdinand 46 (5) 203B
*Joshua D. 28 (5) 234B
Maria 16 (3) 508A
*Mary 50 (5) 204B
Samuel 21 (3) 544B
JOSHUA, Bradford 9 (3) 426A
Elizena 14 (3) 426A
Franklin 19 (3) 426A
Henrietta 40 (3) 426A
Jasper 11 (3) 426A
Lousia 18 (3) 426A
Sarah E. 16 (6) 291B
JOWES, *Cordelia 56 (5)
275B
Ida M 7 (5) 275B
Thomas L. 42 (5) 275B
JOYCE, Addey 5 (6) 446B
Ann M. 22 (6) 446B
Boardly 21 (6) 446B
Cadd 5 (6) 446B
Charley 14 (6) 446B
Ebbe 16 (6) 446B
Harriett 23 (6) 446B
*Harriett 50 (6) 446B
Jane 21 (6) 446B
John 21 (6) 446B
Kennedy 7 (6) 446B
*Martha 52 (6) 446B
Richard 17 (6) 446B
Tobe 20 (6) 446B
JUDKINS, Catharine 5/12 (2)
339A
Mary 22 (2) 339A
*Warwick 24 (2) 339A
JULEN, Caroline 20 (3) 454A

KANE, Ann 26 (3) 541B
*Charlotte 50 (3) 541B
Emmer 8 (6) 377B
Rachel 17 (1) 24B
William 21 (3) 541B
KATE, Ann 58 (6) 305B
Cornelia 25 (6) 305B
Isah 27 (6) 305B
John B. 4 (6) 305B
Mary E. 1 (6) 305B
KEELEY, Alice L. 5 (6)
342B
Amelia 25 (6) 342B
Caroline 3 (6) 342B
*Dennis 35 (6) 342B
Dennis V. 4/12 (6) 342B
Robert 8 (6) 342B
KEENE, Mary 14 (3) 577B
KEEYS, George 16 (5) 179B
KEITH, *Charles 51 (2) 340A
Daniel 19 (3) 517A
Daniel 60 (3) 517A
Elizabeth 49 (2) 340A
*Tabitha 58 (3) 517A
KELL, Amelia 26 (3) 544A
John 9/12 (3) 544A
Julius 3(3) 544A
*Vincent 38 (3) 544A
Vincent 5 (3) 544A
William 7 (3) 544A
KELLEY, Angeline 25 (5)
274A
John A. 9 (5) 274A
Rose 16 (5) 126B
William 7 (5) 126B
*William H. 26 (5) 274A
KELLY, Elizebeth 24 (6)
413A
Hester Ellen 2 (6) 413A
John 6 (6) 413A
Joseph 29 (6) 413A
William 2/12 (6) 413A
KELSO, James 23 (5) 152B
Madora 19 (6) 451B
Maria 18 (6) 451B
Percilla 40 (6) 451B

KELSO (continued)
Samuel A. 10/12 (6) 451B
KELSON, Maria 18 (6) 352B
KENNARD, Caroline 22 (1)
60B
Dina 80 (5) 150B
KENNEDY, Arabell 29 (6)
476A
John 31 (1) 4A
*Levy 35 (6) 476A
Sarah A. 79 (6) 476A
KENT, *Ann M. 34 (5) 220B
Jacob 11 (5) 220B
John C. 14 (5) 220B
John C. 14 (5) 125B
Julia A. 10 (5) 220B
Martha A. 8 (5) 220B
Philip 6 (5) 220B
William H. 2 (5) 220B
KERNAN, Kate 38 (5) 197B
KERSENE, Alexander 4/12
(6) 324B
Joseph 3 (6) 324B
*Richard 37 (6) 324B
Virginia 35 (6) 324B
William H. 6 (6) 324B
KERTIS, Adaline 65 (4) 43B
KEY, Henrietta 19 (5) 162B
*Hiram 30 (5) 150A
Samuel 21 (5) 162B
Sarah 25 (5) 150A
Selden 23 (5) 162B
Susan 59 (5) 162B
KEYS, Abraham 6 (1) 46B
Elizabeth 46 (1) 46B
Elizabeth 8 (1) 46B
Ellen 15 (1) 46B
*James 51 (1) 46B
Robert 85 (1) 23B
KIER, Amelia 65 (3) 520B
KIMBLE, James 21 (6) 331A
KING, *Adam 51 (6) 453A
Adam S. 18 (6) 453A
Ann 35 (3) 592B
Anna 18 (5) 142B
Caesar 28 (5) 274B

KING (continued)
Elizebeth A. 34 (6) 411B
Emily 22 (5) 134B
Ephraim W. 16 (6) 453A
*George W. 38 (6) 411B
George W. 9 (6) 453A
Georgiana A. 39 (6) 453A
Henrietta 30 (3) 592B
Hester 35 (5) 148A
Hester 5/12 (5) 148A
Jemima 28 (2) 247B
Johana Ann 10 (6) 306A
John 5 (2) 247B
Joseph 13 (5) 162B
*Samuel 40 (5) 162B
Sarah J. 30 (5) 162B
St. James W. 3 (6) 453A
Thomas J. 5 (6) 453A
Wayman 14 (6) 306A
William 35 (5) 148A
William 52 (2) 247B
William H. 13 (6) 453A
KIRK, Lizzie 19 (3) 580B
Mary 1 (3) 580B
KIRTY, James 25 (5) 157A
KNOONS, Henry 30 (3) 560B
Henry 5 (3) 560B
Isaac 2 (3) 560B
Sarah 22 (3) 560B
KNOTT, Elizebeth 76 (6)
340A
KOBURN, Emma 21 (4) 102A
Joseph 20 (2) 329A
KRAM, Isabella 22 (3) 521B
Mary 6 (3) 521B
Sophia 4 (3) 521B
LaBARK, Charles 26 (5)
167B
LaBEAT, *Catharine 60 (5)
276B
LACEY, Edward 8 (6) 431B
Louisa 32 (6) 431B
Moses 35 (6) 431B
LACOMPT, Almira 19 (2)
377A
LACOUNT, Albert 5 (3) 520B

LACOUNT (continued)
Charlott 35 (6) 334A
Ellen 30 (3) 520B
George 28 (3) 506A
Maria 9 (3) 520B
Mary Franc 27 (6) 334A
Priscilla 11 (3) 520B
*Rightson 38 (6) 334A
Willie 7 (3) 520B
LaCOURT, Maria 30 (5) 151B
LAKE, Alexander 11 (3) 544A
Alice 4 (3) 544A
*Blaswell 50 (3) 544A
Henry 7 (3) 544A
James 20 (6) 366B
John 9 (3) 544A
Mary 39 (3) 544A
Phebe 1 (3) 544A
LAMBDIN, Sydia 56 (3) 507A
LAMBKINS, Henry 26 (3)
   560A
LAMBSON, Isaiah 19 (5)
   168A
John 16 (5) 168A
LAME, Sidney 22 (3) 452A
LAMPKINS, William N. 23
   (2) 225B
LANDEY, Alexander 7 (6)
   433B
Cornelia 35 (6) 433B
Josephine 9 (6) 433B
Samuel 3 (6) 433B
*Thomas 61 (6) 433B
Thomas 2 (6) 433B
LANE, James 34 (5) 144A
Sidney 18 (4) 94B
*Susan 65 (6) 433A
LANKFORD, Charles 8 (5)
   205A
Eliza 2 (5) 283A
*Freeborn 32 (5) 283A
Gilbert 18 (5) 205A
James E. 3 (5) 283A
John H. 16 (5) 205A
Lavenia 10/12 (5) 283A
Lier 6 (5) 205A

LANKFORD (continued)
Mary 30 (5) 283A
Mary 46 (5) 205A
Sarah E. 5 (5) 283A
LANKFRD, *George 48 (5)
   205A
LANMOTH, Cate 1 (4) 94B
*George W. 45 (4) 94B
Joseph 4 (4) 94B
Susan M. 33 (4) 94B
LANVIN, Emma 6 (3) 542A
George 2 (3) 542A
John 4 (3) 542A
Lydia 36 (3) 542A
Lydia 8 (3) 542A
*LARKINS, Lucy 70 (5) 171A
LATTIENORE, Adel 18 (2)
   382B
Emma 10 (2) 382B
Jane 39 (2) 382B
Mary L. 17 (2) 382B
Robert 40 (2) 382B
LAUDEN, *Elizabeth 37 (3)
   424B
LAUGHLIN, Mary 24 (6)
   318A
LAURENCE, John R. H. 1/12
   (4) 19A
LAURIS, Caroline 36 (6)
   321A
LAW, Angelina 16 (4) 112A
*Harriet A. 37 (4) 112A
LAWRENCE, Eliza 20 (4)
   19A
George 19 (3) 412A
Jane 45 (5) 131A
Joseph 22 (3) 412A
Martha 40 (3) 412A
Mary 63 (1) 54A
*William 46 (3) 412A
LAWS, Alonzo 4 (5) 257A
*Beverly 40 (5) 257A
Edward 1 (5) 257A
Lydia 38 (5) 257A
Margaret N. 6 (5) 527A
LAWSON, George 24 (5)

LAWSON (continued)
  155A
LAYTON, Eliza 10 (5) 168A
 James 35 (5) 168A
LEADER, Ann 31 (2) 384A
LEAKIN, Anna S. 40 (5) 276B
 Cornelius 40 (5) 276B
LEASON, Elizabeth 27 (4)
  86A
LEATHERBERY, Amanda 15
  (5) 138A
LeCOUNT, Sarah A 65 (5)
  161B
LEE, Adam 35 (5) 155B
 Agustus 17 (5) 157B
 Amelia 45 (3) 544B
 *Ann 28 (6) 310A
 *Ann 45 (3) 544B
 Ann 15 (6) 324A
 Ann 45 (3) 544B
 Ann L. 10 (5) 205A
 Anna 25 (5) 282B
 *Anna 36 (5) 205A
 Anna 39 (4) 84B
 Annie 26 (3) 558B
 Charles 10 (5) 158A
 *Charles 39 (6) 324B
 Charles 59 (6) 434B
 Charles H. 10 (6) 324B
 Charles H. 3 (4) 84B
 Clara 53 (6) 409B
 Dennis 40 (5) 170B
 Dennis Jr. 17 (5) 170B
 Eliza A. 52 (5) 159B
 Elizabeth 16 (3) 485B
 Elizabeth 23 (5) 159B
 Elizebath 66 (3) 525A
 Ella 4 (5) 286B
 *Fanny 19 (5) 152B
 Francis 40 (3) 476A
 *George 24 (3) 558B
 *George 30 (5) 282B
 George A. 3 (5) 170B
 Georgeanna 16 (5) 159B
 Grecy Ann 50 (6) 434B
 Harriett 12 (5) 222A

LEE (continued)
 Henrietta 34 (6) 324B
 Henrietta 54 (6) 362B
 *Henrietta 60 (5) 204B
 Henry 22 (2) 382B
 *Henry 40 (5) 158A
 Isaiah 36 (5) 286B
 Jacob 17 (6) 402B
 Jacob 29 (6) 362B
 James 30 (2) 377B
 Jane 40 (5) 157B
 Joanna 15 (6) 310A
 John H. 18 (6) 409B
 John R. 4 (5) 159B
 John T. 14 (4) 84B
 *Joseph 58 (6) 409B
 Joseph 30 (5) 159B
 Joseph 42 (5) 205A
 *Julia 42 (5) 148B
 Kate 38 (4) 106B
 Laura J. 7 (5) 205A
 Levi 10/12 (5) 166B
 *Levi 49 (4) 84B
 Martha A. 7 (5) 170B
 Mary 12 (6) 409B
 Mary 18 (5) 148B
 Mary 24 (2) 382B
 Mary 50 (5) 145B
 Mary 6 (5) 157B
 *Mary A. 30 (5) 170B
 Mary Ann 13 (6) 309B
 Mary Ann 8 (6) 310A
 Mary T. 2/12 (5) 159B
 Nancy 32 (5) 158A
 Rebecca 35 (6) 410A
 Sarah 14 (1) 91A
 Sarah F. 5 (5) 205A
 Sarah Jane 12 (6) 304B
 Sophia 22 (3) 569B
 Sophia 22 (6) 310A
 Susan 16 (6) 409B
 William 2 (5) 205B
 *William 36 (6) 410A
LEGREE, John 26 (5) 234A
 Joseph 6 (5) 234B
 *Mary 57 (5) 234A

LEGREE (continued)
Mary J. 30 (5) 234A
LEMMONS, *Anna 56 (6) 303B
George 8 (6) 304A
Hannah 34 (6) 303B
Lemertine 22 (6) 304A
Louisa 15 (6) 304A
Lydia 38 (6) 303B
Richard 9 (6) 304A
*Sallie 24 (6) 304A
William 6 (6) 304A
LEND, Charles 2 (3) 543B
*Henry 35 (3) 543B
Henry 6 (3) 543B
James 9 (3) 543B
John 4 (3) 543B
Mary 14 (3) 543B
Sophia 2/12 (3) 543B
Susan 37 (3) 543B
LENDER, Ann M. 26 (3) 545A
*James 44 (3) 545A
Perry 4/12 (3) 545A
LEVI, Matilda 70 (5) 158B
LEWEY, Eliza 51 (2) 339A
Henry 11 (2) 339A
*John 52 (2) 339A
John 32 (2) 339A
LEWIS, Alice 12 (6) 431B
Ann M. 7 (5) 276B
Anna 10 (6) 431B
*Casander 56 (6) 415B
Casander 16 (6) 415B
Charlotte A. 25 (4) 94B
*Eliza 46 (6) 431B
Eliza 13 (3) 422B
Eliza J. 45 (5) 276B
Ellen L. 12 (6) 362B
Frank 11 (5) 155A
George 22 (6) 431B
Harriet 24 (3) 422B
Jerry 5 (3) 505B
Jesse 17 (6) 362B
John 12 (3) 422B
John 47 (5) 276A

LEWIS (continued)
Joseph 15 (6) 431B
Joseph 29 (3) 505B
Laura 8 (6) 431B
Margaret 19 (3) 422B
Margaret 45 (3) 422B
Margaret 54 (2) 382B
Maria 30 (3) 505B
Maria 69 (6) 409A
Mary 2 (3) 505B
*Melvina 48 (2) 342B
Nancy 36 (6) 431B
Noah 26 (3) 486A
*Peter 50 (3) 522B
*Peter 50 (3) 422B
*Richard 69 (5) 136B
Sophia 30 (1) 78A
*Thomas L. 50 (2) 382B
William 8 (3) 505B
LIEF, Alice 10 (5) 167B
Henry 40 (5) 167B
Levin 8 (5) 167B
*Sarah 35 (5) 167B
LIGHT, Sarah 18 (4) 28B
LILLY, Anna Jane 13 (4) 6A
*John 32 (4) 6A
Matilda 30 (4) 6A
Samuel 3 (4) 6A
*LINCH, William 40 (4) 6A
LINDSAY, Carrie L. 4 (5) 148B
Cassander 36 (5) 148B
*Joseph 35 (5) 148B
Josephine 2 (5) 148B
LINSEY, Delila 13 (2) 306A
LIVELY, Brackston 17 (4) 112B
Eliza 55 (5) 148B
Gabarella 14 (4) 112B
James 50 (5) 148B
Laura J. 19 (4) 112B
Maria 36 (4) 112B
Mary 16 (4) 112B
Mary 16 (4) 14B
*Statia 35 (4) 112B
LIVERS, Nicholas 80 (5)

LIVERS (continued)
195B
LLOYD, Alexander 17 (2)
306A
Andrew 49 (6) 311B
Anna E. 9/12 (5) 161B
Daniel 13 (2) 306A
Elizabeth 39 (2) 389A
John 8 (2) 306A
Joseph 21 (2) 306A
*Mary E. 21 (5) 161B
Samuel 12 (2) 306A
*William E. 55 (2) 306A
William H. 3 (5) 161B
LOANE, *Ann 77 (6) 435A
Maria A. 27 (6) 435A
Oliver 19 (6) 434A
Oscar 13 (6) 435A
Sarah 50 (6) 435A
LOCKERMAN, Daniel 51 (5)
169A
Joseph 13 (5) 133A
Mary 3 (5) 169A
Mary 51 (5) 169A
LOCKET, Ellen 40 (1) 65A
LOCKETT, Ellen 38 (6) 12A
Ellen 38 (6) 312A
William 71 (6) 312A
LOCKS, Georgeana 20 (3)
426B
John 22 (3) 426B
*John W. 52 (3) 426B
Joseph 18 (3) 426B
Josephine 22 (5) 204A
Margaret 10 (5) 283A
*Margaret 40 (5) 283A
Mary 52 (3) 426B
Samuel 45 (3) 426B
Theodore 16 (3) 426B
LODGE, Eda 82 (2) 335B
*Moses 84 (2) 335B
LONG, Charles 22 (3) 563B
Charlotta 45 (5) 120A
Charlotte 61 (6) 308B
Ellen 19 (4) 29A
*George 40 (5) 146B

LONG (continued)
Grace 29 (5) 146B
Hester 26 (5) 194B
Hester 7 (5) 146B
John H. 5 (5) 146B
Julia 20 (3) 569B
Julia 40 (3) 543A
Louisa 19 (3) 543A
Margaret 10 (5) 146B
Susan J. 11 (5) 146B
William 2 (5) 146B
LOOKS, Margarett 23 (6)
438A
*Samuel 24 (6) 438A
LOUDEN, Levi 55 (2) 336A
LOUDIN, Margaret 25 (3)
423A
Nancy 2 (3) 423A
LOUDON, *Letitia 25 (5)
264B
Laura V. 5 (5) 264B
Mary E. 1 (5) 264B
LOUIS, James 11 (2) 339B
LOUMOIN, Louisa 84 (3)
519A
LOVEDAY, Charlotte 14 (5)
158A
Elizabeth 17 (5) 158A
Elizabeth 50 (5) 158A
Henry 8 (5) 158A
*Henry 56 (5) 158A
Richard 11 (5) 158A
LOVELY, Bellfee 6 (5) 198A
Charles 12 (5) 198A
Jacob 4 (5) 198A
Louisa 34 (5) 198A
LOVING, Anna 20 (2) 388A
LOWDEN, Levi 27 (4) 18B
LOWE, *Elizabeth 30 (5)
156B
Ella 12 (5) 156B
Emily 60 (5) 156B
Hellen 30 (5) 156B
Jackson 9 (5) 156B
Maria 28 (5) 156B
LOYD, Charles 3 (3) 472B

LOYD (continued)
Isabella 26 (3) 472B
LUCAS, *Dilworth 59 (6)
314B
John 21 (5) 147A
John 25 (6) 314B
Malinda 14 (6) 314B
Margaret 48 (6) 314B
Thomas 23 (6) 314B
LUCKET, Agusta 16 (5) 139A
Clara 28 (5) 139A
Joseph 13 (5) 139A
Letha 45 (5) 139A
Lewis 57 (5) 139A
Mary 18 (5) 139A
LUCKETT, Agusta 18 (5)
235B
LUKENS, Adeline 44 (3)
506B
*Isaac 50 (3) 506B
Mary 17 (3) 506B
LUNEBERRY, Annie 17 (3)
416B
Annie 20 (3) 414A
James 18 (3) 414A
Margaret 16 (3) 414A
Margaret 45 (3) 414A
*Robert 50 (3) 414A
LURDON, Silas 25 (5) 249A
LYLE, Jerry 15 (1) 30A
Terry 15 (1) 30A
LYLES, John * 67 (6) 306A
Sarah 56 (6) 306A
MACE, Joseph 15 (3) 525A
MACK, *Alfred 60 (5) 160B
Eliza Ann 24 (4) 88B
Mary 50 (5) 160B
*Nelson 25 (4) 88B
Washington 21 (6) 411B
MACKEY, Joseph 10 (3)
413B
Mary 7 (3) 413B
*Samuel 35 (3) 413B
MACKHENEY, Eliza 45 (3)
506A
*John 53 (3) 506A

MACKHENEY (continued)
John 23 (3) 506A
MACTIMORE, Ann M. 33 (5)
166A
Frances 8 (5) 166A
George 6 (5) 166A
John 48 (5) 165B
William H. 3 (5) 166A
MADDEN, Agness 2 (5) 155B
Agness 38 (5) 155B
Fanny 13 (5) 155B
*French 46 (5) 155B
Jacob 10 (6) 409A
Kate 8/12 (5) 155B
Margaret 36 (6) 409A
Mary L. 8 (6) 409A
Rebecca J. 22 (4) 6A
Samuel 3 (5) 155B
Sarah 9 (5) 155B
Victoria 6 (5) 155B
William 15 (5) 155B
MADDON, Adaline 10 (2)
379A
Elizabeth 12 (2) 379A
*Israel 35 (2) 379A
Mary 29 (2) 379A
Rebecca 3 (2) 379A
William H. 8 (2) 379A
MADDOX, *Carval 35 (6)
411B
Isabela 9 (5) 126B
Marcelis 40 (5) 258B
Mary 33 (6) 477B
Susannah 35 (6) 411B
MADORA, Julia A. 8 (2)
251A
MAJOR, Harriett 20 (4) 9B
MALERY, Joseph 21 (3)
485B
MANLE, Mannela 24 (6)
390B
MANN, *James H. 48 (5)
158A
Margaret A. 40 (5) 158A
MANNING, Emeline 50 (4)
13A

MANOKEY, Charles 50 (2)
  221B
 Elizabeth 14 (2) 221B
 Elizabeth 46 (2) 221B
MANOLDAN, Eliza, 25 (5)
  285A
 Merryman 24 (5) 285A
MARCH, James 21 (4) 18B
MARINE, Joseph 56 (5) 271A
 Laura J. 16 (5) 271A
 Mary 57 (6) 310B
 *Richard 55 (6) 310B
 Robert 18 (5) 271A
 Sophia 56 (6) 310B
 Tresa 47 (5) 271A
MARNIER, Martha 40 (3)
  459A
MARSHALL, William 30 (3)
  524B
MARTIN, *Alexander 30 (5)
  165B
 Alexander 10 (5) 165B
 Alice 3 (6) 465B
 Amelia 3 (5) 149B
 Ann 37 (6) 465B
 *Ann M. 66 (6) 413B
 Ann M. 17 (5) 264B
 Charley 4 (5) 165B
 Elizabeth 14 (5) 212B
 Ellen 33 (5) 149B
 Emma 1 (3) 487B
 *Greenbury 34 (5) 264B
 Hale 10/12 (6) 465B
 Hannah 9 (6) 465B
 Hannah 9 (6) 465B
 Harriett 19 (6) 305A
 Harriett 45 (5) 224B
 Jesse 27 (3) 487B
 John 18 (5) 152B
 John 30 (6) 465B
 John 30 (6) 465B
 John T. 4 (5) 149B
 Leah 40 (3) 496A
 *Louvenia 40 (4) 102B
 Luther 34 (5) 149B
 Martha 88 (6) 347B

MARTIN (continued)
 Mary 21 (3) 487B
 Mary 24 (6) 295B
 Mary 77 (4) 88B
 Mary J. 25 (5) 165B
 Matilda 36 (3) 511A
 *Murray 37 (3) 496A
 Nettie 7 (6) 465B
 Nettie 7 (6) 465B
 Percilla 19 (6) 449B
 Philip 27 (3) 560A
 *Rity 53 (3) 424B
 Sarah J. 35 (5) 264B
 Susan 24 (3) 602A
 Virginia 16 (3) 496A
 Whiloly 50 (5) 161A
 William 90 (6) 347B
 William G. 3/12 (5) 165B
MASON, Cornelius 5 (3) 563A
 Cornelius 50 (4) 109A
 Ellen J. 24 (4) 18A
 Emaline 35 (4) 24A
 Henry 15 (5) 236B
 *Jacob 27 (5) 253A
 Jacob 3 (3) 563A
 Jacob 36 (3) 563A
 Joseph 21 (4) 18A
 Martha 38 (3) 563A
 Martha 39 (5) 236B
 Robert 8 (3) 563A
 Susan 52 (5) 195A
 Susan 52 (5) 275A
 *Susan A. 45 (4) 18A
MATHEW, Thomas 35 (4)
  109A
MATHEWS, Anna 24 (5)
  170B
 Casandra 4 (5) 172B
 Catharine 38 (5) 158B
 *Dela 26 (1) 200A
 *Eliz 42 (6) 378B
 Elizabeth 31 (2) 380A
 Harriett 30 (6) 410B
 James 24 (5) 157A
 James 27 (6) 410B
 *John 40 (2) 380A

MATHEWS (continued)
John 21 (6) 457B
Joseph 13 (5) 172B
Julia 16 (1) 7B
Margaret 36 (1) 200A
Mary J. 33 (5) 172B
Reasin 17 (5) 126B
Robert 12 (5) 172B
Samuel 19 (6) 476A
Susan 25 (3) 543B
*Thomas 40 (5) 170B
Thomas 8 (5) 170B
*Thomas D. 48 (5) 172B
William 13 (5) 172B
William 33 (6) 395B
MATRON, Catharine 26 (4)
  27B
MAULSBY, Mary 21 (5) 171B
MAY, David J. 26 (2) 345A
MAYBRAY, Elizebeth 58 (6)
  413B
MAYDEN, *Eliza 23 (6) 402B
McARY, Eliza 24 (4) 19A
McCABE, Alice 29 (3) 516B
 Annie 9 (3) 516B
 Fannie 7 (3) 516B
 *Jefferson 45 (3) 516B
 Maggie 5 (3) 516B
McCOMAS, Isaac 25 (5) 236B
 Jane 26 (5) 236B
McCOY, Hester 40 (3) 486B
 James 10 (4) 24B
 James 11 (4) 84B
 James 50 (4) 30B
 John 16 (3) 487A
 John 53 (3) 486B
 Mary 21 (3) 486B
 Robert 10 (3) 487A
 Thomas 31 (2) 391B
 Virginia 25 (4) 30B
 William 17 (3) 487A
McDONALD, John T. 2 (5)
  168B
 Mary 30 (5) 168B
 *Richard 35 (5) 168B
McDOW, Ellen 56 (3) 547B

McDOWNEY, Jerry 25 (2)
  308A
McFARLAN, Edward 71 (3)
  423A
McGLACKLIN, *George 43
  (4) 95A
 Henrietta 25 (4) 95A
 John H. 11 (4) 95A
McKINE, Phoebe 18 (5) 271B
McLAUGHLIN, *David 28 (2)
  401A
 Hester A. 25 (2) 401A
McNAMARA, Mary L. 24 (2)
  340B
 Theopolis 35 (2) 340B
McTENNY, John 30 (4) 6A
MEARN, Roda 20 (3) 597A
MEDLEY, *John 30 (3) 503A
 Lavinia 24 (3) 503A
 Margaret 4 (3) 503A
 William 4/12 (3) 503A
MEISTER, Agness 15 (6)
  475B
 Katie 17 (6) 475B
 Mary 12 (6) 475B
 *Mary 41 (6) 475B
MENNIE, George 1 (3) 524B
 Lydia 5 (3) 524B
 Mary 30 (3) 524B
 Rebecca 3 (3) 524B
 Richard 35 (3) 524B
MERRILL, *John H. 30 (6)
  314A
 Violet Jane 30 (6) 314A
MERRITT, Amelia 72 (6)
  412A
 George 81 (5) 161B
 William 45 (5) 161B
MERRYMAN, George 25 (5)
  150B
 Hester 15 (6) 473A
 John 9 (6) 473A
 *John 39 (6) 473A
 Percilla 38 (6) 473A
 Percilla 5 (6) 473A
 Robert 1 (6) 473A

MERRYMAN (continued)
Virginia 14 (6) 473A
William 12 (6) 473A
MEYERS, Amelia 50 (5)
232B
Clara 9 (5) 150B
Cordelia 9 (2) 335A
Edward F. 22 (5) 150B
Emma 5 (5) 150B
Florence 4 (5) 232B
George 12 (2) 335A
Hannah 12 (5) 150B
Henrietta 60 (5) 136B
John 1 (5) 150B
*John 59 (5) 150B
Laura 18 (5) 232B
Mary J. 39 (5) 150B
Matilda 3 (5) 150B
MILBURN, Jane 28 (5) 126A
Louisa 38 (6) 295B
MILES, Alice 12 (2) 384A
Camilla 40 (3) 570B
MILK, Caroline 11 (2) 226A
MILLER, Adam 19 (3) 542A
Caroline 27 (5) 196B
Charlotta 2/12 (5) 196B
Edward 4 (3) 483B
Edward 4 (5) 196B
*Edward 37 (5) 196B
Eliza 48 (5) 167A
Elizabeth 22 (2) 303B
Elizebeth 27 (6) 476B
Ellen 20 (2) 251A
Ellen G. 2 (6) 476B
Florence 6 (3) 483B
George 26 (5) 167A
*George H. 28 (3) 483B
Georgiana 16 (6) 322A
Henrietta 17 (2) 251A
*Henry 53 (5) 167A
Henry M. (6) 476B
Isabella 10 (5) 196B
*James 56 (2) 303B
James 18 (2) 303B
Jane 49 (2) 303B
*John 26 (2) 251A

MILLER (continued)
John 20 (3) 542A
*John E. 35 (2) 222A
*John H. 28 (6) 476B
Julia 10 (2) 304A
Julia 23 (3) 547B
Leah 40 (6) 294A
Lizzie 15 (3) 528B
Lucinda A. 21 (6) 324A
Lucy 25 (2) 222A
Maria 15 (2) 303B
Marion 6 (5) 196B
Mary 2 (3) 483B
Mary 9 (5) 170A
Mary F. 24 (3) 483B
Rachel 18 (5) 167A
Rebecca 30 (5) 147B
Rebecca 7 (5) 170A
Sarah 60 (3) 423A
Sarah A. 14 (2) 222A
Susan 19 (3) 566B
Thomas 48 (5) 147B
Thos. 3 (2) 251A
Tracie 20 (3) 491A
Tricilla 24 (3) 491B
Walter 5 (5) 196B
MILLIGEN, Mary Ann 40 (4)
112B
*William 45 (4) 112B
MILLS, Ann 21 (3) 422A
*Annie 38 (3) 422A
Caroline 11 (2) 226A
Fannie 15 (2) 246A
Fanny 15 (2) 226A
George 32 (2) 226A
Harriett E. 22 (5) 205B
Henry 2 (3) 542B
Isaac 18 (2) 226A
John 23 (3) 422A
John T. 22 (2) 226A
Joseph H. 12 (2) 226A
Lizzie 2/12 (3) 542B
Mary 14 (1) 84A
Mary G. 18 (5) 128A
Mary G. 18 (5) 205B
Nancy 26 (3) 542B

MILLS (continued)
Robert 29 (2) 221B
Robert 30 (3) 542B
Sarah 12 (3) 422A
Sarah A. 41 (2) 226A
*Thomas 54 (2) 225B
MINGO, Frances 65 (6) 318A
James 75 (6) 318A
MINNEY, Anna M. 10 (6)
   453B
Julia A. F. 6 (6) 453B
Margarett A. 33 (6) 453B
*Maria 30 (6) 453B
MINRY, Mary 17 (3) 474A
MITCHEL, Ambrose 25 (4)
   88B
*Harriet 48 (5) 149A
Jane 30 (2) 251A
Joseph 29 (6) 476A
Lizzie 24 (1) 22A
Maria 9 (2) 269A
Martha 20 (4) 88B
Nancy 58 (6) 413B
Rachel 13 (6) 317A
Thomas J. 4 (6) 317A
*Thos. 32 (2) 251A
MITCHELL, Abraham 1 (2)
   269A
Alfred 10 (2) 269A
Amanda 30 (2) 269A
Elijah 2 (2) 269A
Elijah 82 (2) 269B
Elizabeth 30 (5) 274A
Harriet 30 (5) 168B
Jacob 51 (2) 223B
*James 70 (2) 223B
Jane 48 (3) 506B
*John 29 (5) 168B
John 7 (2) 269A
*John W. 34 (2) 269A
Maria 9 (2) 269A
Mary 18 (3) 506B
Mary 22 (4) 20A
Rachel 14 (3) 506B
Susan 65 (2) 223B
William 36 (2) 339A

MOALES, James 40 (5) 148B
MOHLICK, Abraham 23 (6)
   308B
MOLE, Maria 66 (3) 578A
MOMMENIER, Susan 30 (5)
   186B
MONDOWNEY, Martha 29 (5)
   236B
Peter 30 (5) 236A
Samuel T. 2 (5) 236B
Sophronia E. 2/12 (5) 236B
MONK, Margaret 30 (4) 103B
MONROE, Jane 35 (5) 167A
*John 50 (5) 167A
John J. 8 (5) 167A
MONTELL, Mary 35 (5) 203A
MONTGOMERY, Elizabeth
   19 (2) 344B
Sarah A. 51 (2) 344B
*William 28 (2) 344B
MOODY, Sarah 18 (3) 527A
MOON, Julia A. 17 (5) 194A
MOONEY, Ann M. 22 (5)
   179B
Mary L. 11/12 (5) 179B
*Richard 23 (5) 179B
Sarah 60 (5) 179B
William 56 (5) 179B
MOORE, Alexander 25 (2)
   251B
Allice 7 (6) 303B
*Anna 26 (1) 46A
Caroline 30 (3) 571A
Columbus 27 (2) 377B
*Daniel 27 (1) 46A
Dolly 34 (5) 158B
Elizabeth 22 (2) 251B
Ellen 7 (1) 47B
Emilie 44 (1) 47B
Frances 12 (5) 158B
Frederick 25 (2) 309A
Harriet 40 (5) 146A
James 38 (5) 146A
Jane 40 (6) 303A
*Johnny 38 (6) 303B
*Joseph 27 (5) 198A

MOORE (continued)
Joseph 4 (6) 303B
*Levi 45 (1) 47B
Levi Jr. 22 (1) 47B
Mary 15 (3) 542B
Mary 20 (6) 318B
Mary Jane 30 (6) 303B
Matilda 65 (2) 386B
*Murphy 38 (6) 303B
Nora 2 (6) 303B
Richard 30 (5) 158B
Sarah 2 (1) 46A
Sarah 24 (5) 198A
Stella 1/12 (6) 303B
Susan 21 (3) 579B
William H. 5/12 (6) 318B
MORATHIO, Anthony 25 (3)
   567A
MORE, Daniel T. 15 (2) 226A
Elizabeth A. 20 (2) 247B
Frederick 23 (2) 247B
MORELAND, Ann 37 (6)
   455B
Robert 13 (6) 455B
MORGAN, *Arch 47 (6) 435A
Archie 20 (6) 435A
Arietta 15 (6) 435A
Charles 11 (3) 523B
Charles 19 (6) 435A
Charlotte 17 (6) 435A
*Edward 48 (5) 234B
Edward 10 (5) 234B
Hannah 12 (6) 435A
Hannah 48 (6) 435A
Harriet 37 (5) 234B
Ida 2 (3) 523B
*James 60 (5) 172A
*James 40 (3) 523B
James 11 (5) 172A
James 7/12 (3) 523B
John 15 (5) 172A
Mary 45 (5) 172A
Millie 9 (3) 523B
Thomas 13 (5) 172A
Tobias 9 (6) 435A
MORRIS, Annie 52 (3) 520A

MORRIS (continued)
Arabella 46 (1) 133B
Catherine 20 (1) 133B
Charles 3 (3) 485B
Charlotta 23 (5) 148B
Chas. H. 7 (2) 330A
Columbus 5 (1) 133B
Ellen 15 (1) 133B
Emily 22 (5) 150A
*George 50 (1) 133B
George 13 (1) 133B
Henry 10 (1) 133B
*James 47 (2) 384A
*James 55 (5) 150A
*James 70 (3) 520A
James 8 (1) 133B
Jane 18 (3) 507A
Job 2 (1) 133B
John 3 (3) 540A
John 33 (3) 540A
*Joseph 60 (3) 472B
Julia 15 (3) 585A
Kate 12 (3) 491B
Lizzie 5 (3) 540A
Lucinda 54 (3) 472B
Margaret 17 (1) 133B
Maria 34 (3) 540A
Maria 42 (5) 150A
Martha 4/12 (3) 540A
Mary 16 (3) 520A
Mary 41 (2) 384A
Mary 5 (3) 485B
Mary 5/12 (5) 149A
Mary 7 (3) 540A
Robert 9 (3) 540A
Theadore 39 (5) 148B
MORRISON, Charles 36 (6)
   415B
Charlotte 10 (6) 461A
Charlotte 10 (6) 461A
*Ephraim 59 (6) 461A
Harriet 20 (3) 475A
Rachel 20 (3) 563B
Treassa 39 (6) 461A
Treassa 4 (6) 461A
MORSE, Assa 29 (3) 424B

MORSE (continued)
*Joseph 29 (3) 424B
MORTON, Anna 48 (6) 476A
MOSES, Charles 14 (3) 487A
MOSS, Henrietta 2 (2) 257A
Mary E. 24 (2) 257A
MOYERS, Ellen 4/12 (2)
  383A
Mary A. 34 (2) 383A
Mary F. 13 (2) 383A
William 15 (2) 383A
MUFFER, Harry 2 (3) 478A
John 30 (3) 478A
Julia 6 (3) 478A
Mary 28 (3) 478A
MUNDOWNEY, *Edward 35
  (2) 379A
Edward 3 (2) 379A
Eliza A. 11 (2) 379A
Louisa 32 (2) 379A
Susan 9 (2) 379A
William H. 13 (2) 379A
MUNFORD, Minor 22 (5)
  157A
MURDOCK, Katie 3 (6) 454A
*Mary A. 27 (6) 454A
Sylvester 1 (6) 454A
MURRAY, Amelia 30 (5)
  154B
Ann 30 (5) 155A
Anna V. 4 (5) 204A
Daniel 20 (5) 169A
Eliza 55 (5) 169A
Eliza 60 (5) 144A
*George 81 (5) 169A
George 33 (5) 154B
George S. 26 (5) 274A
Hannah 63 (5) 219A
Hester 43 (5) 274A
Laura V. 6 (5) 204A
Mary 35 (5) 204A
Mary E. 20 (2) 377B
Norah 11 (5) 219A
*Robert 70 (5) 219A
*Samuel 60 (5) 144A
Sarah 27 (5) 186B

MURRAY (continued)
Stanley 55 (5) 274A
Thomas 30 (5) 186B
Vance 50 (5) 204A
*William H. 30 (5) 155A
MURRY, Abraham 5 (1) 4A
Ann E. 20 (6) 421A
Ann M. 60 (6) 451A
Caroline 29 (1) 4A
Eliza A. 4 (6) 343A
Estella 5/12 (6) 343A
George W. 16 (6) 343A
James E. 12 (6) 343A
James O. 1 (6) 451A
John H. 9 (6) 343A
Julia 43 (6) 343A
Levin L. 21 (6) 451A
Louisa 20 (3) 506A
Mary E. 7 (6) 343A
Robert H. 26 (6) 451A
Samuel 33 (1) 4A
Sarah 50 (6) 413A
Sarah J. 21 (6) 451A
Susan 30 (6) 413A
Susan A. 2 (6) 413A
*Thomas 49 (6) 343A
William 30 (3) 506A
William H. 28 (6) 413A
MYER, Hester 50 (5) 194B
MYERS, Alfred 35 (5) 159B
Ann K. 2 (6) 434B
Benjamin 19 (6) 306A
Charlotte 40 (3) 505A
Daniel 31 (2) 295B
Elizabeth A. 17 (5) 159B
*George 36 (3) 520B
George 7 (5) 172A
Henrietta 30 (5) 212A
Henrietta 55 (6) 434B
Hester 35 (5) 197A
Isaac 46 (6) 449A
Isaac G. 3 (3) 520B
Jacob 30 (5) 212A
James 10 (5) 172A
John 40 (5) 150B
John 40 (6) 434B

MYERS (continued)
Josephine 31 (3) 520B
Maria 1 (3) 520B
Olivia 27 (2) 295B
Philip S. 20 (5) 171B
*Richard 40 (5) 197A
Richard J. 20 (5) 197A
Robert 8 (2) 295B
Robert 8 (2) 295B
Sarah 5 (3) 520B
*Sarah A. 46 (5) 171B
Sarah E. 21 (5) 171B
Susan 24 (4) 107B
William H. 7 (5) 159B
William H. 22 (6) 434B
MYRES, Harry R. 2 (2) 296B
Mary 39 (2) 296A
NASH, Henna 16 (6) 292A
NAYLOR, *Ann 69 (5) 170A
Jane 27 (5) 170A
Joseph 20 (5) 170A
Joseph W. 36 (5) 170A
Sarah 14 (5) 170A
NEAL, *Anna 25 (5) 234B
Carter 6 (5) 234B
*Emma 24 (5) 234B
Joseph 30 (5) 234B
Mary 1 (5) 234B
Spicer 26 (5) 234B
NEALE, Katie 19 (6) 340B
NEDAB, Sarah 32 (4) 70A
NELSON, Catharine 53 (5) 170B
Henry 24 (2) 222A
*Mary L. 17 (6) 324A
Sarah 64 (3) 423A
Thomas 26 (6) 324A
NERBY, James 40 (1) 89A
NEVERT, Sophia 70 (2) 222A
NEWLUM, Maria 16 (6) 451B
NEWMAN, Catherine 60 (5) 232B
Charles 25 (6) 350B
Daniel 14 (6) 350B
Ellen 40 (3) 440A
Maria 28 (4) 18A

NEWMAN (continued)
Moses 22 (6) 350B
*Sarah 41 (6) 350B
Turner 30 (4) 18A
William 17 (5) 232B
NEWTON, Alexena 37 (1) 80B
Balzell 2 (1) 80B
Georgeanna 7 (1) 80B
Horace 10 (1) 80B
Horace 10 (1) 80B
Jasper 28 (1) 80B
John 14 (1) 80B
*Julia 32 (5) 148B
Margaret 8 (1) 80B
Matilda 3 (1) 80B
William 17 (1) 80B
NICHOL, John 14 (3) 539A
NICHOLIS, Amanda 11 (3) 543A
*Isaaac 40 (3) 543A
Isaac 8 (3) 543A
Joseph 5 (3) 543A
NICHOLS, Alice 6 (5) 149B
Alphonses 14 (6) 475A
*Ann 42 (6) 415B
Ann 58 (3) 476A
*Austin 45 (5) 264A
Carrie 2 (5) 203B
Charlott 19 (6) 475A
Charlott L. 19 (6) 409A
Delia 35 (3) 508B
Delia 35 (3) 508B
Eliza 39 (6) 475A
Eliza Jane 39 (6) 409A
Elizabaeth 33 (5) 203B
Elizabeth 33 (5) 203B
Georgeanna 39 (5) 264A
Georgeanna 4 (5) 264A
Harriet 22 (2) 389A
Harriett 35 (6) 412A
Henrietta 34 (5) 149B
Hester J. 4 (6) 409A
Ida 3/12 (5) 203B
James 19 (6) 433A
James 3 (5) 149B

NICHOLS (continued)
James A. 16 (6) 409A
*John 45 (6) 412A
John 24 (3) 524A
John H. 20 (5) 264A
Julia 23 (6) 475A
Julia J. 22 (6) 409A
Laura 1 (3) 524A
Lavenia 6 (6) 433B
Levin 37 (5) 149B
Lillie 18 (3) 439B
Malvenia 21 (6) 475A
Malvina 20 (6) 409A
Margaret 18 (5) 264A
Mary 21 (3) 524A
Rosa 10 (5) 203B
*Samuel 47 (6) 409A
*Samuel 49 (6) 475A
Samuel 17 (6) 409A
Samuel 18 (6) 475A
Sarah 1 (5) 149B
Sarah E. 9/12 (6) 409A
*William 35 (5) 203B
NICHOLSON, Archabald 12
    (6) 413A
Archibald 87 (6) 70A
Elizebeth 31 (6) 413A
Harriett 68 (6) 470A
Harriett F. 13 (6) 470A
Katie 4 (6) 413A
Samuel 6 (6) 413A
William H. 16 (6) 413A
NICOLS, Ann M. 28 (5) 236A
Annie G. 2 (5) 236A
Charles H. 6 (5) 236A
Hariet 50 (4) 106A
Issabelle 4 (4) 19A
*John W. 60 (4) 106A
*Joseph 30 (5) 236A
Mary 17 (4) 97A
Rachael 45 (4) 19A
Rachael 5/12 (4) 19A
Ruth R 9 (5) 236A
NICOLSON, Caroline 30 (4)
    2A
Charles A. 7 (4) 2A

NICOLSON (continued)
Thomas 11 (4) 2A
*William 35 (5) 264B
NITSON, Jane 30 (3) 475B
NIXON, Charity 50 (5) 186B
NOBLE, Harriet 50 (5) 274A
*John 50 (5) 274A
NOEL, John 88 (3) 519A
NORRIS, Augusta 48 (6) 465A
Augusta 48 (6) 465A
Eliza 49 (5) 160B
Henrietta 20 (4) 48A
*Hester 24 (5) 146A
*John 30 (4) 48A
*John T. 47 (6) 465A
Joseph 23 (6) 465A
Joseph 23 (6) 465A
NOYES, Ellen 19 (3) 582B
NUMAN, Hannah 50 (3) 501A
John 15 (3) 501A
NUTTER, Dennis 35 (5) 148A
Jane 82 (5) 148A
OAKS, Harriett 82 (6) 447A
OFLEY , Charles * 28 (3)
    422B
Ann 29 (3) 422B
Isabella 2 (3) 422B
Martha 9 (3) 422B
OLDHAM, Annett 17 (5) 212A
Caroline 11 (5) 212A
*Lucrecia 40 (5) 212A
Lydia 8 (5) 212A
Victoria 14 (5) 212A
William 20 (5) 212A
—OLIVER, *Alfred 30 (2) 339B
Gennetta 10 (5) 248B
Hester 28 (2) 339B
Mary L. 25 (5) 204B
OREM, Margaret 31 (3) 572A
ORVENS, Harry 7/12 (6)
    350B
OSBORN, Julia 50 (5) 170B
Lydia 39 (5) 143A
OSBORNE, Cordelia 22 (3)
    544B
OSTER, Hannah 52 (6) 455A

OWENS, Allexander 30 (6) 350B
Ann M. 41 (6) 413B
Francis 30 (6) 352B
John C. 6 (6) 413B
*John H. 38 (6) 413B
OXFORD, George 35 (5) 166A
PACA, Harriet 15 (3) 547A
PACEY, Robert 22 (2) 378B
PACK, Henry 15 (2) 387A
Maria 38 (2) 387A
Martha 12 (2) 387A
Nathan 7 (2) 387A
Nathaniel 41 (2) 387A
PAFF, Sophia 20 (3) 473A
PAIN, Mary 47 (1) 177A
PAINE, Amelia E. 15 (5) 162B
Emma 15 (1) 51B
William H. 54 (5) 162B
PAINES, Joseph 46 (5) 146A
Josephine 19 (5) 146A
Lydia 38 (5) 146A
Mary E. 5 (5) 146A
PALMER, Annie 26 (3) 525A
Annie 7 (3) 525A
*Charles 41 (3) 496B
Charles 15 (3) 496B
George 35 (3) 525A
Henry 3 (3) 525A
Jane 9 (3) 525A
Julia 5 (3) 525A
Louisa 39 (3) 496B
Mary 11 (3) 525A
Virginia 26 (6) 306B
PARKER, Anna P 35 (4) 24B
Caroline 18 (5) 242A
*Charles 64 (2) 308A
Charles H. 22 (5) 197A
*Elizabeth 50 (5) 242A
Elizabeth 34 (2) 308A
*George 45 (2) 388A
George 23 (2) 388A
George H. 22 (5) 242A
James 4 (2) 386B
Jane 35 (2) 388A

PARKER (continued)
Jane 39 (2) 386B
John 24 (2) 339B
Julia 19 (2) 388A
Susan 28 (6) 346B
Virginia 16 (5) 283A
PARKS, Sarah 17 (3) 574A
PASAY, Harriet V. 25 (4) 71A
PATTERSON, Alexander 4 (6) 305B
Alfred 4 (3) 522A
*Benjamin 40 (6) 305B
Charles 21 (3) 414A
Daniel 21 (3) 562B
Darrius 23 (3) 414A
Elenora F. 36 (6) 357B
*Eliza 45 (3) 414A
Eliza 30 (6) 305B
Eliza 40 (5) 183A
Eliza 8 (3) 522A
Elizabeth 27 (3) 542A
Ellen 36 (3) 522A
Ellijah 10 (3) 414A
Ely 7 (3) 414A
Fannie 8 (2) 377B
Fannie 8 (2) 377B
Hannah 43 (6) 309A
Isaiah 9/12 (5) 160A
Isaih 14 (3) 414A
James 19 (3) 414A
Jerry 12 (3) 414A
John 6 (3) 522A
*John W. 49 (6) 357B
*Julia 24 (5) 206A
Lizzie 19 (3) 562B
Louise 46 (3) 542A
Mary 2 (3) 522A
Mary 3 (3) 414A
Mary E. 16 (2) 377B
Matilda 26 (5) 158A
Matilda 26 (5) 158A
Minnie 30 (6) 322A
Sarah 15 (3) 522A
Sarah E. 20 (6) 309A
Thomas 23 (5) 206A
Thomas 23 (6) 309A

PATTERSON (continued)
*William 46 (6) 309A
Willie 3/12 (3) 562B
PAYNE, Anna 21 (4) 27A
John 5 (4) 19B
Mary 30 (4) 19B
PEACOCK, Amelia 9 (6)
  338A
*Louisa 32 (6) 338A
PEAK, *John 45 (2) 379B
PEAL, John H. 7 (2) 379B
Louisa 35 (2) 379B
PEARCE, Charlott 19 (6)
  303B
PEDINGTON, Daniel 11 (3)
  559B
Daniel 38 (3) 559B
Emma 9 (3) 559B
Mary 7 (3) 559B
Susan 5 (3) 559B
Susie 37 (3) 559B
PEIRCE, Lewis A. 18 (2)
  219A
Mary L. 20 (2) 219A
PEN, Daniel 4 (6) 312A
George 7 (6) 312A
Hester A. 9 (6) 312A
Julia 25 (6) 312A
Martha Jane 13 (6) 312A
*William H. 42 (6) 312A
William H. 11 (6) 312A
PENBROOK, *Samuel 50 (5)
  194B
PENKENY, Thomas 16 (6)
  293B
PENN, Louiza 15 (5) 131A
PENNINGTON, Ann 25 (6)
  311B
Anna 12 (6) 453B
Anna 26 (6) 453B
*Elizabeth 44 (2) 222A
Ellen 37 (6) 453B
Geo. H. 9 (6) 453B
Harry 1 (6) 453B
Henry 8 (6) 311B
Hester 31 (6) 453B

PENNINGTON (continued)
Lavenia 18 (5) 204B
Mary V. 13 (6) 453B
Virginia 15 (6) 311B
PERKINS, Ann J. 8 (5) 178A
William 21 (3) 525A
PERRY, Alexander 5 (6)
  437B
*Ann Maria 39 (6) 437B
Eliza 26 (3) 561A
Elizebeth 35 (6) 449B
Frances 40 (3) 483B
Frances F. 29 (2) 383A
Griffin 4 (3) 484A
Harriet A. 42 (5) 133A
Joseph 37 (3) 483B
Lizzie 3 (3) 561A
*Major 49 (6) 449B
Mary A. 1/12 (6) 437B
*Ross 40 (5) 133A
William E. 15 (6) 437B
PETERS, Alverta 1 (5) 212A
Catharine 7 (5) 212A
Catherine 60 (3) 528A
Elizabeth 19 (5) 212A
Elizabeth 30 (5) 236B
Frances 7 (3) 542A
John 11 (3) 542A
Julia 30 (3) 542A
Louisa 8 (5) 212A
Mary 9 (3) 542A
Norman 13 (3) 542A
Rosetta 58 (5) 236B
Rosetta 58 95) 236B
PETERSON, James 21 (2)
  328A
PETTY, *Burr 50 (5) 235B
Elsie 50 (5) 235B
Mary J. 14 (5) 235B
PFEIFER, Annie 7 (3) 486A
PHILLIPS, Alice 6/12 (3)
  543B
Carrie 3 (3) 543B
*Charles 34 (6) 330B
Charles 7 (3) 543B
Eliza J. 23 (5) 147A

PHILLIPS (continued)
Eliza V. 2 (2) 344B
George 30 (3) 543B
Louisa 21 (5) 174B
*Loyd 49 (2) 344B
Margaret 2 (5) 147A
Margaret 32 (2) 344B
Morris 9 (3) 543B
Phebe 29 (3) 543B
Rachel 70 (3) 542A
Rachel M. 41 (6) 330B
*Rebecca 46 (2) 252A
*Richard 27 (5) 147A
William 5 (3) 543B
PIERCE, Abraham 4 (6) 342A
Elizebath 22 (3) 488A
George 1 (6) 342A
*John W. 42 (6) 342A
Lotta A. 8 (6) 342A
*Lucinda 40 (3) 488A
Lucinda 24 (3) 488A
Margaret 16 (3) 488A
Martha 20 (3) 488A
Mary Jane 40 (6) 342A
Rose Ann 39 (6) 342A
Thomas 60 (6) 342A
Thomas E. 12 (6) 342A
William 15 (6) 342A
William 15 (6) 342A
PINDEL, *Stephin 31 (1) 4A
PINDELL, Bell 30 (5) 226B
PINDER, Charles 24 (2) 295B
Phillis Ann 25 (2) 295B
PINKET, Alice 11 (5) 171A
Elenora 19 (2) 221B
Elizabeth 28 (5) 171A
John 56 (2) 328A
*Joseph 35 (5) 171A
Rachael 47 (2) 221B
Sally 21 (4) 9B
PINKETT, Amanda 21 (1) 3B
Anna 63 (1) 3B
Celia 19 (1) 3B
Cornelius 27 (1) 3B
Henriette 23 (1) 3B
Martha 20 (1) 3B

PINKETTE, Ellenora 4 (1)
3B
John 17 (1) 3B
Sarah 22 (1) 3B
PINKNEY, Clara A. 70 (2)
377B
Eliza A. 18 (2) 377B
Henrietta 25 (5) 147B
Henrietta 36 (2) 392B
Henry 35 (5) 172B
Isabell 80 (6) 476A
James W. 48 (5) 158B
Jarrett 55 (2) 377B
Jeremiah 35 (5) 147B
Martha 8 (5) 172B
Mary E. 45 (5) 158B
Miranda 26 (3) 563B
Rosa 30 (5) 172B
Samuel 25 (3) 563B
PINNION, Susan 83 (6) 470B
PINYARD, Margaret 61 (5)
151A
PIPER, Tina 42 (1) 2A
PLATO, Ann E 6/12 (6) 348A
John 30 (6) 348A
Mary E. 23 (6) 348A
Nancy 30 (6) 439A
PLUMELL, *Charles 40 (1)
157B
Rachal 38 (1) 157B
POLK, Louisa 50 (3) 585B
Martha 16 (3) 585B
*Moses 49 (5) 133A
POLTERAL, Emeline 20 (5)
127A
POOLE, Anna 17 (5) 125A
PORTER, Charlotta 8 (5)
206A
Harriet 32 (5) 206A
POSER, Eliza 28 (4) 24B
POTTER, Anna 20 (4) 101A
Anna 50 (4) 101A
Sarah 43 (4) 18A
POTTS, Caroline 39 (3) 520B
Edward 5 (3) 521A
Henry 7 (3) 520B

POTTS (continued)
William 3 (3) 521A
POWELL, Anna 28 (4) 20A
Elias 53 (2) 330A
Eliza 52 (2) 330A
James 24 (4) 19B
Joshua 75 (3) 543A
Susan 57 (5) 209B
PRATT, Buddy 4 (6) 433A
Caroline 17 (6) 306A
Christiana 20 (6) 306A
David 16 (6) 433A
David 32 (5) 156A
Elizabeth 24 (5) 178B
Emmer 6 (6) 433A
Estella 2 (5) 156A
*Harriet A. 42 (5) 169B
Hester 60 (4) 111B
Isaac 25 (5) 178B
Jane 58 (5) 156A
John 10 (5) 156A
John J. 22 (6) 306A
John W. 45 (5) 169B
Joseph 8 (5) 156A
Josephine 19 (6) 433A
Katie 11 (6) 433A
Kinsey B. 29 (5) 156A
*Margaret 50 (6) 306A
Mary 28 (5) 273B
Mary L. 1 (5) 178B
Sarah 26 (5) 156A
Sarah 41 (6) 433A
Sarah J. 16 (5) 169B
William H. 27 (6) 306A
PRESCO, Mary J 60 (5) 236A
PRESTON, Susannah 11 (5)
  232B
Susannah 12 (5) 233A
PRICE, *Charles H. 24 (5)
  145A
Frances 14 (5) 212A
James 18 (5) 212A
James 35 (5) 161A
Jane 40 (4) 17B
Kate 18 (4) 103A
*Lucy J. 33 (5) 212A

PRICE (continued)
Mary A. 35 (5) 161A
Mary E. 7 (5) 161A
Mary L. 16 (5) 212A
Robert L. 11 (5) 212A
Ruben M.D. 7 (5) 212A
Sarah 13 (4) 101A
PRICHARD, *Samuel 47 (3)
  580B
PRIMROSE, Alexander 13 (1)
  133B
Amelia 11 (1) 133B
Emiline 3 (1) 133B
Helen 45 (1) 133A
Henny 15 (1) 133B
Henrietta 8 (1) 133B
Nora 5 (1) 133B
Thomas 18 (1) 133B
Thomas 47 (1) 133A
Virginia 1 (1) 133B
William 22 (1) 133A
PRITCHARD, *Frisby 57 (6)
  448A
Hannah 84 (6) 309A
Howard 28 (6) 448A
John 23 (6) 342B
Mary C. 15 (6) 448A
Mary C. 54 (6) 448A
Octavio 18 (6) 448A
Virginia 30 (6) 342B
PROCTOR, Francis E. 31 (6)
  347B
*Robert B. J. 39 (6) 347B
Serenas 7 (6) 347B
Sol J. A. 13 (6) 347B
William E. L. 10 (6) 347B
PUCK, Julia 20 (6) 408B
PULGIN, Henry 23 (3) 525B
PULLEY, Anna 54 (5) 151B
Nathaniel 19 (5) 151B
PULTY, Mary 13 (5) 124A
PUMPEY, Luticia 45 (3)
  522B
PURKINS, Kate 24 (4) 88B
PURNEL, Josephine 19 (2)
  339B

PURNEL (continued)
Levin 22 (2) 339B
Maria 20 (3) 520B
Mary 42 (3) 520B
PURNELL, Amelia 19 (3)
  487B
Ella 6 (4) 95A
Fannie 4/12 (3) 487B
Harriet 1 (4) 95A
John 23 (3) 487B
Juliana 3/12 (2) 392B
Lizzie 30 (3) 507B
Louisa 47 (5) 128B
Margaret 30 (3) 569B
Mary C. 37 (4) 95A
Minta 30 (2) 392B
Sarah 16 (2) 392B
*Stephen 29 (2) 392B
*William 28 (4) 95A
PURNUM, William 24 (3)
  506B
PURVIANCE, Charles H. 21
  (6) 367B
Charlott 6 (6) 367B
Eliza 30 (5) 166A
Eliza J. 11 (6) 367B
Francis 42 (6) 367B
John W. 8 (6) 367B
*Joseph 48 (6) 367B
Joseph 18 (6) 367B
Mahala 13 (6) 367B
Matilda 15 (6) 367B
Sarah E. 22 (6) 367B
Thomas 2 (6) 367B
QUEEN, Eliza A. 50 (6) 347B
*Emanuel 60 (6) 347B
Georganna 22 (5) 197A
John H. 17 (5) 197A
*Lavinia 23 (5) 197A
Mary 22 (1) 37B
Mary J. 47 (2) 330A
Moses 15 (5) 197A
Nancy 45 (5) 197A
Robert 12 (5) 197A
Walter 17 (2) 330A

RAINE, Elizabeth 49 (5)
  197B
RAINER, Eliza 32 (2) 389A
John 2 (2) 389A
Thomas 41 (2) 389A
Thomas 41 (2) 389A
RAKES, *Anna 43 (4) 85A
Harrison 16 (4) 85A
Martinique 17 (4) 85A
Mary 20 (4) 85A
William H. 1 (4) 85A
RALPH, *Ann 61 (2) 378B
Elizabeth 22 (2) 378B
George S. 3 (2) 378B
James M. 32 (2) 378B
Leonnard J. 8/12 (2) 378B
Nancy J. 12 (2) 378B
RAMSEY, Lucinda 70 (5)
  234A
RANSOM, *Mary E. 21 (5)
  167A
William H. 24 (5) 167A
Willie 1 (5) 167A
RAY, Emely J. 1 (5) 152B
Joseph 41 (6) 433A
Mary 3 (5) 152B
Sarah 35 (5) 152B
William 33 (5) 152B
READ, James 20 (5) 175A
Jerome 11 (5) 146B
John 40 (5) 175A
Louiza 15 (5) 146B
*Maria 58 (5) 175A
Nancy 18 (5) 175A
Nancy 32 (5) 175A
Rachel 7 (5) 126B
REASIN, George T. 25 (5)
  149A
Henry 2/12 (5) 153A
Henry 29 (5) 153A
Jane 17 (5) 121A
Margaret 24 (5) 153A
REDDING, Alice 6 (3) 525B
Annie 10 (3) 525B
Emma 23 (3) 525B

REDDING (continued)
 Hannah 60 (3) 525A
 Henry 18 (3) 525B
 Mary 25 (3) 525B
 Rachel 30 (3) 525A
 Solomon 8 (3) 525B
REDRICH, Ann 16 (6) 363B
REED, Carry 17 (4) 85A
 Elizebeth 19 (6) 409B
 Eva 40 (4) 85A
 George H. 13 (6) 409B
 James W. 6 (6) 409B
 *Joseph 50 (6) 409B
 Josephine 4 (6) 409B
 Leonard 13 (4) 85A
 Lewis 2 (6) 409B
 *Maria 27 (6) 409B
 Mary 19 (5) 170B
 Mary A. 40 (6) 409B
 Richard 22 (4) 18A
 Sarah 15 (4) 85A
REESE, Jacob 27 (2) 252A
 *John 29 (5) 235B
 Mary V. 24 (5) 235B
REIDER, Jesse 28 (3) 503B
REILEY, Harriett E. 78 (6)
 414A
RENDY, Clara 14 (1) 25B
RESIN, Mary C. 2 (5) 220A
 Mary M. 23 (5) 220A
 Thomas 7 (5) 220A
REVEL, Ann 19 (5) 252B
REYNOLDS, Richard 33 (5)
 222B
RICE, *Daniel 49 (5) 242B
 Eliza 59 (5) 236A
 Eliza A. 59 (6) 411B
 Lawson 15 (3) 440B
 Nancy 49 (5) 236B
 Richard 35 (5) 147A
RICH, Callie 15 (3) 490B
 William 35 (5) 219A
RICHARD, Addison 12 (3)
 562A
 Andrew 2 (3) 562A
 Catharine 36 (3) 562A

RICHARD (continued)
 Elizebath 28 (3) 505A
 George 11 (3) 505A
 Jacob 14 (3) 562A
 Julia 12 (3) 562A
 Laura 16 (3) 474A
 Laura 16 (3) 562A
 Lizzie 5 (3) 562A
 Margaret 7 (3) 562A
 *Thomas 60 (3) 505A
 William 17 (3) 505A
RICHARDS, Edward 23 (6)
 305B
 Mary Ellen 37 (6) 305B
RICHARDSON, Abarilla 30
 (3) 563B
 Alice 2 (3) 563B
 Ann 37 (6) 322A
 Anna 4 (4) 110B
 Betsy 45 (5) 203B
 Charles James H. 15 (6)
 474B
 Charlott 39 (6) 437B
 Daniel P. 11 (5) 203B
 Eliza 21 (4) 110B
 Emily J. 14 (6) 474B
 Francis A. 11 (4) 88B
 *George 45 (4) 88B
 George 5 (4) 88B
 Harriett 38 (6) 474B
 Harry 6 (3) 563B
 *Henry 30 (3) 563B
 *Henry 34 (4) 110B
 Isabelle 6 (6) 474B
 Isaih W. 4 (6) 325A
 *Jacob 40 (5) 207A
 Lavenia 16 (5) 203B
 *Lewis 53 (6) 437B
 Louvina 4/12 (4) 88B
 Margaret 30 (4) 88B
 Margaret 36 (6) 325A
 Mary 30 (6) 413A
 Mary 5 (5) 142A
 Rachel 4 (3) 563B
 Robert 38 (6) 413A
 Robert 8 (4) 88B

RICHARDSON (continued)
Rosetta 6 (5) 203B
Sarah 26 (5) 162B
Sarah E. 2 (6) 437B
Steven 28 (6) 324B
Susan 18 (5) 146A
*Sylvester 59 (6) 474B
Thomas 4/12 (6) 437B
Thomas 9 (3) 563B
Treassa J. 1 (6) 474B
Victor J. 19 (6) 474B
William 22 (5) 222B
RICHFIELD, Amelia 10 (3)
590B
Amelia 38 (3) 590B
Amelia 7 (3) 590B
Charles 19 (3) 590B
Columbus 17 (3) 590B
George 3 (3) 590B
George W. 23 (3) 590B
*Jacob 45 (3) 590B
Jacob B. 5 (3) 590B
John 5 (3) 590B
Julia 1 (3) 590B
Louisa 12 (3) 590B
Rachel 23 (3) 590B
Sarah 15 (3) 590B
William 8 (3) 590B
RIDGELEY, Ann J. 2 (5)
147A
Mary 24 (5) 147A
William H. 28 (5) 147A
William H. 6 (5) 147A
RIDGEWAY, Anna 88 (5)
205A
Emma 7 (5) 207A
George 17 (5) 207A
George 4 (5) 207A
Joseph 1 (5) 205B
Martha 35 (5) 148B
*Mary 39 (5) 207A
Matilda 56 (5) 151A
*Perry 70 (5) 151A
RIDGWAY, Henry 54 (2)
340B
Margaret 38 (2) 340B

RIGS, Henry 27 (3) 567A
RILEY, Alverta 2 (5) 258B
Caroline 16 (3) 521A
Charles 6/12 (5) 258B
Eliza J. 28 (5) 258B
Emanuel 38 (5) 258B
John 15 (3) 521A
Mary 17 (3) 521A
Mary G. 6 (5) 258B
Nancy 4 (5) 258B
Rachel 35 (3) 514B
RILEY, Rachel 40 (3) 521A
RINGOLD, Anna 6 (6) 458A
Elizebeth 10/12 (6) 458A
Harriett 33 (6) 458A
James 22 (5) 159B
Lewis 13 (6) 458A
Matilda 32 (4) 111A
Moses 40 (5) 170A
William 31 (3) 544A
RINGOLDS, Eliza J. 36 (5)
170A
ROACH, Amelia 19 (3) 544A
*John 56 (3) 544A
Margaret 50 (3) 544A
William 24 (3) 525A
ROANE, *Henry 40 (5) 221A
James 12 (5) 221A
Laura 4 (5) 221A
Priscilla 35 (5) 221A
Rose V. 7/12 (5) 221A
ROBBINS, Ellen 20 (3) 487A
Robert 37 (3) 487A
ROBERS, Fannie 1 (3) 560B
George 7 (3) 560B
Jesse 3 (3) 560B
Julia 36 (3) 560B
*Levin 37 (3) 560B
Levin 5 (3) 560B
ROBERT, Caty 4/12 (3) 422B
Mary 24 (3) 422B
Mary 3 (3) 422B
Orathio 24 (3) 422B
William 5 (3) 422B
ROBERTS, Alexander 12 (5)
274A

ROBERTS (continued)
Elizebeth 44 (6) 413B
Ida 4 (5) 156A
John 28 (3) 559A
John 30 (5) 210A
Louisa 33 (5) 274A
Mary 57 (2) 295B
Moses 20 (4) 22A
Phillip C. 8 (6) 413B
Priscilla 56 (3) 488A
*Robert 60 (3) 488A
Sarah 45 (5) 210A
Susan 32 (5) 156A
*William C. 52 (6) 413B
*William H. 39 (5) 156A
ROBIN, *John 34 (2) 339B
Leah 48 (2) 339B
ROBINS, Georgie 7 (3) 541B
Leah 38 (3) 541B
*William 37 (3) 541B
ROBINSON, Ann 50 (5) 146B
Ann 60 (5) 223B
Anna 13 (4) 112B
Archibald 1 (6) 470A
Arminta 50 (2) 380B
Beckey 11 (6) 447A
Benjamin 27 (6) 438A
Benjamin 9/12 (6) 438A
Benny 13 (6) 447A
Birty 14 (2) 340A
Catherine 27 (6) 451A
Cecelia 52 (6) 451A
Charles 23 (1) 132B
Charles 24 (6) 325A
Charles 37 (2) 401B
Clara 34 (5) 145B
Elizebeth A. 23 (6) 451A
Ellen 24 (5) 153B
Ellen 30 (6) 311A
Ellen 35 (5) 183B
Feeney 2 (6) 447A
Florida 19 (6) 447A
*Gabriel 50 (3) 542A
Gabriel 7 (3) 495B
George 10 (6) 325B
George 3 (3) 559B

ROBINSON (continued)
George 3 (6) 438A
George 7 (6) 311A
Georgianna 10 (2) 340A
Harriet 51 (6) 303A
Harriett 18 96) 451A
Harriett 23 (6) 447A
Harriett A. 18 (6) 325A
Henry 36 (6) 470A
Isaiah 1 (5) 153B
Isaiah 20 (6) 451A
*Jacob 39 (6) 447A
Jacob 6 (6) 447A
James 7 (5) 168A
James B. 13 (6) 325B
Jane 16 (3) 549B
Jane 25 (3) 525A
Jane 48 (3) 495B
Jeremiah A. 2 (6) 325B
*John 26 (1) 40A
John W. 23 (6) 325A
*Josephine 35 (5) 146B
Josephine 24 (6) 451A
*Julia 43 (6) 325A
Julia 60 (5) 248B
Julio 47 (6) 447A
Laura 21 (6) 451A
Leonard 18 (6) 451A
Louisa 17 (6) 303A
Louisa 2 (6) 470A
Louisa 21 (6) 470A
Lucy 47 (3) 542A
Malinda 23 (6) 438A
*Margaret 51 (4) 48A
Margaret 4 (6) 325B
Maria 5 (3) 559B
Mary 10 (3) 559A
Mary 18 (3) 495B
Mary 32 (5) 145A
Mary 36 (3) 559A
Mary 4 (5) 152A
Mollie 8 (3) 559B
Nathan 50 (5) 145A
Rebecca 4 (3) 495B
*Richard 23 (6) 451A
*Richard 60 (6) 451A

ROBINSON (continued)
Richard 25 (6) 451A
Richard 46 (6) 311A
Robert 6/12 (3) 495B
*Samuel 54 (3) 495B
Sarah 31 (6) 447A
Sophia 35 (2) 340A
Sophia A. 27 (6) 447A
*Thomas 24 (5) 145B
Thomas 8 (2) 340A
Tina 9 (3) 495B
Tommy 7/12 (6) 447A
Walker (3) 501A
*Washington 40 (3) 559A
*William 28 (5) 153B
William 20 (6) 447A
William 25 (5) 172A
William 41 (3) 525A
William 6 (2) 340A
*William H. 46 (6) 447A
William H. 5 (6) 438A
Zacharia 9 (2) 340A
ROCKSBERRY, Gordan 28 (5)
  248B
RODGERS, Andrew 10 (2)
  377B
 Edward 1 (2) 251B
 John 25 (2) 251B
 Louisa 25 (2) 251B
RODIN, Barbara 55 (5) 154A
RODNEY, May 18 (3) 509A
ROGERS, Andrew 25 (3) 504A
 Eliza 18 (6) 476A
ROLES, Ann 40 (2) 251B
 Charles 4 (2) 221B
 George E. 1/12 (2) 221B
 *James 39 (2) 251B
 James 5 (2) 386A
 Josephine 20 (2) 221B
 Josiah 26 (2) 339B
 Julia 29 (2) 340A
 Robert H. 5 (2) 251B
 *William H. 21 (2) 221B
ROLEY, Jane 60 (1) 57A
ROLLINS, Alexina 23 (1) 34B
 Alice 16 (5) 160B

ROLLINS (continued)
 Benjamin 30 (5) 160B
 *Edward 40 (5) 160B
 Ellen 21 (5) 160B
 *John 38 (2) 251A
 John 25 (1) 34B
 Laura 8 (5) 160B
 Sarah 10/12 (5) 160B
 Sarah 40 (5) 160B
 Sarah I. 35 (2) 251A
 William H. 4 (5) 160B
ROLLS, *Isaac 70 (1) 110B
 Lucretia 68 (1) 110B
ROOLS, Edward 28 (3) 414A
 Edward 28 (3) 414A
 Edward 5 (3) 414A
 Harriet 3 (3) 414A
 Jane 16 (3) 413B
 Kate 1 (3) 414A
 Laura E 12 (3) 413B
 Mary 14 (3) 413B
 Susan 38 (3) 413B
 Thomas 25 (3) 414A
 *William 50 (3) 413B
 William 7 (3) 413B
ROSCOME, Lucy 4 (3) 487B
ROSE, Hethe 40 (1) 56B
ROSS, Anna 35 (4) 28A
 Julia 2 (6) 437B
 Julia 48 (2) 400A
 *Robert 52 (2) 400A
ROTEN, Ann C. 1 (5) 206A
 Elizabeth 84 (5) 196B
 James 4 (5) 205B
 Joseph 25 (5) 206A
 Louisa 20 (5) 205B
 Oliver 2 (5) 206A
ROYER, Nancy 21 (3) 577B
RUFF, Alice A 7 (5) 235A
 Charles 36 (3) 591B
 Charles McC. 9 (5) 235A
 Georgeanna 26 (5) 235A
 Henry A. 5 (5) 235A
 John 4/12 (5) 235A
 *John W. 35 (5) 235A
 Mary A. E. 11 (5) 235A

RUFFIN, Emily F. 22 (4) 110A
William H. 27 (4) 110A
RUSE, *David 56 (3) 413B
Eliza 56 (3) 413B
Jacob 24 (3) 413B
RUSK, Elizabeth 56 (4) 112A
Charles J. 12 (6) 310A
Harriett 24 (6) 310A
Henry 10 (6) 310A
*James 53 (6) 310A
Martha 8 (6) 310A
Mary 7 (6) 310A
Robert 2 (6) 310A
Rose 3/12 (6) 310A
RUSS, Margaret 39 (3) 591B
RUSSEL, Charles 25 (5) 167A
Mary 33 (5) 167A
William 36 (3) 521A
SALES, *Aaron 29 (6) 438A
Aaron 3 (6) 438A
Charles 14 (5) 286A
Elenora 25 (5) 286A
*Elizabeth 48 (5) 286A
Emily 30 (6) 438A
Eugenia 5 (6) 438A
Isabella 16 (3) 488A
Joseph 12 (5) 286A
Lydia A. 15 (5) 286A
Sophia 2 (6) 438A
SALLERS, Emma 6 (3) 463A
Rebecca 31 (3) 463A
Sarah 26 (3) 463A
Willie 8 (3) 463A
SAMPSON, Catharine 30 (5) 152B
Charles 9 (5) 166A
Charles W. 15 (6) 449B
Charlotta 58 (5) 206A
*Christine 39 (6) 449A
Elizabeth 30 (3) 485B
Feeny 40 (3) 485B
Feeny 40 (3) 485B
*General 60 (5) 206A
James 22 (6) 449B
Jeremiah 1 (5) 152B

SAMPSON (continued)
Joseph 4 (6) 409B
Joseph 66 (6) 409B
Mary 2 (3) 485B
Mary 35 (5) 166A
Mary 65 (6) 304A
Mary 67 (6) 409B
Nathaniel 16 (5) 166A
Rosa 2 (5) 149A
Samuel 5 (3) 485B
Sarah 43 (5) 151A
William T. 21 (5) 151A
SANDER, Catherine H. 37 (6) 333A
William 47 (6) 333A
SANDERS, Ann M. 25 (6) 318A
Caroline 28 (3) 564A
Carrie 3 (5) 234B
Catherine 30 (5) 234B
*Daniel 34 (1) 40A
*Daniel 47 (5) 158B
Edward 23 (2) 409B
Eliza 40 (6) 413B
Elizabeth 1 (5) 234B
Ellen 17 (3) 521B
Emmer 17 (6) 413B
Emmer 17 (6) 413B
*George 35 (3) 521B
*George 35 (6) 318A
George 11 (6) 413B
George 2 (3) 576B
George 6 (3) 504A
George H. A. 6 (6) 318A
Grace 20 (5) 158B
Harry 5 (6) 357B
Henrietta 51 (5) 158B
Henry 49 (6) 357B
Isaac 3 (3) 562B
Isaiah 3 (6) 357B
James E. 8/12 (6) 357B
*John 40 (3) 504A
John 8 (3) 504A
Louisa 24 (3) 576B
Maria 38 (3) 504A
Marsha 19 (1) 74A

171

SANDERS (continued)
Mary 19 (6) 357B
Mary 37 (3) 521B
Mary 4 (3) 504A
Mary A. C. 4 (6) 318A
Nancy 68 (6) 449B
Robert 35 (5) 234B
Robert H. 1 (6) 318A
Sarah 35 (6) 357B
Wilhelmina 18 (6) 413B
*William 46 (6) 413B
William 15 (6) 413B
William 16 (4) 97A
William 4 (3) 576B
William 40 (3) 576B
William H. 17 (4) 94B
William H. 20 (6) 357B
SAPINGTON, Lizzie 15 (3)
    537B
SATCHEL, Alfred 17 (5)
    148A
Ann 30 (5) 148A
Douglas 9 (5) 148A
Fanny 12 (5) 148A
Ida 13 (5) 148A
James H. 18 (5) 148A
SATTERFIELD, Alfred 22 (5)
    283A
SAULTER, Joseph 23 (5)
    169B
*Julia 19 (5) 169B
SAUNDERS, Aresta 2 (5)
    168A
Cecelia 7 (5) 168A
*Charlotta 40 (5) 167B
Eliza 22 (5) 168A
Estella 2 (5) 168A
John 15 (5) 168A
John 45 (5) 168A
Martha 12 (5) 168A
Mary T. 2 (5) 253A
Sarah 19 (5) 168A
Theodore 24 (5) 212A
Theodore 5 (5) 168A
SAYERS, Jane 37 (6) 469A
Mary 35 (6) 469A

SAYERS (continued)
*Sophia 57 (6) 469A
SCHOLFIELD, James R. 21
    (2) 377B
Mary V. 6 (2) 377B
Rebecca 26 (2) 377B
SCOLBER, Irean 27 (6) 296B
SCOTT, Abraham 6 (1) 3A
Alice A. 13 (6) 412A
Amelia 18 (3) 564A
Ann M. 11 (6) 412A
Caroline 30 (1) 35B
Catherine 37 (6) 449B
Charles 14 (6) 310B
Elenora 12 (5) 137A
Elijah 12 (5) 234B
Elizebeth 60 (6) 413B
Ellen 35 (6) 310B
Ellen 56 (4) 84B
Emanuel 38 (1) 3A
Emily A. 21 (6) 306A
George 10 (5) 234B
George 52 (6) 310B
*Henrietta 42 (6) 437B
Henrietta 25 (6) 458A
Henrietta 27 (3) 505A
Henrietta 32 (1) 3A
*Henry 36 (3) 564A
Hester 33 (5) 205B
*Horace 55 (5) 205B
Isabella 1 (5) 204A
James 16 (6) 437B
James H. 10 (6) 412A
Jane 17 (4) 84B
Jane 19 (4) 88A
Jane 5 (3) 505A
*John 37 (6) 412A
*John 50 (6) 303A
John 10 (6) 437B
John 25 (2) 384A
John 45 (5) 234B
John R. 2 (6) 412A
Joseph 17 (6) 449B
Josephine 6 (6) 412A
Julia 19 (5) 205B
Julia 42 (5) 149A

SCOTT (continued)
Lewis 50 (6) 310A
Logan 19 (6) 437B
Louisa 12 (6) 437B
*Maditta 46 (1) 46A
Maria 30 (3) 585A
Maria 7 (3) 505A
Mary 40 (5) 234B
Mary A. 25 (4) 84B
Nancy 50 (6) 413A
*Nelly 26 (5) 204A
Philip 3 (3) 505A
Philip 32 (3) 505A
Phillip 31 (6) 458A
Rachel 51 (6) 309B
*Resin 64 (6) 458A
*Robert 52 (6) 309B
Robert John 14 (6) 309B
Samuel 13 (6) 310B
Sarah 9 (3) 505A
Sarah Ann 36 (6) 412A
Thomas 23 (3) 547A
Thomas 5 (6) 309B
SCROGGINS, George 56 (5)
    204B
*Mary J. 54 (5) 204B
SEAFERS, Ann R 37 (6) 309B
John 40 (6) 309B
Joseph J. 16 (6) 309B
SEAFUSE, Mary V. 10 (6)
    411A
SEAPHUS, Hugh J. 15 (5)
    286A
Solomon 39 (5) 286B
SEASON, Charles 7 (5) 154A
Elizabeth 30 (5) 154A
*William 28 (5) 154A
SEATON, Charlotte 21 (3)
    523B
Charlotte 28 (6) 297A
Eliza 46 (3) 523B
*Jacob 45 (3) 523B
Louisa 70 (3) 523B
William 13 (3) 523B
SECOMPT, Hester 30 (4) 8A
Rachael 28 (4) 8A

SECOMPT (continued)
*Rachael 60 (4) 8A
SEISTLE, Ellen 60 (3) 543A
*Thomas 60 (3) 543A
SEPHIS, Ann 26 (6) 364B
SERANO, Araba 40 (6) 399A
SEVENSON, Caroline 14 (4)
    8A
SEVOY, John 20 (5) 169A
Mary 14 (5) 169A
SEWERT, Eliza 38 (3) 506B
John T. 19 (3) 506B
SEYMOUR, Lewis 25 (5)
    154A
Lewis 26 (5) 144B
SHARE, Mary 26 (3) 475B
SHARP, Alizena 19 (4) 19A
Amelia 37 (3) 485A
Anna E. 8 (4) 19A
*Annie 50 (3) 478A
Charles 6 (3) 485A
Clara 11 (6) 324A
Elizabeth 40 (4) 19A
*Ellis 40 (3) 485A
Georgia 10 (3) 485A
*Henry 70 (2) 338A
Hester 56 (3) 478A
Julia 20 (3) 478A
*Laura 56 (2) 338A
Maria 4 (3) 485A
Mary 18 (4) 92B
Matild 15 (4) 19A
Samuel 14 (6) 324A
Sarah 40 (6) 324A
*William 34 (6) 324A
William 8 (3) 485A
SHARPER, *Lloyd 50 (5)
    219A
SHAW, Amanda 34 (6) 324B
Ann M. 13 (6) 324B
Emma J. 17 (6) 324B
SHAY, Bridget 42 (5) 153B
*James 50 (5) 153B
SHEAF, Agusta 38 (5) 156A
*Joseph 30 (5) 155B
Mary 15 (5) 274B

SHEAF (continued)
Mary E. 23 (5) 161B
William 26 (5) 161B
SHEPARD, Isabella 43 (6)
    413B
*Steven 45 (6) 413B
SHEPOTAN, Antonio 16 (6)
    338A
SHEPPARD, Harriet 20 (5)
    187A
*Jesse 47 (6) 312A
John A. 42 (5) 153B
Martha A. 7 (6) 312A
Susan 40 (5) 153B
SHERWOOD, Charles 20 (3)
    520B
*Lizzie 50 (3) 520B
Lizzie 17 (3) 520B
Mary 24 (6) 318A
Susan 30 (3) 507B
SHIELDS, Angeline 32 (6)
    408B
John F. 8 (6) 388B
John H. 13 (5) 171B
Malinda 8 (5) 175A
*Margaret 33 (5) 171B
Margaret 38 (5) 275B
Margaret A. 2 (5) 171B
Missouri 10 (5) 234A
Perry 90 (5) 234A
Thomas 40 (5) 171B
SHIELS, *Jacob H. 52 (5)
    264A
SHIELS, Susan 62 (5) 264A
SHIRNER, Ellen 13 (1) 34B
Frank 40 (1) 34B
Marcella 23 (1) 34B
SHORT, *Ann 39 (6) 477B
Sophia 5 (6) 477B
SIDES, Elizebeth 45 (6) 366B
Rachel 78 (6) 366B
*Zacharia 50 (6) 366B
SIFERS, William J. 30 (4)
    94A
SILVER, Catharine 36 (2)
    297A

SILVER (continued)
Catherine 28 (2) 384A
SIMMONS, Alice 5 (3) 560A
Amelia 17 (3) 559B
David 41 (3) 559B
George 12 (3) 559B
James 7 (3) 560A
Jane 47 (2) 295B
Julia 37 (3) 559B
Millie 14 (3) 559B
Peter 22 (4) 18A
Walter 10 (3) 560A
SIMMS, *Ann 35 (5) 151B
Eliza 31 (6) 395B
George 56 (6) 431B
Henry 2 (3) 487A
Jacob 28 (6) 434B
Laura 17 (5) 151B
*Lucinda 73 (6) 431B
Mary E. 25 (6) 431B
*Susan 27 (6) 434B
William 53 (5) 283A
SIMPSON, Ann 41 (5) 160B
Hebrew 14 (5) 265A
Hester 37 (3) 503A
Isaac 4 (3) 503A
Issaac 4 (3) 503A
Louisa 7 (3) 503A
Percilla 26 (6) 413A
William 16 (3) 503A
William 27 (6) 413A
William H. 42 (5) 160B
SINCLAIR, Mary 40 (5) 158B
SINGAL, Rachel 24 (6) 387A
SINGELTON, James 49 (2)
    379A
Sidney 39 (2) 379A
SKINNER, Adeline 42 (6)
    362A
Alverta 15 (5) 197B
Atha 35 (4) 94B
Atlass 29 (4) 18A
*Benjamin 30 (4) 94B
Grafton 16 (3) 487B
Henry 50 (4) 6A
Hesekiah 19 (3) 487B

SKINNER (continued)
Hope 65 (6) 326A
Isaac 17 (6) 362A
*James 51 (3) 487B
John 20 (5) 186B
Louisa 12 (5) 186B
Maria 20 (3) 510A
Mary 35 (5) 186B
Rebecca 40 (3) 487B
*Sarah 36 (5) 197B
Thomas E. 39 (5) 197B
*William 40 (6) 362A
SLATER, Harriet 19 (4) 44B
Mary C. 18 (4) 105A
SLAUGHTER, Nelly 75 (4)
  6B
Sarah 18 (3) 467B
SLOCUM, *John 47 (3) 486A
Mary 40 (3) 486A
Mary 40 (3) 486A
SMALL, Harriett 15 (1) 5B
SMALLWOOD, Alice 16 (5)
  212A
Cooper 42 (2) 306A
Elizabeth 8 (2) 306B
Henrietta 72 (2) 295B
Margaret 3/12 (2) 306B
Mary A. 10 (2) 306A
Mary E. 38 (2) 306A
Thomas H. 11 (2) 306A
SMART, Luke 29 (2) 389A
SMITH, Airey 6 (2) 383B
Alexander 46 (5) 156B
Alfred 9 (2) 383A
Alice 18 (5) 161B
Alice 19 (3) 558B
Amelia 24 (5) 149B
Ann 35 (5) 159B
Ann 50 (5) 145A
Ann M. 14 (4) 88B
Ann M. 29 (2) 222B
Anna 1 (5) 158A
Anna 17 (6) 473A
Caroline 20 (3) 488A
Caroline 27 (6) 433B
Caroline 28 (3) 563A

SMITH (continued)
Cassimere 12 (2) 282B
Catharine 70 (5) 154A
Catherine 25 (6) 309B
Cecelia 9 (5) 269B
Cecillia 45 (4) 48A
Charles 1 (3) 523B
Charles 12 (4) 48A
Charles 19 (6) 454A
Charles 32 (1) 47A
Charlotte 40 (2) 282B
Clara 5 (2) 336A
Clara V. 3/12 (5) 149B
Cornelius 26 (5) 158A
Cornelius 7 (5) 269B
Daniel 16 (6) 362B
Daniel 55 (5) 220B
*Daniel J. 30 (5) 204A
David 10 (6) 347A
Doctor 35 (5) 161B
Edward 26 (5) 172A
Edward 53 (4) 48A
Elenora 40 (6) 362B
*Elijah 39 (2) 336A
Eliza 15 (4) 65A
Eliza 34 (5) 269B
Eliza 55 (5) 183B
Eliza J. 18 (5) 166A
*Elizabeth 50 (5) 154A
Elizabeth 40 (5) 156B
Ellen 22 (5) 168A
Emily 23 (4) 40B
Emily 4 (5) 158A
Emma 1/12 (5) 150B
Emma V. 11 (5) 166B
Emmer 36 (6) 431B
Ezedore 3 (6) 309B
Frank 15 (2) 336A
Fredrick N. 23 (6) 362B
*George 23 (6) 470A
George 15 (4) 48A
George 8 (2) 282B
Georgeanna 5 (5) 269B
Grace 32 (5) 207A
Hammond 25 (6) 473A
Hannah 22 (5) 158A

SMITH (continued)
Hannah 24 (5) 178A
Hannah 54 (6) 473A
Harriet 30 (5) 166B
Harriet 66 (5) 168A
Harriet A. 2 (5) 149B
Harriet A. 21 (5) 166A
Harriet A. 7 (5) 166B
Hellen 4 (2) 383B
Henrietta 30 (5) 170A
Henrietta 38 (3) 525B
Henrietta 8 (3) 590B
*Henry 53 (6) 473A
Henry 12 (3) 524B
Henry 23 (6) 473A
Henry 25 (3) 523A
Henry 27 (6) 408A
Henry F. 10 (6) 362B
Hester 30 (1) 47A
Hester 37 (3) 590B
Hester 39 (2) 383A
*Hezekiah 52 (6) 362B
*Hinson 56 (6) 408A
Isaac 45 (6) 312A
Isabella 19 (5) 150B
Jacob 11 (2) 383A
*James 25 (6) 450B
*James 35 (4) 6B
*James 8 (5) 158A
James 21 (5) 161A
James 35 (5) 149B
James H. 19 (6) 362B
*Jane 70 (5) 159B
Jane 20 (3) 493B
Jenny 4 (2) 282B
Jerry 24 (3) 563A
Jerry 6 (3) 563A
*John 31 (2) 222B
*John 31 (3) 590B
*John 37 (3) 422B
*John 42 (2) 383A
John 13 (2) 383A
John 14 (3) 524B
John 14 (6) 347A
John 17 (6) 408A
John 19 (5) 150B

SMITH (continued)
John 20 (3) 521A
John 22 (3) 488A
John 22 (5) 149A
John 4 (3) 590B
John 6/12 (3) 422B
John W. 13 (6) 312A
*Joseph 66 (5) 156B
Joseph 10 (3) 422B
Josephine 14 (2) 222B
Josephine 24 (5) 166A
Josephine 5 (5) 166B
Julia 21 (5) 152B
Julia 22 (6) 368A
Julia 30 (4) 6B
Julia 58 (5) 156B
Kate 4 (3) 563A
Latha 24 (5) 170A
Laura 14 (5) 197A
Laura V. 14 (6) 362B
Lillie 3 (3) 543A
Lizzie 16 (3) 524B
Louisa 18 (5) 197A
Lydia 27 (6) 473A
Lydia 40 (6) 408A
Lydia 49 (6) 433A
Maria 4/12 (3) 543A
Marrietta 4 (5) 204A
*Martha 24 (5) 152B
Martha J. 11 (6) 312A
Mary 1 (3) 590B
Mary 14 (4) 88B
Mary 2 (6) 368A
Mary 20 (3) 543A
Mary 25 (6) 470A
Mary 26 (5) 168A
Mary 27 (2) 380A
Mary 31 (3) 422B
Mary 32 (3) 524B
Mary 36 (3) 485B
Mary 38 (3) 422B
Mary 50 (4) 88B
Mary 56 (4) 97A
Mary 61 (2) 391B
Mary A. 38 (5) 134B
Mary A. 5 (6) 450B

SMITH (continued)
Mary C. 29 (6) 473A
Mary E. 21 (4) 48A
Mary E. 24 (2) 386A
Mary Ellen 12 (6) 347A
Mary J. 30 (5) 197A
Mary L. 38 (6) 391A
Mathilda 45 (5) 264A
Mortimer 21 (6) 473A
*Nathan 55 (3) 525B
Nathan 25 (5) 161B
Nathan 26 (2) 380A
Nathaniel 31 (5) 166A
*Noah 50 (5) 197A
Percilla 26 (6) 435A
*Perry 37 (5) 269B
Philip 27 (5) 159B
Phillip 24 (6) 368A
Pinena 66 (3) 503B
Rachel A. 43 (6) 312A
*Rachel J. 40 (5) 161B
Richard 9/12 (2) 383B
Richard D. 4 (5) 166B
Robert H. 26 (5) 197B
Rosa 16 (5) 197A
Rose 17 (5) 143A
*Sarah 40 (6) 347A
Sarah 24 (6) 450B
Sarah 38 (2) 336A
Sarah A. 6 (6) 362B
Sarah J. 26 (5) 166A
*Solomon 40 (5) 145A
Sophia 24 (6) 362B
Susan 23 (3) 523B
Susan 25 (4) 109A
Susan 3 (3) 523B
Susan 6 (3) 590B
Tangy 38 (5) 168A
*Thomas 38 (3) 523B
*Thomas 38 (5) 207A
*Thomas 40 (5) 166B
Thomas 10 (5) 197A
Thomas 11 (3) 422B
Thomas 17 (2) 383A
Thomas 37 (6) 431B
Thomas 48 (3) 422B

SMITH (continued)
Warner 45 (3) 441A
Wesley 25 (5) 149A
William 12 (5) 197A
William 20 (6) 408A
William 23 (2) 306B
William 24 (3) 422B
William 33 (5) 148B
*William Francis 47 (6) 433A
William H. 13 (5) 154A
William H. 23 (6) 410B
William H. 27 (5) 166A
William H. 8/12 (6) 368A
William H. 9 (5) 166A
Willie 5 (3) 523B
Wilmina 23 (5) 204A
SMUTHERS, Eliza 32 (4) 102B
Martha 27 (4) 102B
SNOWDEN, Amanda 12 (6) 405A
Ann M. 24 (4) 84B
Caroline 43 (4) 84B
Charles 17 (3) 558B
Charles W. 4 (4) 84B
Emily 38 (3) 593B
Henry 12 (6) 405A
*John 40 (5) 160B
John H. 16 (4) 84B
Joseph H. 2/12 (4) 85A
*Mary 42 (6) 405A
Mary 21 (6) 405A
Mary 40 (5) 160B
Mary M. 15 (6) 405A
Rigby 19 (6) 405A
*Samuel 51 (4) 84B
Thomas 13 (6) 405A
SNOWDEN?, Maria 27 (3) 558B
SOIL, Charles 3 (5) 144A
Mary A. 14 (5) 144A
Mary J. 30 (5) 144A
SOLLERS, Sarah 31 (4) 116B
SOLOMON, Deliah 18 (3) 561A

SOLOMON (continued)
Elizabeth 15 (3) 561A
*John 49 (3) 561A
John 3 (3) 561A
Josephine 11 (3) 561A
Mary 5 (3) 561A
Ophelia 7 (3) 561A
Rose 37 (3) 561A
SOMERVILLE, *Barton 37 (3)
 485B
Lettice 39 (3) 485B
SOMERWELL, Charity 35 (3)
 467A
SOMEWELL, *Betsy 47 (3)
 505B
Lavinia 17 (3) 505B
Nellie 17 (3) 505B
SOMMERVILLE, Catharine
 20 (5) 283A
Eliza 12 (5) 209A
Eliza 40 (5) 209A
Elizabeth 1 (5) 209A
Emma 1 (5) 283B
Georgeana 4 (5) 283B
Isaac 40 (5) 209A
*James 40 (5) 283B
Joseph 6 (5) 209A
*Joseph 34 (5) 283A
Joseph 5/12 (5) 283A
Lincoln 10 (5) 209A
Margaret 9 (5) 283B
Rachael 26 (5) 283B
William 3 (5) 209A
SPARRAL, Martha 24 (3)
 487A
SPARROW, Ann L. 18 (5)
 286A
Anthony 13 (5) 286A
Cecelia 35 (5) 169B
Daniel 2 (5) 179A
Emily 28 (5) 179A
Grace A. 25 (5) 172B
*John 30 (5) 179A
*Mary 34 (5) 286A
Mary 6 (3) 422A
*William 65 (5) 169B

SPATE, Caroline 16 (4) 22B
SPENCE, Annie 4 (3) 524A
Annie 40 (3) 524A
Annie 48 (3) 524A
*Benjamin 50 (3) 524A
Benjamin 14 (3) 524A
John 10 (3) 524A
Julia 8 (3) 524A
Mary 6 (3) 524A
SPENCER, Annie 15 (3) 591A
Clara 4 (6) 311A
Elisa 39 (5) 150B
Elizebeth 22 (6) 311A
Emma 8 (6) 311A
*Frances 38 (3) 411B
Fredrick 19 (6) 311A
Henrietta 7 (5) 220A
John 16 (6) 311A
John 18 (6) 390B
*Joseph 55 (6) 311A
Martha 10 (6) 311A
Mary A. 45 (6) 311A
Perry 28 (5) 150B
*Phillip 50 (3) 591A
Susan 53 (3) 591A
Wayman 8/12 (6) 311A
Francis 10 (4) 84B
SPOKS, Anna 20 (1) 35B
SPREIGHT, Eliza 40 (6)
 306A
John 50 (6) 306A
SPRIGG, Daniel 11 (5) 167A
*Elizabeth 40 (5) 167A
Franklin 19 (5) 167A
SPRINCE, Mary 26 (3) 591A
Richard 30 (3) 591A
SPRUCE, Alverta 6 (5) 268A
Emma 23 (5) 268A
*Henry 26 (5) 268A
Henry 4 (5) 268A
Sarah 2 (5) 268A
SPURRIER, Gilbert 24 (5)
 166B
John 40 (5) 147B
Louisa 20 (5) 166B
Rebecca 35 (5) 147B

SPURRIER (continued)
William 13 (5) 147B
William 64 (5) 125B
SQUIRE, Elizebeth 6 (6)
314A
STANLEY, Abraham 28 (6)
325A
Amery 30 (5) 204A
Annie 4 (3) 485A
Annie 7 (3) 591B
Caroline 25 (3) 503A
*Charles 40 (3) 591B
*Charles 48 (5) 204A
Charles 2 (3) 485A
George 2 (3) 503A
George 2 (3) 591B
George 23 (4) 20A
Harriett 23 (6) 433A
*James 35 (3) 487B
Josiah 28 (3) 502B
Josiah 7 (6) 449A
Kate 18 (3) 569A
Kate 34 (3) 591B
Levi 21 (3) 487B
Lidia 25 (4) 20A
Lizzie 4 (3) 503A
Lizzie 5 (3) 591B
Margaret 26 (3) 487B
Margaret 36 (3) 485A
Marian 1 (3) 487B
Martha 30 (6) 449A
Mary A. 24 (6) 325A
Moses 39 (6) 433A
Nanacy 50 (6) 347A
Nancy 50 (6) 449B
Richard 10 (3) 591B
Robert 12 (3) 591B
Sarah J. 4 (6) 325A
Sarah L. 15 (6) 449A
Sedonia E. 1 (6) 433A
*Smart 39 (6) 449A
William 13 (6) 449B
William 40 (3) 485A
STANLY, Edward 29 (4) 18B
Eliza 18 (4) 40B
Francis 21 (1) 4A

STANLY (continued)
John 12 (4) 18B
Laura 24 (4) 18B
Martha 24 (4) 18B
Milly 51 (4) 18B
Moses 20 (4) 18B
William 51 (4) 18B
STANSBURY, Andrew 6 (5)
159B
Mary J. 31 (2) 378B
STANTON, Lizzie 27 (3)
528A
Robert 3 (3) 528A
*Samuel 29 (3) 528A
STARKS, Adeline 4 (4) 88B
*Samuel 29 (4) 88B
Samuel 29 (4) 88B
Susan 30 (4) 88B
Susan 30 (4) 88B
STEPHENS, *Alexander 46
(2) 348B
Alexander 23 (2) 348B
Emma 10/12 (2) 348B
Emma 34 (2) 348B
Gertrude 6 (2) 348B
John E. 25 (2) 348B
Louisa 18 (2) 348B
Rachel 5 (5) 148A
*Sina 50 (5) 148A
Thaddius 3 (2) 348B
Winfield 36 (5) 148A
STERRET, Barbara 35 (5)
133A
Mary E. 11/12 (5) 133A
*William H. 36 (5) 133A
STEVENS, Alfred 23 (3) 521B
Ann 50 (6) 295A
Caroline 16 (4) 6A
George W. 3 (4) 6A
*Hester 50 (4) 6A
Isaiah 22 (4) 6A
Issabella 25 (4) 44A
Josephine E. 19 (4) 6A
Perry 1 (4) 6A
STEVENSON, *Anna 19 (4)
95A

179

STEVENSON (continued)
Susan 40 (4) 95A
STEWARD, Ambrose G. 17
  (6) 367B
Henriett C. G. 18 (6) 367B
John W. 2 (6) 367B
Nancy 40 (6) 367B
Soloner C. 1 (6) 367B
*Theodore 18 (1) 46A
*William H. 39 (6) 367B
William L. 12 (6) 367B
STEWART, Adel 9 (5) 157A
Amanda 28 (5) 275A
*Amos 32 (6) 314B
Catharine 19 (5) 167B
Catherine 20 (5) 238A
Charles 20 (5) 159B
Charloltte 45 (2) 226A
Clara A. 4 (2) 306A
Clinton 11 (5) 157A
*David 40 (5) 157A
Elias 2 (5) 157A
Elisa 15 (5) 151B
Eliza 30 (2) 306A
Eliza A. 10/12 (5) 275A
Ellen A. 43 (5) 151B
Ellen S. 8 (5) 151B
Harrison 13 (5) 157A
*Henry 40 (5) 275A
Jacob 7 (3) 479A
James E. 12 (5) 275A
James W. 22 (5) 157A
*John 53 (5) 151B
Josephine 21 (5) 151B
Louis 5 (6) 314B
Louis A. 20 (4) 9B
Louisa 1 (5) 151B
Mary 7 (5) 157A
*Mary A. 36 (2) 401B
Mary A. 23 (6) 314B
Mary A. 42 (5) 157A
Samuel 46 (2) 226A
Willie 2 (6) 314B
STING, *Elizabeth A. 34 (5)
  236A
George 36 (5) 236A

STOKES, *Adeline 48 (5)
  166B
Adeline M. 18 (5) 167A
Alice 6 (3) 576B
Ann M. 33 (5) 172A
Annie 13 (3) 576B
Annie 17 (3) 591A
Daniel P. 21 (5) 167A
Edward 11 (3) 576B
Ella 10 (3) 576B
*Henry 30 (5) 172A
James W. 15 (5) 172A
*Maria 32 (3) 576B
Maria 8 (3) 576B
Mary 3 (3) 591A
William H. 4 (5) 172A
STOLETON, Henrietta 18 (5)
  197B
James 4/12 (5) 197B
STORK, Mary 11 (6) 441A
STOUT, Emory 53 (5) 169A
STRANISH, Elizabeth 1 (2)
  248A
Jane 30 (2) 248A
William 30 (2) 248A
STRAWBERY, Louisa 15 (4)
  40B
STRONG, Jacob 29 (6) 309B
Julia 27 (6) 309B
STUMP, James 15 (5) 161A
SULLIVAN, *Barney 54 (3)
  426A
Johanna 50 (5) 275A
John 14 (3) 426A
Mary 13 (3) 426A
*Michael 45 (5) 275A
Sarah 40 (3) 488A
Sarah C. 14 (5) 180A
SUMMERS, George 29 (3)
  472B
Mary B. 22 (6) 348A
Steven 47 (6) 348A
SUMMERVILL, Catherine 38
  (6) 346B
*John 33 (6) 346B
Mary F. 5/12 (6) 346B

SUMNERS, Christina 20 (3)
472B
Mary 7/12 (3) 472B
SUNNIS, Eliz 20 (6) 355A
SUTTON, Elizza 6/12 (6)
348A
Iseral 6 (5) 167B
*John 33 (5) 151B
Mary 50 (5) 167B
Phebee 30 (6) 348A
Richard 23 (6) 348A
SWANN, Arimenta 25 (5)
149A
Edward 23 (4) 98B
Hettie 54 (1) 3A
Thomas 2 (5) 149A
William 24 (5) 149A
SWORN, *Edward 30 (2) 306A
Harriet 5 (2) 306A
Hester 2 (2) 306A
Mary 38 (2) 306A
SYDNER, Jane 19 (4) 3B
SYKES, Jupiter 29 (5) 287A
TAILOR, Mary I 24 (4) 94A
TALBOT, Ann 66 (5) 158B
Julia 66 (6) 458A
TALBOTT, Hannah 33 (4) 1B
TARLTON, Hester 36 (4) 18B
TASCO, Agness 10 (4) 112B
Anna 4 (4) 112B
Ellen 35 (4) 112B
Emma 7 (4) 112B
*Frank 30 (4) 112B
Ida 1/12 (4) 112B
Mary 17 (4) 112B
Wilton 13 (4) 112B
TATE, Anna 9 (5) 204A
Emily 17 (5) 272B
Isabella 13 (4) 84B
*James 26 (5) 162B
James E. 7 (5) 204A
Joseph 5/12 (5) 162B
Laura 3 (5) 162B
Mary 26 (5) 162B
*Susan 24 (5) 204A
Zacariah 4 (5) 204A

TAYLOR, *Alford 50 (6) 452A
Alice 1 (3) 506B
Ambrose 20 (5) 168B
Ann 45 (6) 452A
Anna E. 25 (5) 161A
Anna M. 36 (6) 449B
Annie 6 (3) 506B
Charles 26 (3) 506B
Charles 30 (5) 159B
Charlotta 71 (5) 269B
Charlotta A. 21 (6) 452A
Ciscelia 41 (3) 542B
Clara 30 (5) 170B
Clifton 8 (6) 309A
David 22 (2) 303A
David L. 8 (5) 165B
*Edward 45 (6) 449B
Elias 35 (2) 378B
Eliza 45 (5) 168B
Eliza J. 6/12 (5) 168B
Elizabeth 36 (5) 165B
Elizebeth A. 21 (6) 452A
Emily 6 (5) 197B
Emma 6 (3) 542B
Emma J. 25 (5) 168B
Emory 20 (6) 449B
Frances 10 (4) 27B
Francis 22 (5) 170B
George 27 (2) 380A
George W. 60 (5) 166B
Henrietta 26 (5) 151A
Henrietta 60 (5) 220B
*Henry 38 (5) 148B
*Henry 40 (3) 542B
Henry 12 (3) 542B
Henry 7 (6) 292B
Henry 8 (3) 542B
Hester 50 (5) 264A
James H. 12 (5) 165B
*John 48 (5) 165B
John 10 (3) 542B
John 25 (5) 151A
John 25 (5) 161A
John 28 (6) 366A
John H. 3/12 (5) 161A
John W. 13 (5) 165B

TAYLOR (continued)
Lucy 19 (6) 292B
Marceline 11 (5) 197B
Margarett 15 (6) 449B
Martha T. 2 (5) 161A
Mary 4 (3) 542B
Mary 45 (4) 107B
Mary J. 10/12 (5) 198A
Minnie 30 (4) 11B
Nancy 27 (6) 366A
Rachael 56 (2) 303A
Rebecca 25 (3) 458B
Rebecca 25 (3) 458B
Rebecca 3 (3) 506B
Robert 6 (2) 380A
Robert L. 3 (5) 165B
Rosa 25 (2) 380A
Sarah 36 (5) 148B
Susan 27 (3) 506B
Susan 30 (5) 264A
Thadeus 17 (6) 452A
Thomas 65 (5) 159B
Thomas D. 9 (5) 197B
William 10 (6) 449B
William 18 (6) 449B
*William F. 40 (5) 197B
TEIGH, Anna 19 (4) 15A
TEMPLE, *William 34 (2)
  384B
 Zipora 24 (2) 384B
TENANT, Emily 26 (5) 218A
TENEY, George 19 (4) 93B
 John Henry 2 (4) 93B
 Theadore 7 (4) 93B
TENNANT, Addie 20 (2)
  329A
 Liddia 10 (2) 329A
*Robert 35 (2) 329A
TERRY, Jerry 21 (3) 504A
*John 46 (3) 426A
 John F. 9 (3) 426A
 Mary 30 (3) 426A
 Robert 12 (3) 426A
 William 7 (3) 426A
THOMAS, Abraham 4 (5)
  172A

THOMAS (continued)
*Adam 30 (3) 487B
 Adam 25 (3) 496B
 Alfred 13 (2) 335B
 Alverta 16 (6) 362A
 Amanda 39 (2) 335B
 Amanda M. 15 (4) 94B
 Ann 39 (3) 508B
 Ann 4 (3) 484A
 Ann M. 55 (5) 161B
 Anna 20 (1) 47A
 Annie 30 (3) 506B
 Bell 1 (3) 487B
*Benjamin 53 (5) 151A
 Casandria 30 (2) 382B
 Catharine 17 (5) 180A
 Catharine 2 (5) 172A
*Charles 36 (3) 484A
*Charles 66 (5) 172A
 Charles 6 (3) 484A
 Charles 7 (3) 484A
 Charles E. 17 (6) 324A
 Charlotte 8 (4) 94B
*Clara 5 (5) 148B
 Cornelius 3 (2) 382B
*David 37 (2) 335B
*David 40 (3) 484A
 David 32 (2) 382B
 Dawson 29 (2) 222B
 Delia 20 (3) 484A
 Eliza 31 (5) 167B
*Eliza 59 (2) 251A
 Eliza 24 (6) 362A
 Elizabeth 8 (3) 484A
 Elizabeth 39 (2) 299B
 Elizabeth 5/12 (2) 339A
 Fannie 26 (3) 562A
 Fanny 32 (5) 144A
 Francis 20 (1) 18A
 Francis 20 (3) 488A
 Francis 39 (6) 305A
 Francis V. 15 (6) 305A
 Fulton 1 (3) 560B
 George 23 (3) 506B
 George 3 (3) 560B
 George 30 (3) 562A

THOMAS (continued)
George 7 (3) 562A
*George W. 40 (6) 305A
*Georgeanna 28 (5) 161B
Georgeanna 22 (5) 148B
Georgianna 16 (2) 300A
Georgianna 16 (2) 335B
Harriet 60 (5) 161B
Harriett 18 (5) 179B
Henrieta 2 (5) 150B
Henrietta 40 (5) 172A
Henry 12 (5) 144A
*James 40 (5) 144A
James 17 (2) 297A
James 18 (2) 335B
James 48 (2) 336A
James 68 (1) 134A
James H. 25 (5) 161A
*Jane 16 (4) 88B
Jane 50 (1) 57B
Jane 50 (5) 161A
Jane 8 (3) 487B
Jennie 1 (3) 562A
John 13 (2) 335B
*John 30 (3) 414A
*John 54 (3) 559B
*John 65 (5) 255B
John 15 (2) 335B
John 35 (3) 525A
John 7 (5) 167B
John C. 15 (5) 151A
John W. 14 (5) 180A
Joseph 21 (6) 324A
Joseph 30 (3) 560B
Joseph 35 (2) 339A
Julia A. 2 (5) 167B
Levin 26 (2) 222B
Levin 40 (6) 362B
Lewis 14 (5) 144A
Lizzie 25 (3) 414A
*Lucretia 51 (3) 540B
Lucretia 20 (3) 540B
Lucy W. 7 (5) 161A
Maggie 17 (3) 548B
*Margaret 46 (2) 222B
Margret 63 (1) 134A

THOMAS (continued)
Maria 31 (3) 560B
Martha 19 (5) 161A
Martha 47 (1) 47A
Martha 5 (3) 560B
Martha 9 (5) 167B
*Mary 29 (5) 148B
Mary 16 (3) 507B
Mary 29 (3) 487B
Mary 52 (2) 296A
Mary 25 (3) 484A
Mary 26 (2) 296A
Mary 3 (3) 562A
Mary 4 (2) 335B
Mary 70 (3) 542B
Mary 70 (5) 255B
Mary 76 (3) 487B
Mary A. 2 (5) 148B
Mary E. 19 (2) 335B
Mary J. 1 (2) 382B
Mary J. 19 (2) 251A
Mary R. 10 (5) 269A
Melinda 19 (2) 339A
Norah 20 (3) 496B
Olivia 8/12 (2) 296A
Pricilla 17 (5) 154A
Rachael 9 (2) 335B
Rachel 28 (3) 542B
Rachel 50 (3) 489A
Rachiel 60 (3) 475A
Reuben 29 (5) 167B
Rosanna 19 (2) 344B
Rose 18 (1) 28B
Samuel 14 (5) 128A
Sarah 25 (4) 20A
Sarah 29 (3) 542B
Sarah 41 (3) 484A
Sarah 55 (5) 151A
Sarah E. 18 (4) 95A
Sarah M. 7 (5) 151A
Susan 40 (5) 179B
Susan 5 (3) 562A
Susan 8 (3) 560B
Tina 3 (5) 144A
Virginia 27 (5) 183B
*William 31 (3) 488A

THOMAS (continued)
William 14 (5) 151A
William 17 (5) 161A
William 23 (5) 179B
William 27 (3) 562A
William 28 (5) 148B
William 30 (5) 161B
William 39 (2) 340B
William 4 (3) 487B
William J. 36 (6) 362A
THOMPSON, Addie 19 (4)
  109A
Alfred 40 (3) 506A
Annie 21 (3) 490B
Augustene 30 (5) 167A
Balinda 19 (6) 410A
Catharine 29 (5) 171A
Catherine 22 (6) 310B
Catherine 7/12 (6) 310B
Charles 2 (5) 144A
Charles 30 (5) 204A
Charles 7 (5) 285B
Charles H. 26 (5) 170B
Charles W. 29 (6) 415B
Clara R. 4 (6) 435A
Daniel 22 (6) 310B
Edward 1 (5) 207A
Eli 33 (5) 167A
Elisa 20 (5) 150A
Eliza 14 (5) 139A
Eliza 56 (6) 435A
Emily 20 (2) 380B
Emma 11 (5) 148B
Emma 44 (3) 543A
Fannie 22 (2) 380A
George 19 (3) 543A
George 19 (5) 283B
George 25 (4) 6A
George 28 (6) 410A
Geozett 7 (3) 506A
Handy 8 (3) 506A
Harriet 24 (3) 503B
Harriet 30 (5) 285B
*Henry 30 (5) 207A
Howard 1 (5) 150B
Isaac 6 (3) 543A

THOMPSON (continued)
Isabella 25 (6) 379A
James 39 (5) 171A
James 60 (5) 198A
James F. 1 (6) 415B
Jane 29 (6) 350B
Jane 5 (5) 207A
*John 35 (3) 503B
*John 40 (6) 379A
John 1 (6) 350B
John 15 (3) 543A
John 17 (6) 310B
John 18 (5) 198A
John 26 (5) 150A
John 5 (5) 150A
John 63 (6) 465B
John 63 (6) 465B
Joseph 40 (6) 437B
*Joshua 59 (6) 435A
Julia 5 (5) 139A
*Laura 46 (5) 148B
Levenia 25 (6) 415B
Lizzie 39 (3) 567A
Louisa 12 (5) 285B
Loyd 20 (3) 545A
Lucinda 11 (6) 435A
Maria 16 (3) 506A
Mary 40 (3) 543A
Mary E. 3 (6) 415B
Mary E. 30 (5) 207A
Mary J. 8 (5) 275B
Melinda 35 (3) 506A
Nora H. 3/12 (5) 275B
*Perry 39 (5) 198A
Phelix 11 (3) 543A
Rachel 26 (5) 125B
Rachel A. 22 (6) 435A
Richard 19 (3) 545A
Rosa 4 (5) 275B
Samuel W. 6 (5) 275B
*Sarah 29 (5) 275B
Sophia 16 (4) 85B
Sophia 9 (3) 543A
Susan 37 (5) 198A
*Theodore 22 (2) 380A
Thomas H. 2 (5) 275B

THOMPSON (continued)
William 4 (5) 167A
William P. 33 (5) 275B
THORNTON, Edward 32 (2)
335A
Johanna 22 (5) 275A
THORP, Fanny 22 (6) 317B
THURLOW, Sarah 1/12 (3)
491B
TILGHMAN, A. 11 (1) 47A
Alexander 13 (1) 47A
Anna 26 (5) 132A
*Caroline 30 (5) 186B
Caroline 55 (4) 6A
*Eliza 45 (5) 167A
Eliza 40 (5) 275A
Emeline 4 (5) 149B
Emily 23 (5) 241B
Emily 40 (5) 236B
*Francis J. 51 (5) 161A
Frederick 35 (5) 275A
George W. 7 (5) 133A
Henry 47 (5) 186B
*Isaac 60 (4) 6A
Isabella 24 (5) 158B
Isabella 27 (5) 161A
*James 28 (5) 236B
James 1 (1) 47A
James 11 (5) 172B
*John 30 (5) 158B
Mary 4 (5) 186B
Mary F. 15 (5) 167A
*Michael 45 (5) 149B
Perry 7 (5) 186B
Sarah 3 (1) 47A
Tina 80 (5) 147B
William 47 (5) 167A
William H. 10 (5) 186B
TILTMAN, Harman 56 (2)
303A
Hester 27 (3) 412A
Mary 4 (3) 412A
Rebecca 2 (3) 412A
*Richard 55 (3) 412A
TINSON, Mary J. 19 (5) 147A
TIPPINS, Sarah 15 (4) 95A

TITUS, Isaac 6 (5) 146B
*James 50 (5) 146B
John 17 (5) 146B
Margaret 48 (5) 146B
TOADWIN, Ann 43 (5) 147A
Solomon 21 (5) 147A
TODD, Sarah 19 (1) 78B
TODVEN, Edward 25 (2)
319A
James H. 22 (2) 319A
TOHER, Cecelia 42 (6) 450A
TOLIVER, Sydney 25 (5)
227B
TONEY, Charles 1 (3) 469A
Grant 4 (3) 469A
John 8 (3) 469A
Lizzie 2 (3) 469A
Mary 37 (3) 469A
Nathan 40 (3) 469A
Susan 6 (3) 469A
TOOGOOD, *Edward 49 (5)
283B
TORNEY, Ann M. 35 (6)
433A
Caroline 7/12 (6) 433A
Mary E. 7 (6) 433A
Nathaniel 9 (6) 433A
TOWN, Henry 4 (3) 506B
TOWNSAND, Ann 25 (6)
370B
TOWNSEND, *Catherine 50
(6) 410B
Julia A. 24 (6) 410B
TOY, Tobilhia 72 (6) 292A
TRAVERS, Alberta 3 (3)
506A
Eugene 7 (3) 506A
Hester 13 (4) 28B
Mahaley 30 (3) 505B
Maria 1 (3) 506A
Mary J. 39 (2) 345A
Rachael 56 (2) 296A
*Robert 46 (2) 345A
*Solomon 37 (3) 505B
Vina 60 (6) 295B
TRAVERSE, Martha 18 (4)

TRAVERSE (continued)
15A
TRAVIS, *Joseph 35 (5) 204B
Lucretia 38 (5) 204B
TRUETT, *Isaac 26 (6) 314A
Sarah E. 20 (6) 314A
TRUITT, Mary 30 (3) 580A
TRUSTY, Charlott 24 (3)
474A
Charlotte 40 (4) 29A
Diana 52 (2) 306A
Eliza 37 (4) 17A
Enoch C. 14 (2) 306A
Garrison D. 11 (6) 413B
George 4 (4) 17A
John H. 21 (2) 306A
*Jonathan 70 (2) 306A
Josephine 9 (5) 171A
*Lavenia 68 (5) 156B
Lydia 45 (6) 413B
Maggie 16 (1) 110A
Perry 20 (4) 20B
Sarah 6 (5) 126B
Susan 30 (5) 171A
Theodore 16 (3) 485B
William B. 17 (2) 306A
TUBMAN, Charlotte 10 (3)
534A
Emilie 41 (1) 4A
George 40 (1) 4A
George W. 24 (4) 18A
Isabella 24 (3) 504B
John 9/12 (1) 4A
*John T. 55 (4) 18A
John T. 30 (4) 18A
Maria 1 (3) 504B
Mary Elizabeth 24 (4) 18A
Moses 16 (4) 18A
Moses 18 (1) 4A
Robert 23 (1) 4A
Sina 20 (1) 4A
Sophia 13 (1) 4A
Susan A. 50 (4) 18A
William 26 (1) 4A
William 3 (3) 504B
William 31 (3) 504B

TUBMAN (continued)
William H. 21 (4) 18A
TURNAGE, *Allen 23 (4) 19B
Josephine 19 (4) 19B
TURNER, Albert 4 (6) 431B
Benjamin 22 (4) 88B
Elenora 23 (6) 294B
Eliza 27 (6) 431B
Frances 42 (5) 207A
Harry 5/12 (6) 405A
Lillia 1 (6) 431B
Phoebe 15 (1) 59B
Rachel 25 (6) 405A
*Sarah 16 (1) 44A
Susanna 15 (2) 389B
William 11 (2) 392B
William 24 (2) 378B
William 7 (6) 431B
*William H. 50 (6) 431B
TYLER, Alice 35 (5) 219A
Laura 15 (5) 219A
Lavinia 20 (6) 309B
Mary 13 (5) 219A
Milla 40 (4) 104B
*Richard 40 (5) 219A
TYNES, Joseph 21 (6) 415B
TYSON, Malvinia 19 (1) 82B
TYTUS, Sarah 13 (5) 224A
UNDERWOOD, Etta 20 (4)
97A
UTON, George 7 (2) 340A
Henry 12 (2) 340A
*John W. 26 (2) 340A
Lovett 52 (2) 340A
Mary 24 (2) 340A
VALENTINE, Charles 5 (5)
126B
Emily 60 (2) 377B
VALLENTINE, Mary 16 (4)
86B
VANDROSS, William 12 (5)
126B
VARAIR, Matilda 67 (5) 154A
VEAL, Fillica 42 (5) 152B
*James 44 (5) 152B
VENEY, Benjamin 30 (5)

VENEY (continued)
154B
VODERY, Charles 8 (2) 328A
Edward 3 (2) 328A
Flora 1 (2) 328A
George 6 (2) 328A
John R. 18 (2) 328A
*Nathaniel 56 (2) 328A
Sarah C. 11 (2) 328A
Sarah J. 40 (2) 328A
William A. 15 (2) 328A
WADDY, Mollie 20 (3) 474B
WAGNER, Fanny 17 (5) 135B
WALKER, Agness 50 (5)
160A
Benjamin 7 (5) 196B
Cecelia 28 (6) 304A
Charles H. 53 (5) 209A
*Charles S. 37 (5) 152A
*Charlotta 29 (5) 161A
Edward 2 (3) 487A
Elizabeth 28 (5) 219B
George 14 (5) 196B
George E. 6/12 (5) 161A
Hester 33 (5) 209B
*Horace 35 (6) 405A
James 36 (5) 219B
James H. 24 (5) 286A
Jane 19 (5) 286A
John 18 (5) 196B
John 4 (3) 487A
John H. 15 (6) 405A
Lavinia 4/12 (3) 487A
*Margaret 33 (5) 196B
Margaret 45 (6) 410A
Mary 20 (5) 196B
Mary 38 (6) 405A
Mary R. 9/12 (5) 152A
Perry 4 (6) 303B
Peter 8 (5) 196B
Rebecca 60 (5) 198A
*Robert 70 (5) 198A
Rosa 30 (5) 152A
Sarah 30 (3) 487A
Sarah 57 (6) 309B
Susan 4 (5) 196B

WALKER (continued)
*William 30 (3) 487A
William 11 (5) 196B
William 9 (3) 487A
William H. 13 (6) 410A
Willie 3 (6) 405A
Zacheriah 45 (6) 410A
WALLACE, Ann 61 (2) 306B
Charles 10 96) 475A
Elsworth 6 (5) 166A
Emily 39 (6) 475A
Fanny 1 (5) 166A
Fanny 4 (5) 283A
*George 26 (5) 283A
Harriet 38 (5) 203B
*Henrietta 50 (5) 283A
James 22 (6) 452A
Jane 20 (6) 452A
Jane 38 (4) 110A
John 21 (4) 18B
John 23 (3) 545A
Joshua 2 (5) 283A
Joshua L. 22 (5) 283B
Lemuel 44 (2) 383A
Lorenza 5 (2) 383A
Louisa 26 (5) 283A
Mary 6 (6) 475A
Mary 7/12 (5) 166A
Mary L. 25 (5) 166A
Minta 1 (6) 475A
Nathan 58 (5) 166A
Nelly 4 (6) 475A
Robert 12 (6) 475A
Susan 58 (2) 259B
Tudor 16 (6) 475A
Wesley 42 (4) 110A
*William 37 (6) 475A
WALTER, Susan 35 (6) 310A
WALTERS, Clara 50 (6)
323A
Daniel 1 (2) 247B
Ellen 23 (2) 247B
Minta 60 (3) 541B
Sophia 53 (3) 424B
*William 25 (2) 247B
WALTHAM, *Hiram 32 (6)

WALTHAM (continued)
   477B
Caroline 25 (6) 477B
Henry 7 (6) 477B
Pinksy D. 1 (6) 477B
WALTON, Edward 24 (2)
   251B
WANGUST, Mary 26 (6) 448A
Sarah F. 7 (6) 448A
Thomas E. 5 (6) 448A
William 40 (6) 448A
William H. 10 (6) 448A
WARD, *Augusta 40 (3) 545A
*Charles 27 (3) 506A
Charles W. 26 (5) 147A
Effey 40 (3) 506A
Eugenia 14 (3) 545A
George James 5 (4) 112B
Henrietta 40 (4) 112B
James H. 19 (4) 112B
Mary 11 (3) 545A
Mary E. 21 (5) 147A
Morris 7 (3) 545A
*Perry 50 (5) 170B
Sarah 15 (3) 545A
Susan 9 (3) 545A
Thomas 11 (3) 506A
*William 50 (4) 112B
William H. 3 (5) 147A
WARDEN, Annett 27 (5)
   212B
*Jordan 31 (5) 212B
WARFIELD, *Adam 48 (2)
   345A
Alice 3 (2) 345A
Charlotte 18 (2) 345A
George 17 (3) 521B
Gustine 39 (2) 345A
Jerry 40 (3) 521B
Josephine 9 (2) 345A
Maria 15 (3) 521B
Mary 20 (2) 345A
Mary 21 (3) 521B
Sarah A. 66 (4) 102A
WARNER, Easter 30 (4) 19B
Eliza 45 (5) 241B

WARNER (continued)
*Jacob 50 (5) 241B
*Joseph 40 (4) 19B
Louvenia 12 (4) 19B
Margaret 7 (4) 19B
Mary 54 (5) 126A
Mary E. 5 (4) 19B
Sophronia 18 (4) 19B
Virginia 15 (1) 21B
William 1 (4) 19B
WARREN, Annie 3 (3) 506A
Emma 11 (3) 506A
Mary 53 (3) 506A
Samuel 21 (3) 503B
WARRINGTON, Sarah 63 (6)
   417B
WASHINGTON, Adell 20 (5)
   258B
Alice 18 (5) 258B
Alverta 10 (6) 306A
Charles 19 (5) 169A
*Charles 55 (5) 258B
Eliza 4 (6) 306A
Emily 25 (5) 179B
Eva 2 (5) 153B
*Fanny 26 (5) 186B
G. H. 19 (6) 343A
George 10/12 (6) 427A
George 19 (5) 125A
George 22 (3) 563B
George 30 (5) 159A
George A. 27 (6) 451B
Grace 7/12 (5) 258B
Henry 35 (5) 186B
Henry 6 (6) 427A
Howard 15 (5) 258B
James 23 (5) 160A
Johnny 1 (6) 306A
Joseph 24 (5) 179B
Josephine 30 (6) 306A
Lewis 3 (6) 427A
*Lewis 32 (6) 427A
Mary 25 (6) 427A
Mary 3 (5) 186B
Mary 50 (5) 258B
Mary 75 (6) 433A

WASHINGTON (continued)
*Richard 30 (6) 306A
Sapharonia 36 (5) 153B
*Sarah 42 (3) 524A
*Thacker 40 (5) 153B
Virginia 8/12 (5) 186B
William 20 (5) 204A
WATERS, Amanda 17 (2)
    340A
*Charles 24 (5) 179B
Drucilla 18 (4) 99B
Edward 35 (5) 157A
Eliza 44 (4) 110A
*Elizabeth 35 (5) 157B
Elizabeth 57 (3) 485A
Ellen 13 (5) 157B
Gilbert 38 (2) 340A
James 22 (3) 525A
*James 37 (4) 94A
*Job 34 (1) 47A
Laura 15 (3) 562B
Lavina 13 (6) 309B
Levin 30 (5) 168B
Louisa 44 (4) 94A
Mary 12 (2) 340A
Mary 32 (1) 47A
*Mary 53 (3) 562B
Richard 18 (1) 47A
Samuel 17 (5) 167A
Samuel 21 (3) 525A
Sarah 22 (2) 340A
Virginia 9 (2) 340A
WATKINS, Alfred 7 (5) 219A
Amanda 25 (5) 236A
Ann L. 17 (6) 461A
Anna L. 17 (6) 461A
*Benjamin 38 (6) 461A
Caroline 42 (5) 152A
Charles H. 31 (6) 350B
Clara J. 4 (6) 461A
Elenora 11 (6) 461A
Elenora 18 (5) 152A
Elenora J. 11 (6) 461A
Elizabeth 8 (4) 18B
Emma 6 (2) 383A
Fanny 8 (6) 350B

WATKINS (continued)
Francis 34 (2) 383A
Frank 9/12 (5) 152A
Frederick 18 (4) 18B
*George 45 (5) 219A
George 112 (6) 350B
George 13 (4) 18B
George 14 (5) 152A
George 5 (5) 219A
Harriett 10 (6) 350B
John 1 (5) 219A
John 40 (3) 504B
Lewis 15 (4) 18B
Lizzie 39 (6) 461A
Lizzie 39 (6) 461A
Louisa A. 14 (6) 461A
Lyons 1 (6) 461A
Maria 39 (5) 219A
Mary 14 (4) 18B
Mary 40 (3) 504B
Mary A. 16 (5) 152A
Mary A. 35 (4) 18A
Mary M. 27 (6) 350B
Rachael 10 (4) 18B
Robert 30 (5) 236A
Samuel 2 (5) 219A
Savena 17 (3) 504B
Stephen 34 (2) 383A
*Thomas 60 (4) 18A
WATSON, *Charles 54 (5)
    151A
Henrietta 29 (5) 151A
John H. 20 (5) 219B
Nancy 70 (6) 395B
WATTS, Alfred 14 (6) 437B
Anna 6 (6) 438A
Bertha 5 (5) 151A
*Harriet 40 (5) 151A
Harriett 42 (6) 437B
John W. 20 (5) 151A
Josephine 16 (5) 151A
Margarett F. 9 (6) 437B
Mary E. 11 (5) 151A
Mary E. 3 (6) 438A
Rachael 101 (2) 304A
Richard 18 (5) 151A

WATTS (continued)
Sherman 6 (6) 438A
Theodore 8 (6) 437B
*Wesley 39 (6) 437B
William 8/12 (6) 438A
WAY, Jane 42 (2) 305A
WAYMAN, George 25 (3) 487A
Lizzie 26 (3) 487A
WEATHERBY, Sarah J. 25 (5) 206A
WEATHERS, Alexander 30 (6) 448A
Wilhelm 26 (6) 448A
WEAVER, *Benjamin 47 (5) 153B
Carrie 4 (5) 204B
*Charles 34 (5) 144A
Emily 40 (6) 303A
Emma 17 (5) 153B
*Henry 40 (6) 303A
John 15 (5) 153B
Laura 20 (5) 144A
Margaret 8 (5) 153B
Mary L. 8 (5) 204B
Rachel 25 (5) 153B
WEBB, Ann E. 24 (6) 453B
Annett V. 2 (5) 213A
Clara J. 20 (5) 213A
Ella 11 (5) 213A
Emily 22 (5) 203B
Gabriel 3 (6) 453B
*Gabriel 23 (6) 311B
Galoway 24 (5) 203B
*Geo. H. 23 (6) 453B
Harrison 31 (5) 212B
Harry 1 (6) 453B
Laura 7 (5) 153A
Levin 12 (5) 153A
Martha 24 (3) 528B
Martha A. 40 (4) 18A
Mary 49 (5) 153A
Mary E. 5 (6) 453B
Richard 11 (5) 153A
*Robert 70 (5) 153A
Sarah J. 28 (5) 212B

WEBB (continued)
Stephen 27 (5) 153A
WEBSTER, Daniel 12 (4) 71A
Frances W. 23 (5) 252B
Susannah 54 (6) 347A
William 50 (6) 347A
William H. 6 (6) 347A
WEEKS, Abby 50 (6) 395B
Alice A. 100 (5) 145A
*Caleb 70 (6) 395B
WELL, Eliza 22 (5) 157B
William 22 (5) 157B
WELLS, Edward 22 (5) 156B
Emly 28 (6) 449A
George 11 (6) 449A
*George 55 (6) 449A
Henry 18 (6) 449A
James 5 (5) 149B
Jerry 15 (6) 449A
John 7 (5) 149B
Matilda 49 (6) 469A
Thomas 52 (5) 274B
William 34 (5) 149B
WELSH, Mary 45 (6) 412A
WELTHER, Eliza 8 (3) 580B
Henry 6 (3) 580B
*John 49 (3) 580B
John 10 (3) 580B
Lizzie 2 (3) 580B
Robert 4 (3) 580B
Rosetta 43 (3) 580B
WESCOAT, Josephine 20 (5) 169A
Nimrod 30 (5) 169A
William J. 1 (5) 169A
WESLEY, Charley 6 (6) 411A
*Mary A. 51 (6) 411A
WEST, *Charles 29 (4) 19B
Eliza 24 (4) 19B
Josephine 27 (6) 427A
Richard 24 (6) 427A
Susan 34 (1) 50B
WESTLEY, Eliza J. 32 (2) 345A
Frances 11 (2) 345A

WESTLEY (continued)
John 2 (2) 345A
*John 34 (2) 345A
WETHERBY, Sarah J. 30 (4)
  27B
WHALES, George 22 (3)
  411B
WHATTY, Thomas 37 (6)
  408A
WHEATLEY, Ann 50 (6)
  309A
*Daniel 55 (6) 309A
*Edward 40 (3) 516B
Eliza 40 (3) 560A
Elizebath 37 (3) 516B
Susan R. 14 (6) 309A
Virginia 22 (3) 560A
WHEATLY, Alice 10 (3)
  516B
Emily 40 (4) 95A
Estella 6 (3) 516B
Florence 4 (3) 516B
George 2 (3) 516B
Ida 8 (3) 516B
Ophelia 14 (3) 516B
Raymond 12 (3) 516B
*William 35 (4) 95A
WHEELER, Ann M. 50 (2)
  247B
Caroline 9 (5) 133A
Ezekiel 16 (5) 152A
Fanny 25 (6) 364A
Fanny 39 (5) 227B
George 21 (5) 152A
*Isaac 50 (5) 158A
*Isaiah 48 (5) 205A
James 23 (5) 152A
Kate 14 (5) 184A
Louisa 18 (5) 152A
Margareat 16 (2) 247B
Mary 6/12 (5) 152A
*Richard 48 (2) 247B
Sarah J. 37 (5) 205A
Sophia 5 (5) 205A
Susan 20 (5) 152A
Susan 48 (5) 158A

WHEELER (continued)
Thomas H. 14 (2) 247B
Thomas H. 40 (5) 210B
WHITE, Affey 65 (2) 339B
Anna 52 (1) 1B
Asbury 3 (5) 144B
*Caroline 45 (4) 1B
*Caroline 47 (3) 488A
Caroline 50 (3) 508B
Carrie 4 (5) 144B
*Cary 30 (5) 179B
Clayton 27 (3) 488A
David 23 (4) 95A
Desdemonia 10 (3) 524B
*Edward 34 (4) 95A
Elisa 25 (5) 148B
Eliza 13 (5) 144B
Eliza 7 (3) 524B
Elizebeth 6 (6) 448A
*Elizebeth 38 (6) 448A
Grace Ann 27 (4) 95A
*Henry 40 (3) 473A
*Henry 48 (2) 383A
Hester A. 13 (5) 179B
Isaac 32 (6) 324B
John 8 (3) 524B
*John 31 (3) 524B
*John 40 (3) 472B
John Q. 25 (6) 324B
Joseph 13 (3) 488A
Joseph 6 (5) 144B
*Joseph 44 (5) 144B
Jovono 12 (4) 1B
Julia 3 (3) 525A
Kersiah 35 (6) 324B
Maria 20 (3) 508B
Martha 30 (5) 144A
Mary 1 (6) 411A
Mary 23 (5) 200B
Mary 41 (3) 472B
Mary 41 (3) 473A
Mary 7 (3) 488A
Morris 15 (3) 488A
*Nathan 54 (1) 1B
Perry 27 (1) 1B
Pricilla 65 (5) 179B

WHITE (continued)
Rachel 18 (6) 411A
Rachel 8 (5) 144B
Sarah 30 (3) 524B
Sarah 5 (3) 524B
Susan 42 (5) 144B
Theodore 24 (3) 488A
*Thomas 30 (5) 148B
Thomas 33 (3) 544A
William 11 (3) 488A
*William 23 (6) 411A
William 30 (6) 448A
*William 40 (5) 144A
William 9 (4) 95A
WHITINGTON, Aaron 25 (6)
  405A
Eliz 23 (6) 294A
WHITTINGTON, Charlotte 8
  (2) 226A
Eliza J. 10 (2) 226A
Frances 38 (2) 226A
*John 66 (2) 226A
John H. 6 (2) 226A
WHYE, John T. 15 (5) 172A
Susan 36 (5) 172A
William H. 5 (5) 172A
WICKES, *Abraham 35 (5)
  246B
Emma 3/12 246B
John 10 (5) 246B
Mary T. 32 (5) 246B
Richard 15 (5) 246B
William T. 3 (5) 246B
WICKS, Ann M. 3 (5) 122B
Jacob 22 (5) 122B
*Joseph 28 (6) 348A
Mary 21 (5) 122B
Mary E. 28 (6) 348A
WILEY, Elisabeth 29 (5)
  148B
WILK, Louisa 16 (1) 82B
WILKINSON, Caroline 40 (3)
  484A
*John 33 (3) 484A
John 33 (3) 506A
Mary 20 (3) 506A

WILKINSON (continued)
Mary 8 (3) 484A
WILLIAM, George 25 (3)
  504A
*Henry 54 (4) 18A
*Nelson 20 (1) 44B
WILLIAMS, Abrah 35 (6)
  350B
Adeline 5 (6) 408A
Ailey 45 (5) 256A
Alexander 22 (2) 377A
*Alexander 29 (4) 110A
Alexander 35 (4) 111B
Alexander 40 (5) 155A
Alfred 6 (2) 378B
*Alfred 39 (2) 380B
Alice R. 3 (5) 285B
Alverta 2 (6) 450A
Amanda 21 (2) 340A
Amidle B. 2 (6) 395B
Ann 70 (6) 408A
Anna 1 (5) 186A
Anna 20 (5) 186A
Anna 40 (5) 188A
Anna I. 46 (6) 450A
Annie 31 (3) 567A
Ary A. 9 (3) 599B
Benjamin 25 (2) 378B
Benjamin 29 (5) 186B
Celia 45 (3) 578A
Chaney 45 (1) 57A
Charles 10 (6) 450A
Charles 20 (3) 506A
Charles 30 (3) 567A
Charles 62 (2) 393B
Clara 19 (2) 247A
Clara 19 (2) 380A
Clara 26 (5) 234A
Daniel S. 7/12 (5) 161B
David 39 (6) 324B
Dina 97 (5) 157B
*Edward 25 (5) 219B
Edward V. 9/12 (5) 219B
*Elias 60 (3) 542A
Eliza 22 (6) 350B
Eliza 25 (2) 382B

WILLIAMS (continued)
Eliza 27 (5) 167B
Eliza 28 (2) 306B
Elizabeth 61 (2) 393B
Elizebeth 27 (6) 449B
Elizebeth 35 (3) 599B
Ellen 22 (5) 156B
Ellen 7 (3) 599B
Emma 20 (5) 186A
Emma 23 (5) 219B
Fanny 22 (5) 241B
Francis 8 (5) 159A
George 19 (5) 224A
George 2 (5) 186A
George 3 (5) 156B
George 39 (2) 340A
George A. 16 (6) 450A
George W. 20 (5) 197B
Harriet 2 (5) 234B
Harriet 35 (5) 155A
Harriett 47 (6) 324B
Henrietta 2 (2) 339A
Henry 21 (4) 18B
Henry 32 (6) 411A
Henry 42 (1) 24B
*Henry C. 40 95) 285B
Henryet 30 (6) 308B
Hester A. 54 (2) 378B
Howard S. 11 (3) 440A
Ida 24 (5) 196B
Ida T. 1 (6) 308B
*Isaac 50 (2) 339B
James 2/12 (2) 340A
James 23 (2) 389A
James E. 7/12 (5) 156B
John 1 (3) 567A
John 19 (3) 439A
John 2 (2) 380B
John 22 (2) 306B
John 29 (5) 154A
John 31 (2) 339A
John 35 (5) 151B
*John 37 (3) 599B
John H. 3/12 (2) 377B
John J. 9 (5) 199B
John W. 3 (5) 155A

WILLIAMS (continued)
*John W. 53 (6) 450A
John W. 5 (3) 599B
Joseph 25 (2) 247A
Joseph 25 (5) 156B
Joseph 26 (5) 168A
Joseph 3 (5) 156B
Joseph 30 (2) 380A
Josephine 6 (5) 285B
Julia 5 (3) 567A
Kate 3 (5) 151B
Laura 31 (2) 378B
*Lewis 60 (5) 146B
Loander 7/12 (2) 380A
Louisa 19 (3) 542B
Louisa 2 (4) 110A
Louisa 43 (2) 387B
Louisa 45 (3) 476A
Louisa 51 (4) 18A
Lucinda 25 (2) 377B
Lucy 24 (2) 339A
Lucy 35 (5) 151B
Lucy A. 6 (5) 151B
Lydia 46 (5) 215A
Maggie 20 (2) 380B
Margaret 24 (2) 298A
Margaret 29 (5) 161B
Margaret 51 (2) 339B
Maria 17 (2) 339B
Maria 3 (3) 567A
Martha 49 (5) 157B
Martha 6 (2) 339B
Martha E. 11 (5) 285B
Mary 12 (5) 196B
Mary 17 (5) 146B
Mary 17 (5) 151B
Mary 18 (5) 154A
Mary 21 (2) 340A
Mary 21 (2) 387A
Mary 32 (4) 110A
Mary 39 (5) 145B
Mary 63 (3) 542A
Mary 7 (3) 567A
Mary B. 20 (2) 377A
Mary F. 12 (4) 102B
Mary J. 23 (2) 389A

WILLIAMS (continued)
Mary J. 36 (5) 285B
Mary T. 10 (5) 285B
*Mildrett A. 42 (6) 395B
Nathaniel 27 (2) 377B
Nathaniel 3 (2) 377B
Odario 21 (6) 408A
Percilla E. 21 (6) 450A
Pricilla 23 (5) 197B
Priscilla 21 (3) 424B
Rachel 15 (3) 542B
Rebecca 26 (3) 542A
Robert 21 (3) 542B
*Robert 30 (5) 186A
Robert H. 28 (5) 146B
Robert T. 3 (3) 599B
Rodney T. 12 (5) 285B
Rose 5 (4) 110A
Rose 52 (5) 146B
Rose A. 7/12 (6) 450A
*Rosa 63 (5) 197B
S. Mary 26 (3) 577B
Samuel 18 (5) 144A
Samuel 24 (4) 102B
Samuel 5 (5) 234B
Sarah 12 (5) 151B
Sarah 22 (5) 178A
Sarah 33 (5) 137A
Sarah 52 (5) 219B
Sarah A. 43 (5) 199B
Sarah E. 8 (5) 285B
Sebastian 32 (5) 234A
Sophia 11 (1) 44B
Sophia 24 (1) 133B
*Sophia 71 (5) 157A
Steziah 61 (5) 241B
Thomas 28 (6) 449B
Tilley 6/12 (5) 151B
Virginia 13 (1) 37B
Virginia 14 (4) 102B
Walter 11/12 (2) 247A
*Walter 55 (5) 199B
Walter H. 6/12 (5) 285B
Wesley 27 (5) 176A
William 17 (3) 599B
William H. 21 (5) 241B

WILLIAMS (continued)
Woodley 65 (5) 180A
Zacariah 49 (5) 145B
WILLIAMSON, Fanny 8 (4)
 19B
Lloyd 62 (4) 110B
WILLIS, Annie 20 (3) 478A
Charles 20 (4) 88B
George 30 (3) 478A
Henry 12 (1) 44B
Robert 22 (4) 88B
WILLMORE, Buck 4 (6)
 468A
George 6 (6) 468A
Hannah 30 (6) 468A
Jane 12 (6) 468A
John 8 (6) 468A
*John 31 (6) 468A
Louisa 1 (6) 468A
*Mary J. 25 (6) 468A
William 10 (6) 468A
WILLSON, Ann G. 8 (4) 19A
Anna 25 (4) 98A
Anna 36 (4) 19A
Charles 14 (4) 19A
Elizabeth 38 (4) 100B
*George 35 (4) 19A
Henry 36 (4) 1B
Maria J. 31 (4) 1B
Victoria 1 (4) 1B
Virginia 2 (4) 1B
William 8 (4) 1B
WILMAN, Martha 18 (3)
 459A
WILMER, *Henry 58 (3) 503A
John 16 (3) 503A
Louisa 40 (3) 503A
Manuel 9 (3) 503A
Sarah 26 (3) 503A
WILMORE, Charity 11 (5)
 167B
Eleanora 9 (2) 391B
Emanuel 13 (2) 391B
*Emanuel 70 (2) 391B
Emma 26 (5) 145A
Hannah 31 (5) 167B

WILMORE (continued)
Isaac P. 5 (5) 167B
Joseph S. 1 (5) 167B
Mary C. 7 (2) 391B
Mary M. 9 (5) 167B
Mary V. 19 (2) 391B
*Perry 24 (5) 167A
Rosanna 54 (2) 391B
Samuel J. 7 (5) 167B
WILSON, Abraham 21 (6)
  451B
Adeline 15 (1) 36A
Agness 30 (5) 204B
Alice S. 10 (2) 295B
Amelia 23 (5) 151A
Ann M. 15 (5) 205A
Ann M. 20 (5) 206A
*Anna 28 (1) 46B
Anna 13 (6) 308B
Anna 17 (6) 382B
Anna 21 (5) 246B
Anna 22 (2) 222A
Anna 3 (2) 222A
Anna 7 (1) 46B
Anna 73 (2) 345A
Anna 9 (5) 258B
*Anthony 69 (5) 154A
Aretta 62 (5) 154A
*Arrina 39 (6) 409B
Benjamin 50 (2) 335A
Betty 30 (3) 494B
Caroline 44 (1) 46A
Carrie 2 (2) 222A
Cathy 31 (2) 377B
Charice 25 (5) 255B
*Charles 48 (1) 46A
Charles 39 (5) 160A
Charles C. 14 (2) 295B
Charlotta 40 (5) 148A
Charlotte 48 (6) 308B
*Charlotte 56 (3) 412A
Charlotte 7/12 (2) 383A
Cordilea 6/12 (2) 222A
Cyrus 16 (3) 543B
*Daniel 69 (6) 431B
*David 28 (6) 342B

WILSON (continued)
*David 37 (2) 383A
David 3 (3) 484A
David 35 (1) 46B
David 4 (6) 342B
Edward 3 (5) 207A
Eliza 14 (1) 46A
Eliza 17 (3) 487B
Eliza J. 3 (6) 409A
Elizabeth 23 (5) 161A
Elizabeth 27 (5) 153B
Elizabeth 28 (2) 296A
Elizebath 58 (3) 495B
Ellen T. 6 (5) 153B
Emily 17 (5) 277A
Emma 17 (3) 561B
Emma 19 (3) 427A
Emma 26 (3) 478A
Emma 3 (3) 478A
Emory 13 (3) 487A
Emory 18 (5) 154A
Esther 17 (3) 487A
Eveline 27 (6) 410B
Fannie 50 (2) 335A
Fanny 2 (1) 2A
Fanny 50 (1) 88B
Frances 19 (5) 167B
Frances 30 (5) 258B
Frederick 27 (3) 478A
George 19 (3) 543B
George 22 (6) 451B
George 30 (3) 484A
George 36 (5) 204B
George 4 (5) 258B
George 5 (3) 478A
George 7 (3) 484A
George 7 (3) 561A
George 70 (5) 207A
George W. 23 (2) 221B
George W. 40 (5) 258B
Harry 1 (3) 478A
*Henry 55 (6) 451B
*Hester 50 (3) 506A
Isaac 30 (5) 153B
Isaac 74 (1) 44B
James 37 (2) 383A

WILSON (continued)
James 6 (1) 46B
James 7 (2) 383A
James 8 (6) 305B
James 9 (5) 126B
Jane 28 (2) 383A
Jane 4 (5) 153B
Jennie 6 (1) 47A
*Jeremiah 30 (1) 46B
John 15 (3) 487A
John 15 (6) 305B
John 19 (3) 544B
*John 40 (3) 487B
*John 48 (5) 148A
*John H. 34 (6) 305B
*John H. 30 (2) 222A
John H. 8 (2) 222A
John T. 27 (5) 148A
John W. 9 (6) 410B
Joseph 13 (6) 305B
Joseph 6 (1) 46B
Laura 19 (5) 151B
Laura J. 20 (5) 284A
Lawrence 21 (3) 563A
Leander 22 (5) 274A
Lewell 19 (3) 487A
*Lewis 36 (6) 409A
Lizzie 20 (3) 525B
Louisa 32 (6) 305B
Lucretia 10 (2) 383A
*Lucy A. 52 (5) 171A
*Lydia 48 (5) 207A
Margaret 26 (3) 484A
Margaret 37 (6) 411A
Margaret 8 (5) 207A
Margarett J. 25 (6) 476B
Maria 15 (3) 512A
Maria 21 (3) 544A
Maria 25 (6) 367B
Maria 65 (6) 451B
*Martha 37 (3) 487A
Martha 1 (5) 147A
Martha 16 (3) 495B
Mary 14 (3) 487B
Mary 15 (3) 505B
Mary 17 (3) 563A

WILSON (continued)
Mary 18 (3) 459B
Mary 23 (3) 506A
Mary 23 (6) 409A
Mary 26 (6) 342B
Mary 3 (5) 161A
Mary 35 (5) 160A
Mary 40 (5) 205A
Mary 47 (3) 563A
Mary 48 (3) 537B
Mary 5 (3) 484A
Mary 5 (3) 561A
Mary 8 (3) 495B
Mary A. 11 (5) 258B
Mary E. 9 (5) 207A
Mary F. 12 (5) 205A
Mary R. 9 (2) 222A
Mary V. 2/12 (6) 342B
Matilda 36 (3) 487B
Milkie 31 (2) 383A
Moses 11 (5) 198A
Raachel 35 (1) 46B
Rachel 35 (1) 46B
Raymond 3 (6) 305B
Rebecca 21 (5) 156B
Reuben 40 (5) 215A
Reuben 40 (5) 224A
Richard 21 (6) 350B
Robert 2 (5) 161A
*Robert 22 (2) 296A
*Robert 25 (5) 161A
Rosa 17 (5) 148A
Rosetta 42 (6) 413A
Sarah 20 (3) 487A
Sarah 26 (3) 506A
Sarah 28 (3) 561A
Sarah 30 (6) 356B
Solomon 12 (5) 258B
Sophia 22 (6) 350B
Susan 15 (4) 15A
Susan 25 (3) 493B
Thomas 26 (2) 385A
*Thomas 51 (6) 308B
*Thomas H. 24 (5) 156B
Thomas L. 1 (5) 156B
Thomas S. 3 (5) 151B

WILSON (continued)
William 1 (3) 561A
William 10 (5) 207A
William 22 (5) 151B
William 30 (3) 561A
*William 52 (6) 413A
*William 62 (3) 495B
*William E. 28 (5) 151A
William H. 16 (6) 411A
William H. 2 (6) 350B
William H. 32 (6) 410B
William J. 6 (6) 342B
WIMSLEY, Eliza 18 (4) 2A
WINDEER, Martha 2 (3)
  560B
Mary E. 23 (3) 560B
WINDER, Susan 30 (5) 147A
WINDSOR, *Whitfield 22 (5)
  144A
WINFIELD, George 25 (2)
  389A
*William 23 (5) 158B
WING, Ann 19 (3) 433B
Carmilla 39 (2) 345A
Elverta 6 (3) 520B
Emily 4/12 (2) 345A
George 10 (2) 345A
*George 44 (2) 345A
John 12 (2) 345A
WINGATE, Louisa 11 (6)
  301A
WINKLER, *Mary 36 (6)
  367A
WINTER, Rebecca 20 (5)
  276B
WISE, Ellen 33 (6) 457B
Enock 35 (6) 457B
George 2 (6) 457B
Jane 28 (6) 340A
John 20 (4) 112B
Mary 14 (4) 118B
Sarah 32 (5) 187A
WISHER, *Andrew 63 (5)
  139A
Ann B. 64 (5) 139A

WOLFORD, James 17 (3)
  504B
WOOD, Ellen 22 (5) 162A
Mary A. 35 (5) 149A
*Stephen 52 (5) 149A
WOODBRIDGE, Hait 16 (1)
  49B
WOODLAND, Agness 1 (5)
  160A
Hannah 10 (5) 160A
John 25 (5) 160A
WOODS, Anna 40 (5) 224A
John 30 (3) 485A
Lewis 22 (5) 134B
Maria 27 (3) 485A
Mary A. 27 (6) 455A
William 3 (3) 485A
WOOLFORD, Ann M. 42 (5)
  197B
*Bartholomew 30 (5) 197A
Emm. E. 7 (5) 197A
Henrietta 22 (5) 145B
Horace 38 (5) 145B
James E. 7 (6) 312A
Jeffery J. 19 (5) 197A
John 9 (6) 312A
*John 40 (5) 197B
Joseph H. 8 (5) 197B
Levin J. 30 (5) 197A
Linton 10 (5) 197B
Lucinda 58 (5) 197A
Maria J. 14 (5) 197B
Martha 24 (5) 197A
Mary 26 (6) 312A
Mary E. 4 (5) 197B
Mary V. 6 (6) 312A
Steven 28 (6) 312A
William R. 2 (5) 197B
WORDEN, Charles 3 (3)
  541B
Edward 5 (3) 541B
Lucy 9 (3) 541B
Mary 37 (3) 541B
William 38 (3) 541B
William 7 (3) 541B

WORLEY, Anna L. 16 (4) 9B
WORSHAM, Amander 22 (6) 409B
*Isaac 38 (6) 409B
James H. 4 (6) 409B
WORTHERLY, Caroline 21 (6) 332A
Robert E. 2/12 (6) 332A
Train 26 (6) 332A
WORTHEY, Bertha 17 (5) 148B
James 27 (5) 148B
WRIGHT, Alice 31 (3) 520B
Augusta 29 (3) 520B
Charles C. 12 (6) 408B
*Charles W. 32 (5) 180A
Elisa J. 37 (5) 180A
Eliza 37 (6) 408B
Eliza A. 6 (6) 408B
Elizabeth 13 (2) 335B
Elizebeth 10 (6) 415B
Elizebeth J. 18 (6) 434B
Emory 29 (3) 414A
Fannie 35 (2) 335B
Frances 14 (2) 335B
Francis 25 (3) 479A
Francis 29 (5) 186B
G. S. P. 32 (4) 19B
Garrison S. 11 (6) 434B
George 10 (6) 408B
George W. 8 (4) 19B
Hellen 1 (6) 408B
Henrietta 30 (3) 502B
Henrietta W. 8 (6) 434B
*Isaac 80 (4) 94B
James 17 (6) 408B
James 3 (3) 479A
John 22 (5) 155B
John F. 1 (2) 335B
Joseph R. 22 (6) 434B
Kate 5 (3) 479A
Margarett 15 (6) 408B
Mary A. 25 (3) 414A
Mary E. 27 (4) 19B
Mary T. 4 (6) 408B
Nancy S. 35 (6) 434B

WRIGHT (continued)
Pacience 28 (5) 139A
Rebecca 25 (6) 408B
Richard 18 (3) 422A
Robert 6 (2) 335B
Sarah 48 (6) 411B
Sarah J. 8 (6) 408B
*Thomas 42 (3) 479A
Thomas G. 23 (6) 408B
William 16 (2) 335B
William 20 (5) 161B
*William 37 (6) 408B
*William 62 (6) 434B
*William T. 36 (6) 434B
WYE, *Abraham 38 (5) 149A
Catharine 35 (5) 149A
Charles H. 33 (2) 306A
George 12 (5) 149A
Harriett A. 21 (2) 306A
Hester 56 (2) 306A
Jane 31 (2) 306A
Jarrett 13 (5) 149A
John 25 (5) 150B
Maria 23 (5) 150B
Martha 1 (5) 150B
*Philip 56 (2) 306A
YORK, Sarah 61 (6) 331A
YORKMAN, Harriet 50 (3) 525A
YOUNG, Alice 40 (3) 476B
Alverta 6/12 (5) 156A
Ann 16 (5) 144B
Ann 18 (2) 385A
Ann 45 (5) 195A
Anna 24 (1) 78B
Anna M. 28 (5) 151A
*Annetta 30 (5) 156A
Benjamin 21 (5) 153A
Betty 14 (5) 207B
Charles 1 (3) 446B
Charlotta 2 (5) 169B
Daniel 38 (5) 169B
Elizabeth 36 (5) 169A
Elizabeth 50 (5) 171A
Ellen 70 (5) 151A
Ellen P. 40 (5) 152B

YOUNG (continued)
Emily 60 (5) 144B
Francis M. 16 (6) 310B
*George 32 (5) 144B
George 12 (5) 171A
Harriett 3 (5) 152B
Henry 23 (6) 325A
*Henry 46 (5) 180A
Hester 12 (6) 322A
Hester 14 (6) 403B
Hester 17 (3) 504B
Hester A. 7 (6) 311A
Horace 35 (5) 212A
*Iggy 80 (3) 503B
Isaac 39 (3) 504B
*Jacob 56 (5) 162A
Jacob Jr. 22 (5) 162A
James 28 (3) 503B
*James 54 (5) 171A
James Jr. 26 (5) 171A
Jane 11 (6) 421A
Jane 50 (5) 162B
John 30 (3) 446B
John J. 28 (2) 222A
John W. 25 (6) 310B
Joseph 17 (5) 207A
Joseph 3 (6) 311A
Julia 14 (5) 162A
Julia 47 (5) 162A
Laura 12 (5) 156A
Louisa 12 (6) 311A

YOUNG (continued)
Louisa 25 (5) 212A
Louiza 14 (5) 156A
Lucretia 8 (5) 156A
Margaret 40 (3) 503B
Maria 35 (3) 504B
Maria J. 39 (6) 310B
Martha 1 (3) 503B
Martha 21 (3) 503B
Martha 5 (5) 151A
Mary E. 1/12 (5) 151A
Mary E. 18 (6) 310B
Peter 49 (5) 152B
Priscilla 49 (3) 503B
Rachael 26 (2) 222A
*Rachel 38 (5) 169B
Ruth 40 (5) 180A
*Samuel 32 (5) 151A
Sarah 6 (5) 156A
Sarah J. 8 (5) 124B
Susan 35 (5) 162B
Susan 7 (5) 151A
Tallis 16 (3) 601B
*Thomas 49 (6) 310B
Thomas H. 9 (6) 311A
William 29 (3) 503B
William 3 (3) 446B
William 3 (5) 153A
William H. 2 (5) 212A
*William H. 47 (5) 169A